You will find many books on the biblical and practical importance of the local church. But few can match the way Brad Edwards shows us the need for the church amid rampant anxiety, division, and individualism. Not only our churches but even whole societies would be transformed by implementing the wisdom found in this book.

Collin Hansen, vice president for content and editor in chief, the Gospel Coalition; author, *Timothy Keller: His Spiritual and Intellectual Formation*

At a time when trust in institutions is low and when professing Christians across the political spectrum are "loving Jesus but not the church," this book is a refreshing apologetic for the body of Christ. *The Reason for Church* combines biblical exegesis, sociological insights, and a tone that connects to the doubts of today's generation. If you are skeptical of the church, you should read this book before you empty the pew, and if you love the church, you should read this book to strengthen your arguments. And church leaders should immediately put it on top of their reading lists.

Daniel Darling, director, the Land Center for Cultural Engagement; author, *Agents of Grace*

The Reason for Church is one of the most important books of the year. An incisive, insightful analysis of the acids eroding institutional health today, from the heart of a pastor who loves Jesus and his bride and wants to see disciples made and formed in Jesus's likeness. Brad Edwards is a gift to believers struggling in an era of loneliness.

Trevin Wax, vice president of research and resource development at the North American Mission Board; visiting professor, Cedarville University; author *The Thrill of Orthodoxy*

Late modernity isn't working as individualism, therapy speak, technology, and secularism have all overpromised and underdelivered. The good news is that we don't have to be hollowed out by the cross-pressures of late modern life. Brad Edwards shows how the church provides us with an identity, belonging, and cultivation against this stark and unlivable modern backdrop. Picking up where

Timothy Keller's *The Reason for God* left off, Edwards uses Keller's "defeater beliefs" framework to show the reasons for rekindling our love for the church.

Michael Graham, program director, The Keller Center; executive producer and writer, *As in Heaven* podcast; coauthor, *The Great Dechurching*

The church is the mother of Christians. Without her, there is no ordinary way of being saved. Christians have affirmed this for millennia. But in our day these claims are often questioned or rejected, angrily denounced, or met with an indifferent shrug. At a time when the church is viewed with suspicion and associational life is in decline, such claims can sound strange or even offensive. Brad Edwards's book explains why church can be hard and why common life is in decline and then offers a constructive path forward, starting with a return to Mother Church. Why is the church so important? Why have Christians across time spoken so strongly in her favor? Brad's book addresses these questions. If you (or a loved one!) have struggled to understand why going to church matters, you should read this book.

Jake Meador, editor-in-chief, Mere Orthodoxy

There are two ways Christians can bear witness to the truth in a disenchanted age. The first way is to angrily react to every outrageous thing around us. The second way is to diagnose our society's crises and joyfully show why the gospel was always the cure. Brad Edwards offers here a masterclass in the second way. Here is an example of cultural apologetics that is intelligent, artful, and convincing in pointing modern readers to the beauty and purpose of belonging to God's church. This is a book for those who need to belong but don't yet know *whom* to belong to. In the same way that Tim Keller's work tilled the ground for Christian belief, Brad's work will prepare both the hurting and the cynical to receive the amazing gift of the local church. Read and share.

Samuel D. James, author, *Digital Liturgies: Rediscovering Christian Wisdom in an Online Age*

The Reason for Church

The Reason for Church

*Why the Body of Christ Still Matters
in an Age of Anxiety,
Division, and Radical Individualism*

Brad Edwards

ZONDERVAN
REFLECTIVE

ZONDERVAN REFLECTIVE

The Reason for Church
Copyright © 2025 by Christopher Bradley Edwards

Published in Grand Rapids, Michigan, by Zondervan. Zondervan is a registered trademark of The Zondervan Corporation, L.L.C., a wholly owned subsidiary of HarperCollins Christian Publishing, Inc.

Requests for information should be addressed to customercare@harpercollins.com.

Zondervan titles may be purchased in bulk for educational, business, fundraising, or sales promotional use. For information, please email SpecialMarkets@Zondervan.com.

ISBN 978-0-310-16669-6 (audio)

Library of Congress Cataloging-in-Publication Data

Names: Edwards, Brad, 1984– author.
Title: The reason for church : why the body of Christ still matters in an age of anxiety, division, and radical individualism / Brad Edwards.
Description: Grand Rapids, Michigan : Zondervan Reflective, [2025]
Identifiers: LCCN 2024047429 (print) | LCCN 2024047430 (ebook) | ISBN 9780310166672 (paperback) | ISBN 9780310166689 (ebook)
Subjects: LCSH: Church. | Church renewal. | BISAC: RELIGION / Christian Church / Growth | RELIGION / Christian Theology / Ecclesiology
Classification: LCC BV600.3 .E375 2025 (print) | LCC BV600.3 (ebook) | DDC 262.001/7—dc23/eng/20241113
LC record available at https://lccn.loc.gov/2024047429
LC ebook record available at https://lccn.loc.gov/2024047430

Published in association with the literary agent Don Gates @THE GATES GROUP.

Cover design: Darren Welch Design
Cover art: Getty Images
Interior design: Sara Colley

Printed in the United States of America

25 26 27 28 29 LBC 5 4 3 2 1

*For Christ's bride, whose goodness and beauty
made writing this book worthwhile*

*For my Hannah, whose love and sacrifice
made writing this book possible*

Contents

Part 1: Babel's Brick and Mortar

Part 2: The Body and Bride of Christ

Foreword

When I was involved in college ministry in New York City, many students would say, "I don't believe in any religion or that anyone possesses the truth." When I felt a bit snarky, I'd respond, "Except for that statement, right?" Others would claim that the goal in life is to "follow your heart," and I would counter, "What about that kid who used to beat you up in school? They were being pretty true to themselves." They'd reply, "No, they weren't, because they were harming others. You're free to do as you wish, as long as you do no harm." But who defines what is harmful?

These phrases are not just harmless mantras; they are cultural narratives.

In today's culture, which Charles Taylor refers to as "A Secular Age," many of our most common narratives push us toward radical individualism, leaving us feeling empty, lonely, burned-out, and searching for a sense of belonging. Brad Edwards has written a terrific and well-resourced book that helps us see that the real solution to our deepest longings for meaning and significance is not found in turning further inward or liberating ourselves, but rather in devoting ourselves to a redemptive community: the local church.

It is a brave but crucial endeavor to convince those suspicious of authority, glued to their phones, and seeking comfort anywhere else that the solution to our ailments lies in an institution they've already dismissed as irrelevant. To do so, we have to critically examine individualism's "defeater beliefs," which prevent us from grasping a true and better identity, formation, narrative, belonging, and purpose found within the church.

For example, we crave the absence of all constraints, allowing us to forge our own paths. Brad argues that while we are blazing our own futures, without any obligations to others or communal ties, we are not truly free, but rather in bondage to ourselves.

Our society rightly condemns the abuse of power but struggles with its right use. In a time when it seems that every public act is a performative power play, of course we distrust all authority figures and shy away from discussion and engagement.

Even for Christians, our culture's individualistic narrative about identity as something to be discovered and achieved and expressed is more influential than we think. It creates a subtly consumeristic mindset that sees church more as a service provider than as a spiritual family.

I could go on.

However we try to elevate our personal experience of identity, it is a counterproductive and fragile project that makes us crave validation, increases anxiety and uncertainty, and ultimately hinders our growth in community. And as Brad notes, the most heartbreaking part is that "withdrawal most often comes on the cusp of transformation. . . . We can't avoid dying to ourselves anymore" (p. 41).

After Brad carefully deconstructs these and other "defeater" narratives and acknowledges the valid human longings they represent, he doesn't stop at mere critique. He emphasizes that these narratives resonate with us because we are shaped by stories. The solution to our problems lies not in seeking more autonomy or self-discovery but in placing ourselves within the larger story of redemption. All other stories are incomplete, but inside the local church, we come together to remember and embody this narrative.

We don't have to achieve our identity or invent our own names; instead, we can live into the names given to us. By committing ourselves to the local church, we become rooted in the broader story of redemption and freed from the burden of needing to be more than who we were created to be. True freedom is not about autonomy but about learning how to live humbly and nonanxiously within the beauty of our design. Brad shows how Jesus fulfills these universal longings, and the church is the way we live them out.

Throughout the book, Brad is clear and honest that the church has not always been the community it ought to be. We've often given in to our culture's incomplete narratives. But the beauty of the church lies in the fact that it ultimately depends not on the performances of its members but on the person it points us to: Jesus Christ. As my mother used to say, "The church is not so much a museum for saints but rather a hospital for sinners." Brad's book is both a love letter to the church and a call to recognize how, in a world of commodification and dehumanization, the covenant community found in Christ offers a way forward.

For people caught up in self-interest and minimal commitment, the local church built on grace and service will radically show forth not with coercion but with care. In the church, we collectively rest in the finished work of Jesus, knowing he, unlike a world enslaved to performance, is our true freedom. He is the only one who will always accept and welcome exiles into belonging around his table. *The Reason for Church* edified me. It reminded me that, as a Christian, I am not accepted because of what I do. I live and do because I'm already accepted. And that makes all the difference in the world.

Michael Keller

Introduction

The Tower of Babel and the Body of Christ

> Perhaps a new generation of leaders will arise who want to build for
> posterity, to plant seeds that will take generations to bear fruit, to
> nurture forms of culture that will be seen as blessings by our children's
> children. If we are serious about flourishing, across space and through
> time, we will be serious about institutions.
>
> —Andy Crouch

F̲ew statements have been more validating for pastors ministering in
our cultural moment than when, in an early 2021 interview, Tim
Keller recalled telling his wife, "I got pancreatic cancer, but at least I'm
not actually a working pastor right now."[1] Keller wasn't just describing
pastoral ministry during the coronavirus pandemic. He was keenly aware
that the American social and cultural consensus was shifting rapidly and
understood that these changes would have profound implications for the
future of evangelicalism.

For many pastors and lay Christians across the country, the pandemic confirmed a growing sense that we have been ministering with

---

1. Carey Nieuwhof, host, *The Carey Nieuwhof Leadership Podcast*, Episode 583, "Tim Keller
on How He Would Preach If He Was Starting Over, His Biggest Regret, The Decline of The
Evangelical Church, and How Culture is Changing the Future of the Church," July 12, 2023,
2:31:38, https://careynieuwhof.com/episode583/.

one hand tied behind our backs. We've been missing *something*—in Scripture, culture, church, or all of the above—that made ministry feel even more like walking through a minefield than it usually did. It took the American evangelical church failing the pandemic's stress test to start questioning whether we've taken the institutional church for granted.

Early in ministry, I expected that the hardest part of being a pastor would be persuading non-Christians that God exists. By several orders of magnitude, it has been much harder to persuade *anyone* that church is good or beautiful. Some of our skepticism is rooted in bad church experiences, but this is an even greater cultural phenomenon than it is individual or personal. Overwhelmingly, distrust is now our society's default posture toward all institutions (including the church). Because I didn't even have a category for the church as an "institution"—let alone an awareness of my own anti-institutional bias—I was woefully unequipped for shepherding our church through what I only now understand as the beginning of an age defined by countless and often conflicting flavors of radical individualism. Although it sure seemed like that shift happened gradually and then suddenly during the pandemic, the signs and symptoms of change had already been spreading for several years. I just didn't recognize them as such.

My wife and I met Maria[2] over ten years ago, in the very early days of planting our church, The Table, in Lafayette, Colorado. Then, as now, she was one of the most well-connected and passionate advocates for our city. Her enthusiasm was as informed as it was infectious. So hiring her as our real estate agent to help us find a home in the community she so obviously loved and knew so well was a no-brainer.

During one of the first few days she scheduled tours of several potential houses, she asked a question I'd been (anxiously) anticipating: "So why are you moving to Lafayette?"

"Well," I said, "it might sound a little crazy, but I'm a pastor, and we're hoping to start a church here."

We knew she wasn't a Christian but not a whole lot else about what

---

2. Name changed.

she believed, spiritually or otherwise. We were moving from just outside Boulder County, so we knew the area pretty well—culturally progressive, hyperspiritual, and critically underchurched. I was prepared for all kinds of objections and negative reactions we might get along the way, but her reaction left me dumbstruck and speechless: "Oh, wow! Good for you for following your dreams!"

Friends, there are many ways to describe what motivates someone to start a church from scratch, and I can assure you that "following your dreams" is rarely one of them. Church planters belong to a unique species of "gluttons for punishment," but that's not because we *like* the sometimes-hostile reactions our vocation provokes. Jesus is simply *worth* it. I was pleasantly surprised that her reaction was so effusively positive, but I was more than a little unnerved that I had no idea how to explain why Jesus was a true and better reason for planting a church. For years I couldn't stop thinking about that conversation. It was only because of the pandemic's acceleration of existing cultural trends that I was able to see and understand the lens through which Maria viewed the world. Her reaction could not have been more faithfully delivered if she were reading directly from individualism's script.

I don't remember how I responded in the moment, but it was probably a supremely awkward version of "Gee, thanks." The only thing I knew for certain at the time was that I would be ministering in a subtly yet powerfully different world than I'd prepared for.

The Need for a New Apologetic

Thoughtful pastors and writers have spent the better part of the last century equipping the saints with apologetic tools and theological resources for communicating the Gospel in a post-Christian culture. They have blessed countless Christians, myself included. I came to faith shortly after reading C. S. Lewis's *Mere Christianity* in a single sitting. Then I read it again, cover to cover, just a few days later. I devoured Tim Keller's *The Reason for God*, wide-eyed and open-mouthed as I marveled at the intuitive simplicity of his explanations. No book outside of Scripture has more powerfully shaped my preaching and philosophy of ministry. As a former-skeptic-turned-new-believer, apologetics were more than tools for ministry and evangelism, they were sense-making ciphers that caught my mind up with what God was doing in my heart.

Imagine my bewilderment when, seemingly overnight, such incredible resources fell flat with my skeptical neighbors. In 2016, a non-Christian friend told me, about halfway through reading *The Reason for God* together, "It's fine, I guess. These are good answers. They're just not answers to the questions I'm asking." His response put flesh to Maria's reaction a year earlier and helped me understand that Christians are relatively well-equipped for a post-Christian world that objects to the existence of God. But we are wholly unprepared for a postinstitutional world that rejects any need for church.

Not having an answer to that objection has made ministry of all shapes and sizes much, much harder. And whether it's because we failed to appreciate individualism's pervasive influence (syncretism) or because we naively thought we could co-opt it for ministry (pragmatism), our discipleship might have suffered even more than our evangelism. We've equipped countless Christians to give "a reason for the hope that is in [them]" (1 Peter 3:15), but not how to *get* that hope in them. Precious few Christians understand that our hope in Christ is collectively and ordinarily experienced and derived from within his Body. That omission has become so implicitly embedded in the DNA of our spiritual formation that we've made multiple generations of very lopsided disciples who are church agnostic at best: they know and love Jesus but could take or leave his bride. And for many who grew up in church, leaving has even become a virtue and mark of spiritual maturity.

They leave for the same reason Maria didn't really need to know why we wanted to start a church. It was enough to know that we wanted to. What more reason does one need than to follow their desires wherever and however they lead? Whether they lead us into church or out of church, we assume by default that desire is our purest guide to what is true, good, and beautiful.

In 2016, when my friend said *The Reason for God* didn't seem to answer his questions, like any halfway decent pastor, I asked what some of those questions were. Every one shared a root skepticism of institutions. To my surprise, he was open to God. Eager, even. It was church he couldn't get on board with. *The Reason for Church* is the product of my wrestling with those questions in the decade since, and an initial answer to them in the form of a cultural apologetic for the institutional church.

The Tower of Babel and the Roots of Radical Individualism

Sometime after Adam and Eve's rebellion got them kicked out of Eden but right before God promised to redeem it all through the descendants of a childless geriatric named "Abram," a fall-weary humanity came upon a wide, flat plain that seemed like prime real estate for building an Eden of their own. The horizon-spanning open space would afford them quite a view from which to see any approaching threats, but it could also *be* seen from far and wide. "We could build such a tower," they might've thought to themselves, "that our fame will spread even farther than the eye can see, drawing more people to establish our fledgling society. We can finally have *a refuge of our own making*."

Most Christians familiar with the Tower of Babel in Genesis 11 have heard it told as a cautionary tale of human hubris and ambition. While that's true, it isn't the full story. God's primary concern wasn't that their aspiration outpaced their ability. It was the exact opposite: ". . . this is only the beginning of what they will do. And nothing that they propose to do will now be impossible for them" (v. 6). God wasn't surprised by what his own creation was capable of. He made humanity in his own image. They might not have been able to literally build the tower all the way up to the heavens, but they were on the verge of achieving something significant, something that required God's direct intervention before it was too late. The hubris he was most worried about was not architectural or vocational, but existential and related to their post-fall *nature*. They wanted to "make a name for [themselves]" (Genesis 11:4).

Our name is about far more than just our reputation or notoriety. It's about identity. The tower, with all its height and grandeur, was just a means to that end. A source from which they could draw dignity, value, and worth like water from a tap. To "make a name for [themselves]" is to say they do not need the power, resources, or reputation of any *other* name to go on existing. It's about independence and self-reliance. That venture didn't end any better for them than it does for us. Still, God was gracious. Confusing their language, and thus their ability to communicate or connect with each other, was a severe mercy that ultimately prevented them from existing apart from God and their creaturely design.

Historically speaking, Christendom often gets a bad rap for valid reasons, but it undeniably inculcated a very good and biblical individuality—the assumed value of individual dignity, agency, and conscience—into the DNA of Western society. Those values can, by common grace, be found in other societies and cultures, but none nearly so consistently or comprehensively as those where the church has a significant historical presence.

The more post-Christian society becomes, the more our individuality is rapidly metastasizing into individualism—an ideological, moral, and even religious commitment to self-definition. Whatever adjective we attach to it (e.g., expressive or radical), individualism aspires to *achieve* rather than *receive* our identity.[3] Though Babel's builders were the first to make a name for themselves, modern individualism bears an uncanny spiritual resemblance.

Where individuality is the right and good implication of being created in the image of God, individualism is an ideology amplified by the fall (Genesis 3). It melts down God's good gift of an individual's inherent

---

3. This concept and definition comes from Robert N. Bellah, Richard Madsen, William M. Sullivan, Ann Swidler, and Steven M. Tipton, *Habits of the Heart: Individualism and Commitment in American Life* (University of California Press, 2007).

dignity, value, and worth to reshape and recast it in our own image and on our own terms. Though Babel's means may differ, our motives are eerily consistent across time, place, and circumstance. Whether via family or career success, online platforms or in-person activism, winning championships or elections, self-expression or self-liberation, or following our dreams or following our desires, someone who grew up in an individualistic culture like ours will default to ordering their lives toward making a name for themselves.

But there are *always* trade-offs. There are always unforeseen costs in leaving old ways to forge new paths. Over and over again, Scripture uses every creative and literary means possible to explain that even when we think we've found what we're looking for, apart from God, it rarely makes us happy for long. Genesis follows the implications of the fall from our individual relationships with each other (Cain and Abel, Genesis 4) to humanity's relationship with creation (the flood, Genesis 6). The Tower of Babel is an equally tragic story that explains how sin compromises our collective relationship with God. In other words, it shows the fall's impact on institutions and the relationships they're built out of. Straying from God's design and purpose will inevitably lead to the fracturing and scattering of *what we make of each other*.

An Institutional Meta-Crisis

The implications of a churchless Christianity are legion, and none of them offer the goodness or beauty we're made for. The widespread erosion of mental health, a worldwide loneliness epidemic, unending political turmoil, and the fastest dechurching movement in American history are not a perfect storm of coinciding crises, but symptoms of a single meta-crisis: a growing inability to solve collective problems collectively. Ours is in an institutional crisis, and one largely of our own making.

But before you start gathering populist kindling to burn institutions at the stake, realize they're also our only way out of this mess. I am fully aware that few words cause more eyes to glaze over or induce more naps than the word "institution," but that's primarily because we've completely forgotten the vital role they play in our search for identity.

Andy Crouch says institutions are arenas, not unlike a football stadium: "An arena provides the context where all the participants in a football game, not just players but coaches, crew, referees, broadcasters and fans, can participate most fully and wholeheartedly, and where the artifacts associated with the game are used most skillfully and meaningfully."[4] There are very real differences between various football arenas, but because they are all built for the same purpose and share the same norms, anyone can step into a new stadium and know how to play their role. A quarterback traded to a new team might have to learn new plays, but stealing second base won't be in any playbook. Similarly, a Christian walking into a new church might have to learn new songs, but Madonna's "Like a Virgin" won't be one of them.

Most institutions aren't nearly as exciting as a football game. They are slow-moving, inconsistent, and messy because people are. Human formation is rarely linear and doesn't happen overnight. It never happens on our own. We need time and space to grow together in an environment organized by consistent expectations and mutual reciprocation. The institutions of marriage, family, and higher education are all examples of social spaces and guardrails that, when healthy and not straying from God's design or their shared purpose, guide and nurture everything that makes us most beautifully and wonderfully made.

We desperately need more and healthier institutions because, at their core, institutions are a culturally adaptive and common grace social technology—a means for groups of people to cultivate and preserve values, organize themselves for specific ends, and steward power that individuals can't (or shouldn't) on their own. Municipalities solve crime problems that residents can't solve on their own. Nonprofit organizations solve economic, housing, medical, and other problems that the poor can't solve on their own. Universities solve all kinds of problems, but especially

---

4. Andy Crouch, "Football and the Gift of Institutions by Andy Crouch," Qideas.org, archived December 13, 2023, at https://web.archive.org/web/20231214110140/http://208.106.253.109/blog/football-and-the-gift-of-institutions.aspx.

the vocational and research variety that the uneducated can't solve on their own. Congress solves legislative and societal problems that neither citizens nor politicians can solve on their own (hypothetically). As our ordinary means of grace, every local church is a *redemptive* institution: God's ordained vehicle for making himself known to our neighbors and making disciples of all nations. In and through the body of Christ, God applies grace to the problems of sin, brokenness, and alienation that none of us can solve on our own.

We dramatically overestimate technology's ability to solve those problems.

We've always had a love-hate relationship with institutions, but long-standing expectations over the speed of social change, reform, and progress are increasingly reshaped by new tech and media that promise to deliver answers and solutions like magic. And sometimes they do. But having our expectations met at the speed of light isn't always good. It can feed resentment and distrust of anything that seems slow to change or accommodate our desires. Without at least some institutional participation, we will inevitably forget that some good only comes slowly, that constraint might flourish rather than oppress us, and that rights incur a responsibility to consider others in how we exercise them. Instead, we will come to see that anything less than instant gratification is sclerotic, "bureaucracy" is an irredeemably dirty word, and that all our problems would be solved if (insert institution here) would read the room and stop harshing our mellow.

Just look to the unraveling of journalism for the consequences. We now distrust the few remaining journalists still bound by such outdated traditions as checking facts with multiple sources. In our bias toward speed, we place our trust in independent journalists and freelancers. We assume they're more reliable because they aren't beholden to any institution. Yet truth is too easily sacrificed in the rush to shape a narrative or have ours confirmed. Getting what we want when we want it has only reinforced confirmation bias, fueled polarization, and further eroded our trust in all institutional journalism.

That same pattern is playing out in varying degrees across every social and spiritual institution in America. The resulting meta-crisis is more than our abandonment of institutions; it's also the unraveling of the social cohesion and formation they provide. We can all feel it—the atmospheric suspicion and cynicism infiltrating every nook and cranny of society. In less than a decade, we went from fighting to believe we can thrive together to settling for surviving on our own.

Many of our institutions are riddled with abuse and corruption and in desperate need of reform, but throwing the baby out with the bathwater doesn't solve our problems; it guarantees we won't. Being utterly free to achieve our individual identities isn't delivering greater personal peace and security, but systemic depression and anxiety. Self-definition is self-defeating. Without the mediating institutions that make up our social fabric and obligate us to one another, we feel tossed to and fro by every wind of change. Every election cycle feels like living through an existential hurricane, each requiring an escalation in dehumanizing rhetoric to gain the attention of a desensitized and burnt-out populace. Institutions that haven't cracked under that pressure are often too worn out and/or divided by culture wars for us to feel like we can rely on them for the shelter and stability they provided in previous periods of social upheaval.

Repairing that damage takes decades, if not generations, and building healthy institutions is challenging under ideal circumstances. Circa 2015, church planting was said to have a 50 percent failure rate. I shudder to think what it might be in an era of exponentially higher baseline skepticism of pastors. In this environment, running for election to your local school board, city council, or even *dog catcher* is signing up for verbal abuse, if not worse. No matter where we turn, we can't seem to get past the misinformed certainty that nothing we build will be true, good, or beautiful enough to last or be worth the effort. Burning down the wrong, unjust, and ugly things others have built is much easier and offers us a temporary high of having done something to make a difference. Whether that difference is a net good rarely crosses our minds. It feels too good not to be. Long term, it only divides us further.

Nascent reservoirs of individualism are no longer dammed up or held back by the counterbalancing sociocultural values, virtues, or incentives historically formed and shaped by institutions. None of us can say whether that's a result of God directly inflicting a Babel-like confusion upon us or if we're just experiencing the inevitable consequence of a zero-sum competition for dignity, value, and worth. Regardless, our society seems hell-bent on making a name for ourselves apart from God—often in his name but always at each other's expense—and it's tearing us apart.

But it doesn't have to.

The Church Is Our Way Out

Unsurprisingly, God has already given us the means we need to address this crisis: the body of Christ. By that I mean much more than the sum of individual believers across time and space. And I also don't mean that our collective action problem can be solved by Christians acting collectively. The confusion fueling our division is deeper than that. If institutions are, generally, "what we make of each other," then the specific spiritual institution we call the church is *what God uses to make us more like Jesus*. We don't need better answers or faster technology. We'll just use it to further dehumanize ourselves and each other. We need to be rehumanized. To become, individually and collectively, a more Christlike people. Only within God's redemptive institution— the church—can sinners and sojourners be brought in, built up, and sent out to spiritually, socially, and culturally terraform a world made inhospitable by radical individualism.

For anyone who sees the church as a major (if not primary) reason for our dysfunction, that probably sounds ludicrous. If that's you, I get it. You're not wrong, but you might still be missing the bigger picture. What if your skepticism is at least partly the result of cultural assumptions you don't even know you have? What if we are all suffering from Stockholm syndrome with individualism, and that's why it's so hard to see or trust any true, good, or beautiful reasons for church? Whatever your answer, you have nothing to lose and everything to gain in asking questions like these.

If I'm right, and our institutional meta-crisis isn't limited to the church, then connecting the dots between major cultural undercurrents should make it much easier to see where deep-seeded assumptions are diminishing the place and purpose of the church in our lives. We can rectify that by apprehending the reasons for church, but those reasons won't be fully believable until we are freed from our cultural captivity.

Toward that end, **part 1** of this book examines several "church defeaters" of individualism—the implicit cultural beliefs that make church seem like an implausible, if not impossible, refuge for human flourishing. Their power is in sounding compatible enough with Scripture or common sense that most Christians uncritically embrace them and most church leaders struggle to explain why they shouldn't. Unaddressed, they can even lead us to believe we're being *more* faithful or spiritual by keeping Christ's bride at arm's length. I spend the first half of the book evaluating these church defeaters on their own terms because they are culturally upstream of conscious belief. Showing that they *can't* deliver on their promise is essential for fully seeing the true, good, and beautiful reasons for church.

Therein lies the beginning of good news: our hunger to build a modern Tower of Babel proves the existence of a received identity greater than any we can achieve. Each church defeater is an implicit admission that modern life has become inhospitable to human flourishing and is unable to offer the lasting dignity, value, or worth we're made for. With fresh awareness of individualism's pervasive influence, **part 2** will then explore five especially acute and neglected ways the body of Christ is, surprisingly, exactly the refuge we're searching for.

God gave us an incredible gift. Within the body of Christ, God's means of grace are ordinarily found and our existential longing satisfied.

PART 1

Babel's Brick and Mortar

> Come, let us build ourselves a city and a tower with its top
> in the heavens, and let us make a name for ourselves, lest we
> be dispersed over the face of the whole earth.
>
> —Genesis 11:4

I was first introduced to the idea of "defeater beliefs" by Tim Keller's seminal book, *The Reason for God*, where he addressed the ten most common intellectual objections to belief in God that he encountered in his day-to-day ministry in New York City. He clearly and graciously demonstrated that despite each objection's very intuitive and common-sense reasonableness, the vast majority of us don't arrive at our conclusions by evidence, reason, or any other purely rational process. Instead, defeater beliefs operate at the level of cultural assumption. Taken on the basis of faith, they "automatically make Christianity seem implausible to people,"[1] or preclude Christian faith altogether.

---

1. "Every culture hostile to Christianity holds to a set of 'common-sense' consensus beliefs that automatically make Christianity seem implausible to people. These are what philosophers call 'defeater beliefs.' A defeater belief is Belief-A that, if true, means Belief-B *can't* be true." Tim

Similarly, our modern Tower of Babel is constructed out of five defeaters that operate on the same level (cultural assumption) and function in the same way (precluding other beliefs), but with respect to church instead of God. They're not theological[2] as much as ecclesiological and experiential in their downstream impact, and they reflect our culture's ongoing transition from modernity to post-modernity. Where Tim Keller's original defeater beliefs were primarily objections birthed from enlightenment rationalism, church defeaters are rooted in biblical values that have become so distorted by secularism that they're now Christian in name only (i.e., post-Christian). On their own or together, these church defeaters are components of individualism's implausibility structure,[3] inoculating us from God's institutional means of grace (the church) and stunting our discipleship. And while God is certainly not limited or unable to save image bearers apart from the church, according to the consistent witness of the Old and New Testaments, that is clearly an exception[4] and not the rule. Our discomfort with the necessity of church is itself a symptom of our cultural conditioning and assumption that our identity must be individually achieved rather than received from Christ through his body and bride.

Each of the first five chapters will cover a different defeater that makes church seem an implausible or impossible refuge in our age of radical individualism. Some are primarily systemic with profound implications downstream (e.g., chapters 1 and 3), some are more purely cultural (e.g., chapters 2 and 5), but all involve an interplay between cultural and spiritual formation (especially chapter 4). I'll explain throughout how church defeaters, despite seeming compatible with Christian beliefs, are better understood as expressions of individualism—the brick and mortar we've used to build our own Tower of Babel. But they're also inferior materials. They're unsustainable and unsatisfying replacements for what

---

Keller, "Deconstructing Defeater Beliefs: Leading the Secular to Christ," 1, https://www.goodsoil .com/docs/DeconstructingDefeaterBeliefs.pdf, emphasis original.

2. This is a bit of a false dichotomy in that there is no ecclesiology that isn't essentially theological. My point is more about how the defeater operates and its implications.

3. Keller, "Deconstructing Defeater Beliefs."

4. For example, Philip and Ethiopian eunuch in Acts 8:26–40.

is true, good, and beautiful. And so much so, in fact, that they don't hold up even by their *own* standards.

Keep in mind that these are defeater *beliefs*, not defeater *behaviors*. We need a fresh perspective more than new application. Debunking a church defeater isn't a matter of changing what we do in church so much as it is about changing how we *see* church. For that, we first need to zoom out far enough to see where individualism has distorted how we view our relationship with God and each other.

The primary application for part 1, then, is twofold. First, use each chapter like a magnifying lens for intentionally examining your own heart. Do you see patterns of self-actualization (chapter 1) in what you expect from your church? Has intuitional spirituality (chapter 2) made it harder for you to ask for help or hear loving rebuke from those who know you well? To what degree has anti-vision (chapter 4) made you frustrated with other believers who vote differently than you? After that, put on each chapter like a pair of prescription sunglasses as you go about daily life. Do your convictions reflect God's good news or an anxiety-fueled newsfeed (chapter 3)? Where do you see virtuous victimhood (chapter 4) weaponized by public figures?

Second, notice and grab hold of whatever questions come to mind as you read. It's a safe bet that they are signs that your own Tower of Babel is being dismantled and you're starting to see Jesus, his bride, and yourself more clearly.

Despite all my doom and gloom, viewing our cultural moment through the lens of Genesis 11 offers at least one surprising hope that's easy to miss. The fall of Babel was "both preventative (he stops them from achieving the unified and centralized closure that they desire) and compulsory (he forces them to scatter across the earth, as originally intended ...)."[5] The consequences were undoubtedly painful, but God knew that allowing Babel to use their God-given ability to build a city (institutions) and make a name (identity) for themselves would only

---

5. Christopher J. H. Wright, *The Mission of God: Unlocking the Bible's Grand Narrative* (IVP, 2006), 197.

further entrench them in rebellion. God confused and scattered Babel to frustrate their autonomy and force humanity back onto the path he designed for their flourishing—the cultural mandate he first gave Adam and Eve in Genesis 1:28.

What if, whether by direct intervention or natural consequence, God is allowing our modern Tower of Babel (individualism) to collapse under its own weight and for the same effect? What if he intends to use all our dysfunction and polarization and stubbornness to ultimately restore something we've lost, even if nothing about our present moment feels especially redemptive? Only God can say for sure, but God's intervention at Babel implies that the unsustainability of our current trajectory isn't all bad. It could be a severe mercy that reintroduces redemptive guardrails that God will use to put us back on track. If we're learning anything through our cultural moment, it's that we definitely cannot flourish apart from God, either as individuals or as a society. And even if we could, he loves us too much to let us. That means, at the very least, that we can't mess this up. No matter what happens, we can rest assured that God is steadfast in his love and faithfulness to his people (the church) and that Jesus is, even now, making all things new. Nothing is too far gone for God to co-opt for our redemption, including our own rebellion. And if that's the case, then he will even prevent even our *dismantling* of our modern Babel from being another way we make a name for ourselves. The point isn't to build a better tower and call it church but to entrust ourselves to Jesus in and through his broken but beloved people.

With that freedom, let's begin.

1

Spiritual Pragmatism

*How Seeker Sensitivity and
Self-Actualization Reduce the
Church to a Spiritual Nonprofit*

Why is religion less popular with Millennials? In short, because it is not compatible with individualism—and individualism is Millennials' core value above all else. Individualism promotes focusing on the self and finding your own way, and religion ... promotes focusing on things larger than the self and following certain rules.

—Jean Twenge

Church Defeater 1: Spiritual Pragmatism. Because churches exist to facilitate our personal spiritual growth and help us fulfill our unique potential, following Jesus faithfully may require leaving or switching churches for one that better meets our spiritual needs.

I t was largely despite the church that I came to faith my junior year of college at Truman State University—a public liberal arts university in Missouri. Up to that point, I'd proudly considered myself a skeptic of all organized religion, especially Christianity. I skipped class to argue with the open-air preachers and evangelists that a few local churches often invited to yell "repent!" at students as they walked to and from classes. When a very kind, well-intentioned Christian tried explaining the gospel to me over lunch in our dorm's cafeteria, I rudely told him he could tell me about Jesus only after he explained how a global flood could be reconciled with the geological record (I've since apologized). It was only after a failed relationship and a year-long depression that I ran out of answers, swallowed my pride, and got desperate enough to walk into the auditorium where a campus ministry met for Sunday worship.

It's very possible I still oozed more skepticism than openness, but I went three times before someone other than a greeter spoke to me. Jared lived in the dorm room next to mine, and I still remember the surprised look on his face when he saw me standing in the back where I was trying not to stick out like a vegan at a Texas BBQ.

"Brad! I didn't know you were a Christian!" I'd invited him to my fraternity's parties a few times the previous semester, and he'd seen me emerge hungover from my room enough that his surprise was more than fair.

"Well, uhh, I'm not actually . . ."

"Wait, then why . . . *oh*. Uhh, you want someone to sit with?"

I didn't mention that I'd angrily told God the night before that this was his last chance to prove he was real, that if I had to go to church one more time without anyone talking to me or inviting me to sit with them, I was done. Instead, I asked him about our dorm's Bible study mentioned during announcements. "You're interested in that?" he asked. "I mean, you want to come with me tomorrow night?" Just a few months later, Jesus saved me from myself and I was baptized into new life.

I'm both a Christian and a pastor because God used Jared to answer my (angry) prayer that morning, but I became a church planter because

Jared should not have been the first to notice and welcome his neighbor. For years afterward, I was convinced that Christians struggled to invite or welcome our non-Christian neighbors to church because we were too comfortable and too consumed with "church stuff." In my early days as a pastor, I regularly encouraged Christians to spend less time in church so they would have more time with their neighbors. I could not have been more misguided.

According to Jim Davis and Michael Graham in *The Great Dechurching*, we are in the midst of the largest and fastest religious shift in US history. As the title suggests, it's not a good shift. Forty million American adults have stopped going to church over the last twenty-five years. That's more than came to faith "during the First Great Awakening, Second Great Awakening, and the totality of the Billy Graham Crusades combined."[1] Perhaps even more surprising is *why* people are dechurching. Contrary to the impression given by viral posts and headlines, the single most common reason people stop going to church isn't political disagreement, spiritual abuse, or any other headline-topping or attention-grabbing controversies . . .

It's because *they moved.*

That's right. They moved to a new city or state, and they either never tried looking for a new church or lost hope of finding one that fit.

Think about that for a second.

Most of us can empathize with the very real challenge of restarting your life in a new place or the weird awkwardness of "church shopping." It's not a quick or easy process. But you wouldn't stop going to grocery stores if you couldn't find one you like as much as your old one. No one can go without food. Yet if "man shall not live by bread alone, but by every word that comes from the mouth of God" (Matthew 4:4), how have so many Christians come to see participating in the community birthed, nourished, and matured by the Word of God as any less essential for survival? Whatever our specific reasons might

---

1. Jim Davis and Michael Graham with Ryan P. Burge, *The Great Dechurching: Who's Leaving, Why Are They Going, and What Will It Take to Bring Them Back?* (Zondervan, 2023), 5.

be, something has changed that makes us think that we either don't need what churches are offering, or that we can find it elsewhere and by some other means.

That reasoning is the essence of our first church defeater: spiritual pragmatism.

The Oxford Dictionary defines pragmatism as "an approach that assesses the truth of meaning of theories or beliefs in terms of success of their practical application." *Spiritual* pragmatism goes beyond a simple assessment of a church's effectiveness. It is the unexamined assumption that churches exist to meet our spiritual needs and help us grow into our full potential. Fueled by individualism's need to achieve identity and make a name for ourselves, this utilitarian mindset values a church by how well it serves as a vehicle for our self-actualization. Wherever spiritual pragmatism takes root in churches, Christians will be implicitly, if not explicitly, taught to view discipleship, and faith itself, through a self-centered and transactional lens.

We'll get back to spiritual pragmatism in a moment, but it's helpful to start with self-actualization because it's easier to see for most of us. Secular self-actualization embraces almost any means of fulfilling one's potential. What matters most is that you are in the driver's seat and not some other person, institution, or tradition. The "how" must be up to you. Self-actualization is so baked into American culture that it has subtly influenced evangelical approaches to discipleship, making one's own spiritual growth the *telos*, or purpose, of the Christian life, instead of the fruit or by-product of following Jesus. Self-actualizing "discipleship" isn't more than what Scripture calls us to, but less. It reduces the scope of Christian faithfulness to personal spiritual practices like Bible study and prayer.

Now, don't get me wrong—individual spiritual disciples are very good and essential ingredients of healthy Christian piety. But it's a sure sign that we are slipping into self-actualization when piety becomes an imbalanced piet*ism* that overvalues individual spiritual practices to the neglect of more outward-facing (e.g., evangelism) and communal acts of faithfulness (e.g., weekly worship) that aren't necessarily meeting our "spiritual needs." We are called to be faithful and trust God to give the growth, but evangelical self-actualization functionally puts the ultimate responsibility for both on our shoulders. Because we are at least intuitively aware that we can't carry that burden on our own, we expect our church to make that burden easier to carry. We will become convinced that it is impossible to faithfully follow Jesus if our church doesn't make it easy to pick up our cross.

These expectations may not prevent us from joining a local church, but they will keep us from *staying* in one. As long as a church's ministries feel like they're sufficiently supporting our spiritual growth, life is good! But if that doesn't happen on our terms or on our timeline, we project our disappointment onto our church—saying it's inadequate or has failed altogether. At that point, being faithful means leaving our church for one with ministries more aligned with our expectations of spiritual growth.

You might've already identified the flaw in that reasoning: no matter how well a church meets our needs at any given moment, a church filled (never mind *staffed*) with sinners saved by grace is bound to disappoint and fail us eventually. So when our disappointment is so closely linked to how we understand the *telos* of the Christian life (self-actualization), the temptation to leave for another church starts lurking sooner with every iteration. Even if a given church actually has enough resources to meet and satisfy our spiritual pragmatism, it will unintentionally reinforce and perpetuate our self-actualization. With enough repetition, our attachment to *any* church can dissolve completely.

So, how did we get here? How did self-actualization become so embedded in the DNA of our discipleship? Ironically, our obsession with our own individual growth is the product of evangelical churches using corporate growth strategies (bad means) to reach non-Christians (good end). Much like the tension experienced between a parent and their teenager as they come of age, modern spiritual pragmatism is both the progeny of the seeker sensitive movement and a generational reaction against it. To illustrate that paradoxical relationship, let me introduce you to Luke and Sarah.

The Paradox of
Spiritual Pragmatism

"It's just too . . . I don't know, *institutional*. You know what I mean?"

Sarah and her husband, Luke, had moved to the Boulder area several months earlier and, like many coming from more churched contexts, they were really struggling to find a church that felt like a good fit for both of them. The church they'd been attending was big but not huge, with several full-time staff, a thriving children's ministry to serve the area's many young families, and a new building they were filling faster than they could add services to accommodate the growth. They were one of the better seeker sensitive churches in our area, whose sermons, worship services, and ministry programs were all designed to reach non-Christians seeking deeper spiritual truth.

"And that's great," she reassured me, "but I'm just in a really different place. I need something with more *depth*." She went on to describe a false dichotomy that's common among Christians coming from seeker friendly churches. Namely, the false choice between depth and breadth of growth. The assumption that we have to neglect or set aside our own spiritual growth to reach non-Christians isn't the fruit of emphasizing evangelism but of discipling Christians to see themselves and their neighbors as consumers of spiritual goods and services. So if a church is trying to reach non-Christian "customers," it's easy for Christians to feel left out or neglected. But that doesn't need to be the case.

"Well," I replied, "that doesn't sound too institutional to me. What you're describing sounds more *corporate*, like a church trying to offer spiritual fruit to customers instead of cultivating it in disciples." Even though that distinction was still under-developed in our fledgling church plant, I explained that helping Christians see and understand the difference was quickly becoming a major emphasis in The Table's ministry. It had the encouraging and clarifying effect I'd hoped for.

Not long into my explanation, Sarah elbowed her husband in the ribs as if to say, "See! This is what I mean!"

Let's pause for a moment. Until now, I've left out a pretty important bit of information. I failed to mention why they moved to the area: Luke was hired as one of the pastors of their church. During our conversation, I assumed Luke was planning to resign and wanted to explore whether our church might be a good place to worship until they figured out what was next. That's why, after I'd briefly described how our church has tried to avoid the pitfalls Sarah described, I was shocked when Luke smiled and said, "It sounds like you've finally found a church home, honey!"

Sarah apparently noticed my confusion in Luke's use of "you" rather than "we"—I have a terrible poker face—and explained, "Oh, it'll just be me. Luke will still attend [the church he serves as a pastor] on Sundays."

It turns out that Luke was quite happy in his role as a pastor and liked their current church just fine. He was just there to support Sarah and help her find a church that would help her grow in her walk with Jesus.

Like most pastors, I take a day off other than Sunday to Sabbath because it's hard to fully turn off and rest the same day you're preaching or leading worship. There are all kinds of ways vocational ministry makes being a "normal" Christian more difficult and requires creative adaptation. This isn't one of them. When I asked if they were worried that attending different churches could put their marriage on different formative trajectories of growth, they expressed confusion. It hadn't even occurred to them, and they wondered what made me think it was even possible in the first place.

If that's confusing for you too, it's likely that most or all of your church experience has been in a church that was highly influenced by the seeker sensitive movement. Indeed, even if seeker language is brand-new to you, the movement's philosophy of ministry has been so dominant within evangelicalism that very few *don't* view their church through a similar lens. To change that, we have to understand just how much our modern view of church has been culturally, historically, and generationally conditioned whether we realize it or not.

The Lasting Influence of Boomer Pragmatism

It was Sarah's first description of their current church that first got my attention. "Too institutional" is a critique now so common that it's cliché, but it was first used by young baby boomers to describe any community or organization they saw as too slow to reform or allergic to change. While they were mostly right about the symptoms of that allergy, they misdiagnosed the underlying cause.

Most churches in the mid-20th century weren't too institutional. They were simply too exhausted. Boomers are the children of "the Greatest Generation" (born between 1901 and 1927), who endured several lifetimes-worth of hardship and sacrifice to bring the world back from the brink of disaster after disaster: WWI, the Spanish Flu (which killed 5% of the world's population), the Great Depression, and WWII. They, and the institutions they led, already had their fill of conflict, change, and revolution. So, of course, their churches were allergic to change. They more than earned the right to a long nap.

Baby boomers could not have experienced a more different childhood and adolescence. They grew up during a veritable explosion of economic growth that definitively reshaped American norms and expectations. The "war dividend" set baby boomers up as a market force unto themselves. In the roughly two decades after they were born (1946–1964), car and home ownership became the norm. College became an option not just for white collar elites but for hard-working blue-collar Americans as well. Over the course of a single generation, becoming a cultural elite first became possible for the average American. As the largest generation ever born, boomers were also the first generation to be collectively targeted by mass media and marketing as a unified (and therefore, predictable) demographic. The post-war reordering of nearly every economic incentive around boomers' needs and dreams infused individual achievement and fulfilling one's potential with the weight of a moral imperative. Ever-greater access to consumer products and services cultivated parallel expectations of ever-greater vocational opportunities, social standing, and political influence (e.g., the civil rights movement and the sexual revolution). If you couldn't make something of yourself, you were either lazy or ate too much avocado toast. Either way, something was wrong with you.

It is impossible to overstate how much the baby boomer experience still dominates the American consciousness. As Yuval Levin writes in *The Fractured Republic*, we all "see our recent history through the boomers' eyes" and "have no self-understanding of our country in the years since World War II that is not in some fundamental way a baby-boomer narrative."[2] That self-understanding isn't limited to historical musing; it has been passed on, forming and shaping the interpretive lens of subsequent generations. Over approximately two decades, stretching from the late '50s to the early '70s, almost every dimension of American life went through a generational metamorphosis that has lasted into the present day, including the local church. We inherited our distrust of institutions like any other family trait.

The Birth of Seeker Sensitivity

Discouraged and frustrated with denominational churches that seemed more concerned with preserving tradition and cultural preferences than reaching the lost, baby boomer pastors like Bill Hybels, the founding pastor of Willow Creek Community Church, sought a more modern, nimble, and culturally relevant (i.e., more familiar and less alienating to non-Christians) expression of church by incorporating new ideas, research, media, and technology. In an interview with *Christianity Today*, Hybels summarized that aspiration as trying to create a more "biblically functioning community that has a full-orbed approach to bringing people to Christ, assimilating them into the body of Christ, discipling them, helping them find their spiritual gifts, and sensitizing them to the needs of the world."[3] The churches that resulted

---

2. Yuval Levin, *The Fractured Republic: Renewing America's Social Contract in the Age of Individualism* (Basic Books, 2016), 27.

3. Michael Maudlin, Edward Gilbreath, Kevin Miller interview with Bill Hybels, "Selling Out the House of God?, Part 1," *Christianity Today*, July 18, 1994, https://www.christianitytoday.com/ct/1994/july18/4t820a.html.

were driven by a straight-forward pragmatism: do whatever it takes to reach non-Christians with the gospel and deepen discipleship within the church.

While the aspirations behind seeker sensitivity were noble, a "whatever it takes" pragmatism turned out to be a Trojan horse. When an institution (e.g., a church) uncritically adopts or adapts to present cultural norms and fads, it can inadvertently smuggle in other assumptions that seem innocent at first yet prove dangerous over time. I took great pains to describe the historical background, economic forces, and generational dynamics above to explain why boomer pragmatism naturally gravitated toward corporate growth strategies yet didn't foresee the downstream consequences. The same pragmatic strategies that produced multiple decades of explosive growth also smuggled *marketplace logic* into the church.

In a near-perfect illustration of that blind spot, Bill Hybels reportedly hung a quote from management guru Peter Drucker right outside his office at Willow Creek Community Church: "What is our business? Who is our customer? What does the customer value?"[4] Such marketplace logic is entirely appropriate for a business or for-profit corporation. But churches are supposed to assume the logic of the kingdom. The questions hanging outside Hybels office should have read, "Who is our king? What does he value? Who must we become to love our neighbor?"

The Failure of Marketplace Logic

If W. Edwards Deming's popular adage that "every system is perfectly designed to get the result that it does" is accurate, then the upstream incorporation of marketplace logic both supercharged ministry innovation and fundamentally reshaped the evangelical church. Executive Pastor Greg Hawkins articulated that very spirit in Willow Creek's commitment to "fundamentally change the way we do church" by replacing "all of our old assumptions . . . (with) insights informed by

---

4. "Trusting the Teacher in the Grey-Flannel Suit," *The Economist*, November 17, 2005, https://www.economist.com/special-report/2005/11/17/trusting-the-teacher-in-the-grey-flannel-suit.

research and rooted in scripture."[5] That dream, in many ways, became a reality. The modern praise band and Contemporary Christian Music (CCM), as well as youth pastors, small groups, and life-stage-based ministries are just a few of the era's ministry innovations now considered typical (if not essential) contours of the evangelical landscape. Countless books were written advocating for one model or another as the most effective evangelistic or discipleship strategy.

Unfortunately, in discarding so many traditions, these new churches lacked the historical perspective needed to understand which insights are truly *rooted in* Scripture and which they had merely *read into* Scripture. Perhaps counterintuitively, neglecting that distinction compromised seeker sensitivity's long-term ministry on multiple levels, but especially in basic discipleship.

For decades, Willow Creek Community Church and thousands of seeker sensitive churches emulating them operated off a fundamental premise: greater participation in ministry programs and activities (input) would result in greater spiritual growth and maturity (output). Wash. Rinse. Repeat. Except that the results of Willow Creek Association's own comprehensive multiyear qualitative study showed that "increasing levels of participation in these sets of activities does NOT predict whether someone's becoming more of a disciple of Christ. It does NOT predict whether they love God more or they love people more."[6]

Just let that sit for a minute.

At the time that article was published, Hybels had spent thirty years successfully spreading the seeker sensitive way of doing church. In the article, he dubbed this *generational* effort to fundamentally change the way we do church a "mistake" that bore no discernible fruit in discipleship.

Can we be honest? That's not a mistake. It's a catastrophe. Drucker's logic may have made church more accessible for seekers—those who are considered "of the world"—by remaking church in their own (baby

---

5. C. M. S. Admin, "Willow Creek Repents?," *Christianity Today*, October 18, 2007, https://www.christianitytoday.com/2007/10/willow-creek-repents/.

6. Admin.

boomer) image, but it also emptied church of what makes it "not of the world" and, therefore, what non-Christians are seeking in the first place.

Shortly after moving to the area where we were hoping to plant a church, a neighbor invited us to join them and some friends for dinner at a local BBQ joint. Upon learning that I was a pastor, one of them immediately asked what I thought about the nearby megachurch. Their worship services are a particularly well-orchestrated example of the seeker sensitive brand you'd expect of most megachurches: an inspiring-yet-practical sermon bookended by worship music performed by a professional band, all excellently produced with dazzling lights and smoke machines. Or, as it has come to be (disdainfully) known, "a Coldplay concert with a TED Talk."

When I asked why she was asking, she explained without hesitation that she wasn't a Christian, had only ever set foot in a church for weddings, and "didn't believe any of that stuff" largely because of polarizing political differences constantly amplified on cable and social media (which she thought this church exemplified the worst of). However, she figured that if she was going to be critical of a church, the least she could do was visit on a Sunday morning to make sure she was being fair. So she did. Not once or twice but *three times*. That coincidence with how I came to faith more than got my attention.

Her primary takeaway surprised her as much as it did me. Something bothered her even more than having her suspicions about the church's politics confirmed, and she'd been thinking about it ever since: "If faith is about something bigger than everyday life, shouldn't Sunday look and feel different than Monday through Saturday?"

Friends, forgive me for pointing out the obvious, but is this not the very problem seeker sensitivity has spent decades reinventing church and ministry in order to solve? Here we have a non-Christian willing to visit a church (three times!) despite her skepticism, and her overall experience was essentially too familiar to be compelling or attractive.

After decades of telling our neighbors that church is just like everything they're already familiar with, they're starting to believe us.

In 2013, Andy Crouch saw this writing on the wall: "One of the great tragedies of the church in America is how many of our most creative leaders poured their energies into *creating forms of church life that served just a single generation*. Even when these efforts were built around something larger than a single personality, they were doomed to seem dated and 'irrelevant' even to the children of their founders."[7]

Churches are formative institutions. They will shape disciples to become more—or less—like Jesus. Changing institutional forms overnight will have unpredictable long-term consequences that only years or decades of hindsight can make apparent. Treating disciples as customers may not have turned churches into businesses, but it has arguably blurred the lines. Filtering ministry through customer values has trained multiple generations of Christians to see every local church as a provider of spiritual goods and services. Unless churches exert tremendous effort to resist it, that demand then incentivizes churches to compete to be the supply for seekers. We cringe while uttering the phrase church shopping because we know how consumeristic it sounds, but we do it anyway because we have been so shaped by marketplace logic that we really truly don't have any other way to describe it.

In other words, we've been supplying something that's no longer in demand, and we stopped supplying what is always in demand to do so.

Because I'm a millennial, it physically pains me to say this, but in that sense, we're all boomers. We always have been. And like boomers, we may update the church's style or expression, but we are nevertheless remaking church in our own image every bit as much as they did. If we want to resist that impulse, we must first have compassion for baby boomers and learn from them. We are no less shaped by our environment. No generation is immune from the self-centering temptation Dietrich Bonhoeffer described in his book *Life Together*: "Those who love their dream of a Christian community more than they love the Christian community itself become destroyers of that Christian community even though their personal intentions may be ever so honest, earnest and sacrificial. . . . It is

7. Andy Crouch, "Football and the Gift of Institutions by Andy Crouch," Qideas.org, archived December 13, 2023, at https://web.archive.org/web/20231214110140/http://208.106.253.109/blog/football-and-the-gift-of-institutions.aspx, emphasis added.

not we who build. Christ builds the church. Whoever is mindful to build the church is surely well on the way to destroying it, for he will build a temple to idols without wishing or knowing it."[8]

Reshaping the church without successfully discipling a generation of Christians is far worse than failing to do both. Seeker sensitivity may not have cultivated deeper Christlikeness in Jesus-followers or grown their love for God and neighbor, but it did accomplish something. Specifically, three decades of steeping our discipleship in the logic of the marketplace has subtly repurposed discipleship for self-actualization and reduced the church to a spiritual nonprofit.

The Consequences of Reducing Church to a Spiritual Nonprofit

Like most Gen Xers and millennials, Luke and Sarah rejected the rank consumerism often associated with their baby boomer parents but kept the foundation of pragmatism it was built upon. We now want to be empowered instead of entertained, equipped instead of fed, shepherded instead of engaged, and authentically known instead of lost in a crowd.

"Wait," you might be thinking, "what's wrong with being empowered, equipped, shepherded, and authentically known?" Nothing! Those are all very good things one should experience in a church. That's not the problem. The problem is that it's putting lipstick on a pig. Self-actualization and seeker sensitive consumerism are just two different expressions of the same spiritual pragmatism that enables us to remake church in our own image. Even if we now cringe at the thought of finding a new church home like we would pick one of many chain stores in a mall, we still treat the local church like a nonprofit offering spiritual services. The consequences aren't trivial.

Think about it this way: If the local church is merely a spiritual nonprofit, one should simply "drive to the place with the best demographically appropriate programming for your family and the best

---

8. Dietrich Bonhoeffer, *Life Together* (HarperOne, 2009).

Sunday morning experience."[9] If no church can scratch everyone's itch at the same time, you can always supplement by live streaming the sermons of the really gifted preacher who wrote that book you really liked. Or, if you experience deeper connection to God by being in nature, just grab a good devotional and go for a hike on Sunday mornings. Do whatever works best for you. What matters most to God is your spiritual growth, that you're becoming the kind of person *you* believe he created you to be, and anything that doesn't support your (self-actualizing) spiritual journey is optional. If, for whatever reason, your church no longer aligns with your values or helps you fulfill your potential, simply find one that does. It's nothing personal. After all, how would it not be unfaithful to stay at your current church if another just down the street more effectively or conveniently supports your relationship with Jesus? Through this lens, you and your spouse and your kids attending different churches is an entirely reasonable (and practical!) course of action. If we're all just different people with different spiritual needs and it's the church's job to meet them, then Luke and Sarah were being perfectly consistent and faithful.

Here's why any form of spiritual pragmatism is so tragically misguided: the local church isn't a spiritual nonprofit, it's nothing less than God's broken-but-beloved family. The difference is more than semantic. Where our primary reason for church is pragmatic, our relationship with God will feel equally tenuous, transactional, and impersonal. An otherwise biblically faithful church that we feel isn't meeting our spiritual needs is a worthwhile, if challenging, opportunity to follow Jesus and grow in our trust of him. If he promised that those who lose their life for his sake will find it, then how could he not also be faithful to meet our needs through (and not despite) doubling down on our commitment to our spiritual family? If we wouldn't be okay with our kids leaving our family for one they think will better help them grow, then we shouldn't leave our church for one with a better youth ministry.

9. Jake Meador, "Church as NGO," Mere Orthodoxy, April 21, 2023, https://mereorthodoxy.com/jake/church-as-ngo.

Spiritual Pragmatism Doesn't Work

When we feel like we have the opportunity and means to fulfill our potential, we feel genuinely blessed. Spiritual pragmatism reassures us that God loves us and we're "doing it right." Nobody can tell us we're doing it wrong because it's working, obviously. Until, that is, we're too busy #winning to take our blood pressure or notice the clumps of hair falling out of our head due to all the stress. *It's fine. Really.*

Spiritual pragmatism isn't sustainable because it barely works when all our circumstances cooperate to support our self-actualization. Which is never. What can spiritual pragmatism offer us when, hypothetically, a global pandemic takes away our hobbies, leads to the loss of our job, minimizes human contact, and otherwise forces us into the exact opposite circumstances needed for our self-actualizing? When nothing works, anxiety creeps in. If we keep trying and failing anyway, anxiety gives way to frustration and anger. But anger isn't sustainable, so depression starts knocking on the door because the spiritual growth and personal fulfillment we were previously in complete control of (or at least had the illusion thereof), is now undeniably unachievable however we defined it before. The more you believe self-actualization is possible, the more disturbed you will be when it's out of reach. The pandemic is obviously an extreme and (I hope) unique example, but the same existential roller coaster plays out over the smaller hills and valleys of everyday expectation and disappointment.

At the end of the day, spiritual pragmatism stunts our growth because the church is not a transactional organization but is rather—like any other family—a formative institution. Spiritual pragmatism can't help but undermine our experience of God's love and our belonging to him because how we relate to church and how we relate to God are indelibly linked. That's how God made us. It's why we call the church the body of Christ, and why the New Testament is utterly saturated with familial language and imagery. We can no more detach and reattach to the body of Christ at will than a limb can be amputated and sewn back on without consequence.

Over time, treating the church lightly in the name of taking our faith seriously will inevitably weaken our attachment to church and, therefore, to the ordinary means of experiencing the love and belonging for which we are "fearfully and wonderfully made" (Psalm 139:14)—his own. Every time we detach from one church, reattaching to the next church and restarting deep relationships becomes progressively harder. Every time we believe the lie that it won't be, that this time is different, we desensitize ourselves to familial connection. We make the deep community (horizontal connection) and meaningful spirituality (vertical connection) we long for even more elusive.

It's all quite the catch-22, isn't it? We can't flourish without church, but it is the American church's complicity with individualism that discipled us into thinking we can live without her. I wish I could tell you that we've figured it out at The Table, that we've discovered and finely tuned the (conveniently book-sized) formula for success. But we can't resolve pragmatism with more pragmatism. That's what makes recovering a multidimensional discipleship such a generational challenge, and one that will only worsen the longer we take to be disabused of our pragmatism.

Still, it is no small thing to realize that most of our discontent isn't with the water we've been swimming in (church), but with the pollution making it so hard to breathe (spiritual pragmatism). If we didn't even know we've been viewing church through such a pragmatic lens, seeing her clearly for the first time can change everything about our experience . . . so long as we allow it to also change our posture. And there is no better place to start that transformation than changing how we approach the Sabbath.

Reconnecting to Spiritual Family Through Sabbath Rest

Like church in general, spiritual pragmatism views the weekly worship service as just one tool in our toolbox for meeting our spiritual needs.

Sure, we could go to church, unless we're too tired and need to sleep in, or our kids have a soccer game, or we had a long week and just need some "me" time. After a long week of self-actualizing, going to church feels too much like work, not rest. We might even quote Jesus's teaching that "the Sabbath was made for man, not man for the Sabbath" (Mark 2:27) to justify seeking spiritual refreshment with a weekend in the mountains. As a Colorado transplant, believe me, I can relate to that temptation.

But self-care isn't Sabbath rest. Jesus invites us into more than rest from work; Sabbath is also a rest "*to* the LORD your God" (Exodus 20:10, emphasis added). Sabbath is rest in and through God's worship among God's people. Weekly Sabbath (rest-through-worship) will, like binoculars, magnify God in our lives and fill our vision with his glory. Conversely, spiritual pragmatism looks at worship through binoculars backward: it minimizes God by making our good, rather than his glory, our lens for weekly worship. A self-actualizing worship won't feel restful at all, and Sabbath without worship is just R&R. Neither are the life-giving gift that God intends Sabbath to be. While undoubtedly refreshing, our souls need mere refreshment like a bleeding artery needs a bandage. It might stop us from bleeding out, but it won't help us heal.

How does that help us reconnect to spiritual family? Just as a transactional horizontal relationship with church spills over into our vertical relationship with God, a change in our posture toward worship will spill over into our posture toward our church family.

Shortly after admonishing readers about the dangers of our dream of community in his classic book, *Life Together*, Dietrich Bonhoeffer described the beautiful inseparability of rest-through-worship from God's spiritual family: "Do what is given to you, and do it well, and you will have done enough . . . Live together in the forgiveness of your sins. Forgive each other every day from the bottom of your hearts."[10] That's it. Show up with what you have, not what you wish you had or think you should have even if all you have left is a weak grasp on Jesus. That's more than enough; in God's family, it's everything.

---

10. Bonhoeffer, *Life Together*.

What if our loneliness isn't something you need to fix or optimize but an invitation into what I'm describing? What would it look like to simply accept that you're lonely by processing it in prayer among those with whom you long to feel closer? Family is rarely effective or efficient for much of anything, but that is a miserable, soul-crushing standard of value anyway. Pragmatism doesn't determine whether anything is true, good, or beautiful. God does. In Christ, accepting that our growth isn't all on us *is* realizing our full potential. Being slow to learn or change doesn't mean God isn't at work in our lives. It means he's growing us in ways, means, or areas of life outside of the narrow scope of our conscious awareness (including spiritual pragmatism). With resurrection promised on the other side of dying to ourselves, what we perceive as a lack of growth might be one of the surest signs of God's faithfulness. Discipleship is so much bigger (and better) than self-actualization. That it is frequently confusing and uncontrollable is how we know we're following God and not something we've conjured up ourselves.

Likewise, our church's failure to get that promised ministry off the ground isn't just cause for leaving, it's an invitation to deny ourselves, take up our cross, and follow Jesus into the unknowable in the sure hope of resurrection life. For if "it is finished" as Jesus proclaimed from the cross (John 19:30), then all that's left for us is to rest-through-worship in that finished work. All that's left is to enjoy God and abide in him where he is most ordinarily found—his broken-but-beloved family—and trust him for our growth, because "in him you also are being built together into a dwelling place for God by the Spirit" (Ephesians 2:22).

Reflection Questions

1. Where might you believe the lie that your spiritual growth is the *telos* (purpose) of the Christian life—that what matters most to God is your spiritual growth? Have you ever left or switched churches for that reason? Whether you have or not, what would it take to more

fully embrace a vision of discipleship that instead trusts God for your personal growth as a by-product of faithfulness?

2. How has the pursuit of personal spiritual growth shaped your expectations of the church? In what ways might you relate to your church more as a service provider than as a spiritual family? In hindsight, how might spiritual pragmatism have blinded you to the needs of others (e.g., your neighbors, church, or other Christians)?

3. Does going to church every Sunday feel more like work or rest? Answer as honestly as you can, then try to analyze your answer. Is there a part of your answer that assumes worship is about meeting your spiritual needs? How would you reverse engineer your answer if you started with worship as a grateful response to God for his steadfast love?

2

The Sacred Self

How Intuitional Spirituality and Therapy-Speak Make Us More Fearful, Fragile, and Alone

Religious man was born to be saved; psychological man is born to be pleased. The difference was established long ago, when 'I believe' lost precedence to 'I feel,' the caveat of the therapeutic. And if the therapeutic is to win out, then surely the psychotherapist will be his secular spiritual guide.

—Philip Rieff

Church Defeater 2: The Sacred Self. Because our fragile intuitions are our only reliable source for spiritual truth, we become hypervigilant of any potential harm and use therapeutic culture to keep ourselves safe—at all costs.

It's always been hard, but something has shifted . . . This isn't the usual kind of hard."

A friend and fellow pastor—we'll call him Andrew—called me to process a particularly painful pastoral care situation. A twentysomething dating couple in his church—we'll call them Tom and Heather—couldn't escape a particularly nasty cycle of conflict between them. After more than a year of on-and-off fighting, Tom called it quits because he felt like everything he tried to fix in their relationship caused more hurt and made it worse. He was far from innocent in their conflict, but Andrew supported Tom's decision because they were stuck in a feedback loop of only ever confessing each other's sins, with neither party taking responsibility for the reactivity they contributed to the cycle.

"Did you tell them that?" I asked.

"Yes," Andrew sighed. "Not in as many words, but as clearly and gently as I could."

"How'd they take it?" I asked, fearing the answer.

"Not well."

Heather reminded Andrew of previous conversations where she vulnerably shared that she has chronic anxiety and a history of trauma. She said that Tom "avoids conflict because he grew up in a volatile home," and so Andrew supporting Tom in his decision to break up with her only "retraumatized" her and "bordered on spiritual abuse." Andrew asked Tom, who was sitting right next to her, if he agreed with her assessment. "I mean, it hurt her even more than arguing did, so yeah. I just want her to be happy."

Andrew was taken aback. He felt like he had more than enough understanding and trust to offer this couple difficult feedback. Andrew and his wife loved Tom and Heather deeply, and they were regular fixtures in their home, around their dinner table and at their daughter's soccer games where they cheered her on from the bleachers. Heather had come to trust them enough to share a long and tragic history of hurt and betrayal. They regularly and tearfully prayed with her. Over many late-night beers, Tom openly processed the grief of growing up without a father and the confusion of trying to figure out his first serious relationship without one. Surely a relationship like that could withstand honest yet gently delivered feedback, even if it was difficult to hear. Tom and Heather genuinely wanted (and needed) a church community. But like most of the millennials and Gen Zers who attend Andrew's church, they had very idealistic expectations about what a church should provide for them and how comfortable they should feel along the way.

Heather may have used more therapeutic language than most, but they followed a well-trodden path. I've seen it too, and with unnerving predictability. No matter how much trust a pastor has earned, care given, safety demonstrated, or time spent doing all of the above, there is an invisible boundary that, if transgressed, has become a relational point of no return. It varies only slightly from person-to-person, at or shortly after the point where you suggest that how they feel is valid and understandable yet may *not* fully or accurately represent reality. Even when the hurt it is genuinely accidental and the pastor's contrition is immediate, *intent* no longer matters, only *impact*.[1]

It is never easy to feel misunderstood or not receive the compassionate balm you hope is offered in the wake of sharing hurt or struggle. Even when others respond well, vulnerability hangovers are real. But I still have whiplash from how quickly and easily we are now willing to cut off longtime friends, family, and churches at the slightest hint of invalidation or transgression.

Our next church defeater, the sacred self, is the belief that we, individually, are our only reliable source for truth and, especially, identity. Functionally, it's the next evolutionary phase of expressive individualism. Self-definition is no longer merely a social effort but an ultimate quest with our very sense of self on the line. To navigate that journey, we've turned our intuitions into a self-contained and self-protecting spirituality.

But the problem with building a sacred refuge out of our oft fickle and fragile internal world is that it requires a hyper-vigilant sensitivity

---

1. See chapter 2 of Greg Lukianoff and Jonathan Haidt, *The Coddling of the American Mind: How Good Intentions and Bad Ideas Are Setting Up a Generation for Failure* (Penguin Random House, 2018).

to emotional safety. Whereas traditional Christian language catechizes belief in an external authority (God) and defines boundaries for orthodox belief (Scripture), the sacred self repurposes therapeutic language to catechize belief in internal authority and set whatever boundaries are necessary to prevent harm. Where Christianity breaks down walls of hostility, the sacred self builds them in the name of safety.

In an article for *Wired* magazine, tech and culture commentator Katherine Alejandra Cross explains why a self-protective posture amplifies rather than heals hurt, making deep, meaningful community or relationships practically impossible: "Reconciliation is simply compromise and the acceptance that one is not always right and that one's feelings should not always prevail or be seen as objective truths. Compromise doesn't invalidate your worth as an individual; in exchange for tolerating the eccentricities and foibles of others, you get to be in a real community that will sustain and support you."[2]

The sacred self doesn't just make staying in a church more difficult; this church defeater will utterly preclude church to the degree that emotional comfort is a condition of our openness to vulnerable intimacy. For those who have experienced truly abusive relationships (whether with a church, parent, or significant other), the sacred self experiences God's healing refuge as an existential threat.

Although this is a relatively recent phenomenon, it has proliferated quickly through social media because it is deeply embedded in the psyche of American culture. Understanding it's historical and cultural development is the first step in inoculating us from its false promise of safety.

The Origins of Intuitional Spirituality

Carl Trueman's *The Rise and Triumph of the Modern Self* argues that we live in the wake of a 20th century therapeutic revolution that can be

---

2. Katherine Alejandra Cross, "All the Feels: Therapeutic Language Is Proliferating on Social Media. No, That's Not a Good Thing," *Wired Magazine*, n.d., https://apple.news/Ar0Yzs W03Sk2PPqtKc3cvhQ.

traced all the way back to the 18th century Romanticism of Jean-Jacques Rousseau. The connections are anything but a stretch. Rousseau was vehemently skeptical of institutions, convinced that they were irrevocably compromised by materialistic incentives and incompatible with individual freedom. "Man is born free, and everywhere he is in chains."[3]

His ideas were radical for his time, but we've come to likewise reject the empirical Rationalism encapsulated by Descartes's thesis *Cogito Ergo Sum* ("I think, therefore I am"). We now accept as common sense the Romantic notion that *intuitionism* ("I feel, therefore it's true") is a purer and more reliable compass in life. Without Rousseau, we wouldn't over-value authenticity, the pursuit of happiness, or self-expression. His contributions are baked into almost every dimension of Western art, literature, and film. That is perhaps most consistently and obviously true in children's movies, and there is no better Romantic storyteller than Disney.

Social pressures preventing you from being your true self? Just "Let It Go."[4] Obligation got you down? Simply "Hakuna Matata" and escape to nature where life is more noble and pure.[5] Your problem isn't a lack of character, maturity, or wisdom, but that nobody sees the specialness inside of you. Thankfully, "The key to being special is to believe that you can be."[6] The rare but refreshing outlier *Encanto* celebrates the goodness and beauty of family identity as greater than the crushing weight and loneliness of individual identity.

Disney isn't the only well-known name in animated storytelling, but it has a monopoly on our imagination because all parents are unavoidably nostalgic. Who wouldn't want to relive and share the stories that shaped

---

3. Jean-Jacques Rousseau, *The Social Contract*, Penguin Books Great Ideas (Penguin Books, 2006).

4. From Disney's *Frozen* (2013).

5. "Hakuna Matata" from Disney's *The Lion King* (1994) is a remarkable (if unintentional) parable of Rousseau's noble savage argument that civilization corrupts individuals. Similarly, Mufasa's tender yet powerful rebuke to Simba ("Remember who you are! You are my son, and the one true king!") is strangely undercut by where he tells his son to look for his identity ("Look inside yourself, Simba.").

6. As said to Emmet, the protagonist, in *The Lego Movie* (2014). Although not a Disney production, it was wildly successful in replicating the same expressive individualism formula.

us with our kids? But movies are more than artifacts of our childhood. Each is an episode of a larger cultural narrative (expressive individualism) that finds its genesis in Romanticism. Even if it's not terribly logical (by definition), intuitionism makes sense to us because it is baked into Western culture and society and then reinforced by countless narratives that praise and celebrate those living according to its script.

Rousseau and Jiminy Cricket agree: always let your conscience be your guide. Unless it tells you to rob a bank . . . or neglect your family . . . or torch local businesses . . . or launch an insurrection . . . or, on second thought, perhaps our conscience alone isn't a sufficient guide . . . ?

Within a larger institutional landscape and as part of a shared consensus of what is at least minimally true, good, and beautiful (e.g., freedoms of speech, religion, and association), intuitionism is a helpful, tempering influence. It serves as healthy guardrails within institutions, preventing us from being hoodwinked by those without our interests at heart. But we also can't live without institutions. The more we distance ourselves from institutional involvement, the less our intuitions are collectively shaped by civilizing communities like church, school, marriage, family, and others. Without institutions serving as guardrails for our intuitions, social consensus gives way to culture wars. We start coming apart at the seams. Our individual intuitions alone are simply too finite, fickle, and frivolous to serve as social, never mind spiritual, anchors or guides.

Intuitionism also wouldn't have nearly as much cultural influence if we didn't have the economic margin to freely explore it. As the world has become wealthier in the last half century (and faster than the previous 2,000 years combined), we feel less day-to-day need for society's middle layer of mediating institutions that kept those with less means from falling through the cracks. Without a doubt, that's a good problem to have! A privilege, even. But as late 1990s rapper The Notorious B.I.G. wisely proclaims in his song "Mo Money Mo Problems," there are very real trade-offs to having more economic margin.

The more our material needs are met, the more our existential problems feel more urgent and significant. We slowly start expecting governmental, social, and spiritual institutions to adjust accordingly and pick up the slack with our existential needs. But the consequences of failure being more psychic than tangible doesn't mean they aren't incredibly significant. Assuming faithful institutional leaders don't capitulate to pedaling in vibes and performative tribalism (see chapter 4), they will find themselves bombarded by expectations they can't possibly meet even if they wanted to. This pressure is especially acute in local churches:

> Ministry defined as "meeting people's needs" is dangerous in a society where the more affluent and privileged among us have solved with a credit card most of our biblical needs like food, housing, and clothing. So we move on to assuaging personal needs the Bible doesn't give a rip about—*meaning making, a purpose-driven life, balance, freedom from anxiety, or a sense of personal well-being.* Fulfillment of desire becomes elevated to the level of need, and need gets jacked up to the status of a right.[7] (emphasis added)

As churches stray from their God-ordained purpose of glorifying God, making disciples, and loving our neighbors into meeting needs they aren't equipped for, pastors and congregants alike will find themselves in a vicious feedback loop of disappointment and distrust not unlike the one in which Tom and Heather found themselves. Whether those expectations are reasonable is irrelevant. They are needs, and needs are sacred. And you can't take issue with needs because you can't argue with what's sacred. Institutional trust will erode whether a church fails to meet them by trying and failing or not trying at all. So we abandon any authority outside ourselves and seek guidance from the only source that still makes sense to us: our intuitions. At that point, it is only a matter of time until self-guidance becomes self-definition and intuitionism becomes a spiritual identity. That shift has grown more common in parallel with growth of the demographic we refer to as the Nones—those who classify themselves as spiritual but not religious.

---

7. William H. Willimon and Stanley Hauerwas, "The Dangers of Providing Pastoral Care," *The Christian Century*, 138, no. 16 (August 11, 2021), https://www.christiancentury.org/article/interview/dangers-providing-pastoral-care.

How Intuitional Spirituality
Functions as a Religious Identity

As a description for everything from nominal evangelicalism to an unhealthy obsession with essential oils, to say that you are "Spiritual but not Religious" (SBNR) unapologetically proclaims faith *not* in Christian doctrines received externally from the church, but in one's *intuition* as the default for discerning what is true, good, and beautiful. Like a choose-your-own-adventure version of the Apostles' or Nicene Creeds, it serves as a foundation upon which all intuitional spirituality is built: "True spirituality transcends organized religion, so I don't need anyone to tell me what to believe or how to live."

In her excellent book, *Strange Rites*, religious scholar and commentator Tara Isabella Burton distills multiple sociological approaches into four dimensions or handholds for explaining how social and especially religious identity is formed: community, ritual, meaning, and purpose. SBNR's specific beliefs and practices are not manifested from within so much as they are cobbled together from a smorgasbord of options for each dimension. Where prior generations received religious identity institutionally (with all four dimensions experienced within a single institution), Burton argues that SBNR could be more accurately described as a religiously remixed approach where one builds their own bespoke identity from multiple unrelated sources of community, ritual, meaning, and purpose:

> Today's Remixed reject authority, institution, creed, and moral universalism. They value intuition, personal feeling, and experiences. They demand to rewrite their own scripts about how the universe, and human beings, operate. . . . Today's Remixed don't want to receive doctrine, to assent automatically to a creed. They want to choose . . . the spiritual path that feels more authentic, more meaningful, to them. They prioritize *intuitional spirituality* over *institutional religion*.[8]

---

8. Tara Isabella Burton, *Strange Rites: New Religions for a Godless World* (PublicAffairs, 2020), 10, emphasis added.

Some degree of intuitional spirituality has been a part of faith and life in America from the beginning. Settlers fleeing religious persecution in Europe founded new churches and denominations in trailblazing antithesis to those they left behind. The pietism that fueled the First Great Awakening quickly evolved into a more organized revivalism by the Second Great Awakening, with figures like Charles Finney trying to recreate conversion experiences with emotionally manipulative tactics. But unlike the first and second iterations, what Burton insightfully labels the Third Great Awakening (the Jesus movement of the 1960s and '70s) happened *precisely* at the same time Rousseau's nascent skepticism of institutions was supercharged by the war dividend and exploded across American culture. Americans started questioning and rejecting the institutional anchors that historically tempered and matured revivals. While almost all revivals begin outside the institutional church and culminate with a return to the fold, the Jesus movement only partially returned, and even that was to a church that had been largely stripped of institutional depth (see chapter 1). I'd argue that the seeker sensitive movement largely tried to recapture (at best) or manufacture (at worst) the magic of the Jesus movement with branded worship experiences, but inadvertently produced a different flavor of the same nominalism dogging churches in the decades *prior* to the First Great Awakening. But without institutionally-robust churches to mature, deepen, and pass newfound faith on to the next generation, that nominalism is proving to be fertile soil for a very different kind of conversion experience: deconstruction.

So much of what we now refer to as deconstruction[9] is the downstream, next-gen fruit of the Jesus movement's institutionally thin revival, and the unintended consequence of teaching Christians to secure their faith in individual experience rather than the institutional church. That experience can be offered in many different forms, ranging from in-depth Bible studies (for cognitive certainty) to heartfelt worship (for emotional

---

9. For a more in-depth exploration of this topic, see Ian Harber, *Walking Through Deconstruction: How to Be a Companion in a Crisis of Faith* (InterVarsity Press, 2025).

comfort). Whatever its shape, tying our assurance to personal experience, even an experience of love for Jesus, is still a house built upon sand. It leaves our sense of self vulnerable to changes in everything that shapes and influences our experience—our circumstances, culture, or social norms. Weathering the impact of those changes can be an incredibly disorienting journey without someone (e.g., a church) to help you understand and navigate it. That's why most deconstruction is a very unwanted crisis of faith—in church, God, or both—that happens *to* you, not one you initiated or went looking for.

Many exvangelicals describe a similar in-flooding of doubt—of a faith understandably shaken within the church or by her abuse or neglect—but relieve the pressure by explicitly rejecting American evangelicalism and fully embracing Romantic, intuitional spirituality. Some outright deconvert, but most dechurch to embark on a self-directed journey to discover their true self—one that doesn't feel as blindly assumed from tradition or received from institutions. That too is a conscious effort to build a remixed spirituality that's less culturally captive than American evangelicalism but, in the process, swallows whole the intuitional spirituality that most makes American evangelicalism so, well, American.

Rejecting institutional religion to embrace intuitional spirituality just isn't nearly as revolutionary as we think it is. It is every bit as inherited as any faith, just from our broader cultural experiences rather than from within a particular institution. But because intuitional spirituality is so overwhelmingly celebrated and reinforced by Romantic narratives, it will be our default spiritual trajectory to the degree that we're not countercatechized within a community, ritual, meaning, and purpose (i.e., a church) shaped by a Better Story (i.e., the gospel).

Like all religions, intuitional spirituality needs a place of worship. And so, unanchored from institutions, we build bespoke cathedrals out of the only materials we believe are reliable and worthwhile: our self, however we define it. We make our intuitions as central to our spiritual (but not religious!) identity as Notre Dame or any other religious architecture. Despite seeming to offer more spiritual freedom and flexibility, canonizing our intangible and subjective intuition leaves us hopelessly undefined and fragile. We will feel more sensitive and protective of our identity—as we do of anything we feel slipping through our fingers.

On their own or in contrast to institutions, our intuitions simply are not the safe refuge or more reliable guide we think—or rather, feel—they are. Worse, their fragility and risk-aversion requires those who care for us to walk through a minefield of invisible assumptions and changing, subjective instincts just to get past the foyer (if they ever do). That hyper-vigilance leaves us only more insecure and isolated. Spiritual intuitionism lacks a language to articulate signs, symbols, and boundaries that traditional religions use to cultivate community and connect through shared ritual, meaning, and purpose. The language and categories of therapeutic culture provides those tools, but using them doesn't move us any closer to healing—or hope thereof.

How Therapy Speak Catechizes Hopelessness

What our new identity really needs are flying buttresses. Not literally, of course. Like all religious identities, the sacred self needs support and reinforcement. Christian faith is reinforced through confessions, creeds, and catechisms that introduce the doctrines of the faith and instill faith's language into our everyday life. Likewise, the sacred self needs a catechism to support and shape the world within intuitional cathedrals. Australian pastor and author Mark Sayers uses very catechism-like questions and answers to illustrate how the therapeutic worldview is a secular departure from historic Christianity:

Q: What is the purpose of life and/or faith?
A: *Achieving internal peace.*

Q: What is sin?
A: *Anything that causes mental or emotional discomfort or pain.*

Q: What is the world?

A: *A dangerous place filled with pain, trauma, and discomfort that I must control or avoid to stay safe.*

Q: What is the solution to the moral ills of the world?

A: *Harm minimization. Create and preserve a place that's safe from harm and free of risk.*

Q: What is the church?

A: *Ideally, church is a refuge. But in light of the church's track record, anything but shallow attachment to church is high risk, low reward. If I do risk it, I will be extremely hesitant and guarded until I know it is safe (if it ever will be).*[10]

Even if it isn't as explicitly structured as Sayers's example, so-called therapy speak has proven remarkably well-suited in providing the categories and language for organizing and communicating a sacred internal reality. Like a religious catechism, it functions as a secular shorthand representing and conveying (pseudo-)transcendent meaning. It provides a coherent plausibility structure that supports—or buttresses—intuitional spirituality. But unlike a religious catechism that has been painstakingly derived from a sacred text, therapy speak repurposes a litany of therapeutic terms and clinical language that were never meant to be used outside the confines of a counseling session. Therapy speak isn't therapy, but rather the use of therapy's technical language, categories, and even specific diagnoses to describe more mundane situational or relational stress and prescribe how others relate to us.

Granted, a lot of therapy speak is little more than innocuous, pop-culture shorthand. For example, I know the 2004 movie *Meet the Fockers* starring Ben Stiller is supposed to be hilarious. Me, I'd rather be punched in the face than ever watch it again. As the child of a messy and often

---

10. I modified and expanded the chart by Jake Meador, "Mark Sayers's 'Sin Chart,'" Mere Orthodoxy, September 16, 2022, https://mereorthodoxy.com/jake/mark-sayerss-the-sin-chart.

manipulative divorce, I've described *Meet the Fockers* as "triggering" more than a few times. Is it possible to be physiologically triggered by a movie's association with a traumatic event? Of course it is. Was I? Not even close. To be triggered in this context is just a simple and humorous way to communicate that I don't enjoy movies that use escalating levels of deceit to get a cheap laugh. But my discomfort falls far short of the technical definition: "A trigger is a stimulus that sets off a memory of a trauma or a specific portion of a traumatic experience."[11]

That kind of therapy speak is more of a linguistic fad than anything we should lose sleep over. What I'm more concerned about is an equally widespread but far more harmful variety used as leverage to manipulate others. Almost overnight, the weaponization of terms like trauma, boundaries, harm, and abuse in both personal and professional settings went from niche to normalized. The Oxford Dictionary declared "toxic" the word of the year in 2018 due to the "sheer scope of its application."[12] It can describe "workplaces, schools, cultures, relationships, and stress," but is most often used to describe particular expressions of masculinity, and a wide array of political "rhetoric, policies, agendas, and legacies of leaders and governments around the globe."[13]

Ideas can now be declared irretrievably harmful merely for their *potential* impact—although that idea somehow gets a pass—and people or groups are considered unsafe for believing them regardless of whether or how they're lived out. One can pathologize a friend or family member to justify cutting them off. "Setting boundaries" is used more often to avoid conflict than resolve it. Calling someone a narcissist if they aren't one can be a *highly* manipulative no-win Kafkaesque trap—where any attempt to deny or defend yourself is a textbook DARVO (Deny, Attack,

---

11. "Understanding the Impact of Trauma," in *Trauma-Informed Care in Behavioral Health Services* (Substance Abuse and Mental Health Services Administration, 2014), chapter 3, https://www.ncbi.nlm.nih.gov/books/NBK207191/.

12. Elizabeth Schulze, "'Toxic' Is Oxford Dictionaries' Word of the Year, Beating 'Techlash' and 'Gaslighting,'" *CNBC*, November 15, 2018, https://www.cnbc.com/2018/11/15/toxic-is-oxford-dictionary-2018-word-of-the-year.html.

13. Oxford Languages (@OxLanguages), "The Oxford Word of the Year 2018 is . . ." X, November 14, 2018, video, https://x.com/OxLanguages/status/1062846136388476928?s=20.

and Reverse Victim and Offender) response that only confirms the accusation. I'm just scratching the surface here.

Sometimes we do have a clinically narcissistic boss. Sometimes people do respond to an accusation with DARVO tactics. But innocent people can DARVO too. My point isn't that abuse never happens or that it is always overblown, but that unless we are trained to diagnose clinical pathologies or distinguish abuse from run-of-the-mill conflict between sinners, we ought to be incredibly hesitant to jump to conclusions likely to perpetuate harm in the name of preventing it. Therapy speak also risks neglect—of cutting ourselves off from care by making it much harder for the average person to know how to help (i.e., "If they're OCD/bipolar, how could I possibly help? I'm not a therapist!"). Whether intended or not, it effectively communicates, "Look, don't touch."

This has theological implications too. If a therapeutic methodology assumes or incorporates any vertical relationship with the Divine, it is agnostic at best. Unless a therapist actively integrates faith, mere therapy is only equipped to navigate our horizontal relationships. So, when Christians are more deeply catechized by therapy speak than, for example, the Westminster Confession or the 1689 Baptist Confession of Faith, it will reshape our perceptions and expectations of church—and, as we discussed in the previous chapter, eventually God.

One symptom of that reshaping is the increasingly blurred line between the roles of pastor and therapist. Therapists (or at least good therapists) point you inward to explore emotional realities to gently bring them out for deeper healing. Pastors (or at least good pastors) absolutely facilitate and support healing, but they do so by pointing you upward to the greater spiritual reality of Christ. Both empower us to face a broken world with greater resilience, but they do so by deepening our understanding of overlapping yet distinct realities (subjective vs. objective), which require different approaches. Though related and complementary, pastors who function like spiritual therapists and therapists who take on the role of secular priest are both operating out of their depth. The former risks limiting God to what "makes sense" and the latter risks making a god out of our experience—two forms of the same intuitional spirituality.

Sadly, those lines had become blurred beyond recognition for Tom and Heather, and they soon left Andrew's church to find "a more trauma-informed church." Andrew has a master's degree in both divinity (MDiv) and counseling (MAC), so he is more trauma-informed than most. Yet, by most definitions, trauma-informed is essentially another way of saying that someone has the compassion and sensitivity that individuals need to heal in the aftermath (and ongoing experience) of trauma. Any biblically ordainable pastor or elder should have at least that in their fundamental disposition and character.

Ideally, therapy increases our capacity *for* love and our ability *to* love, as C. S. Lewis so beautifully articulated in *The Four Loves*: "To love at all is to be vulnerable. Love anything and your heart will be wrung and possibly broken. If you want to make sure of keeping it intact you must give it to no one, not even an animal. Wrap it carefully round with hobbies and little luxuries; avoid all entanglements. Lock it up safe in the casket or coffin of your selfishness. But in that casket, safe, dark, motionless, airless, it will change. It will not be broken; it will become unbreakable, impenetrable, irredeemable. *To love is to be vulnerable*."[14]

To those of us who feel perpetually beat up, unable to trust, and hopeless that the future might hold anything but more trauma, therapy speak offers "language to distance [ourselves] from reality."[15] Co-opting therapy's empathetic motive and social cache without accepting its purpose provides a blameless cover to withdraw into so-called safer spaces or relationships—but at the cost of truly thriving in community. Over time, confusing "self-preservation for emotional maturity,"[16] capacity, or resilience creates an anxious feedback loop, cutting us off from the means of our growth and conditioning us to settle for being *merely seen* (transparency) when we could be *fully known* (vulnerability). For if everything

---

14. C. S. Lewis, *The Four Loves* (HarperOne, 2017), emphasis added.
15. Mia Staub, "Be Quick to Listen, Slow to 'Therapy Speak,'" *Christianity Today*, May 22, 2024, https://www.christianitytoday.com/ct/2024/may-web-only/quick-to-listen-slow-to-therapy-speak-toxic-trauma-abuse.html.
16. Staub, "Be Quick to Listen."

is trauma then no one is safe, and we can never let our guard down. That, truly, is heartbreaking.

Therapy speak may indeed have extraordinary power to explain our inner world, but little—if any—power to redeem us. In an *Atlantic* article on the sudden popularity of polyamory, Tyler Austin Harper sources therapeutic culture in a growing existential hopelessness: "If we are fixated on finding fulfillment and endless self-reinvention, it is because our own inner lives feel like the only thing most of us have control over. The therapeutic cult of personal growth is a response to external problems that feel insoluble, a future that feels shorn of causes for hope."[17] Rather than delivering us from existential despair, therapy speak inculcates despair with a kind of post-Christian rationalization of narcissistic self-focus—not by directly making too much of *ourselves*, but by indirectly making too little of *everyone else*, including God. That stunting of our redemptive imagination can't help but catechize the hope out of us and leave us more fragile. We certainly won't look for healing where God promises it is most ordinarily found—the body of Christ.

Why the Sacred Self Can't Replace the Church

So many of us, shepherds and sheep alike, fear to speak truth-with-love deeper than surface level symptoms because crossing the threshold into another's cathedral without proper consecration is trespassing. You'll get thrown out. Quick. Even if it is painfully clear that their current path will lead a loved one further into misery, we hesitate to say so for fear of being cut off from them (and therefore from any future opportunity we might have to care for them). Even if that line weren't invisible and subjective, it would still be an impossible one to walk. Love can't stay only

---

17. Tyler Austin Harper, "Polyamory, the Ruling Class's Latest Fad," *The Atlantic*, February 1, 2024, https://www.theatlantic.com/ideas/archive/2024/02/polyamory-ruling-class -fad-monogamy/677312/.

skin deep and still be love. Just as no surgeon can remove a tumor using only anesthesia, no one can love others without risk of hurt.

Still, I genuinely don't blame anyone who thinks leaving church is easier than staying to resolve conflict. Mostly because it *is*. I have a world of compassion for anyone, for example, wanting to start afresh in a community unaware that their spouse had an affair. Who wouldn't want to flee feeling so exposed? "When the crisis ends, they sometimes excommunicate those who have been present during the crisis because they fear we have seen them when they were so vulnerable."[18] Even if every knowing look is saturated with tender grace, it would be hard not to feel defined by the persistent fear, guilt, or shame they battle every day.

But that is the most heartbreaking part of this church defeater: withdrawal most often comes on the cusp of transformation. It is only after having the time and opportunity to do the work of addressing our wounds that we realize we are still bleeding out, that our *wound* healing is not the same as *us* healing, and we finally run out of options. We can't avoid dying to ourselves anymore. It often takes every bit of that journey, of our unasked-for vulnerability, to be open to Jesus's promise: that on the other side of death to our desires, our safety, our intuition, and everything else we might rely on to make sense of our suffering apart from Christ's, is a resurrection life more sacred and safe than anything found within ourselves. It is at that point, when Jesus starts making more room for himself and leaving muddy footprints in our pristine cathedral, that we will most want to quit. Yet C. S. Lewis assures us that it is the point where healing starts feeling a little scary that our redemption begins:

Imagine yourself as a living house. God comes in to rebuild that house. At first, perhaps, you can understand what He is doing. He is getting the drains right and stopping the leaks in the roof and so on: you knew that those jobs needed doing and so you are not surprised. But presently He starts knocking the house about in a way that hurts abominably and does not seem to make any sense. What on earth is

---

18. Willimon and Hauerwas, "Dangers of Providing Pastoral Care."

He up to? The explanation is that He is building quite a different house from the one you thought of—throwing out a new wing here, putting on an extra floor there, running up towers, making courtyards. You thought you were being made into a decent little cottage: but He is building a palace. He intends to come and live in it Himself.[19]

To get within sight of that reward only to restart the renovation of our hearts even once is a travesty of the highest order, but the way we spin fearful retreat into courageous self-care is one of the most egregious examples of self-imposed (and actual) gaslighting imaginable. We're every bit as complicit as Rousseau and Disney.

Conscience is an important guardrail, but it's a terrible north star. Our intuitions are not *utterly* untrustworthy, but they aren't *ultimately* trustworthy either. Far from it. Because the world, our hearts, and our faculties are objectively compromised by sin, defining reality by our experience thereof will inevitably careen us down dark and fearful paths. No pastor, no church, no friend will ever feel sufficiently safe or without risk. That's partly why we make our intuitions sacrosanct: we sense, or at least suspect, that our intuitively built identity is far more fragile than the churches we used to entrust ourselves to. And on that point, at least, our intuitions are correct. The sacred self trades a house of worship for a house of cards.

Institutions are far from perfect, and the church is no exception. However, at their best, they are external and shared ways of embodying community, ritual, meaning, and purpose so that anyone who wants to be invited in, can be. The how and why of participation is clear and tangible, if not in the brick-and-mortar architecture, then in how life is ordered and shared among its members. Finding our place in the ordered life of a congregation can still be confusing, scary, or strange, but that doesn't imply an absence of hospitality or welcome. If anything, we tend to call "strange" those experiences that transcend our ability to make sense of them. Sometimes a disturbed intuition can be a sign that there

19. C. S. Lewis, *Mere Christianity* (Touchstone, 1996), 175–76.

is a God around here somewhere, One who isn't just a figment of our imagination or emanating from our intuition. It's good that we can't shake the strangeness of that experience. It's how we know we've found a refuge that transcends both our self and our experience.

Recapturing Vulnerable Intimacy

Have you ever noticed that if you try to look directly at something in the dark the most you can make out is a silhouette? That's not just your imagination. If you look at something indirectly, using your peripheral vision, the details and texture will be noticeably clearer. Likewise, peace and safety are best seen in the periphery, where we have much better night vision. Fixing our gaze upon peace, rather than its Prince, only fills our gaze with its opposite. The presence of brokenness, sin, and death can seem so pervasive and inevitable that they overwhelm any hope of experiencing redemption in this life altogether—and possibly the next.

That's a startling claim, but here's an example of how I've seen it play out on more than a few occasions.

No child should *ever* have to experience abuse at the hands of their father. And it is immanently understandable that an adult with such childhood trauma might find relating to God as a Father to be extremely painful or scary, if not actually triggering. It might even "make sense" to us that God wouldn't want to retraumatize anyone by insisting we call him Father. If God is good and loving, how could he not? But refusing to relate to God as Father because it's painful won't, no matter how hard we try or how firmly we believe it will, bring healing or redemption to that horrific experience. He wants so much more for us than to make us safe or heal our wounds. Our Father wants to make his children *new*. The sacred self remakes God in the image of our wounds. And no path can lead to resurrection, in this life or the next, if it accredits more power to a broken world than to the God who has vowed to redeem it.

In an alternate universe, where Tom and Heather had welcomed Andrew's shepherding, he would have carefully and compassionately explained that any relationship focused on preventing harm or staying safe more than cultivating vulnerability and intimacy only exacerbates hurt feelings and neglects real needs. Neither party can be fully honest or vulnerable with each other. Neither of them will know or be known more than skin-deep. Not if what is true, good, and beautiful is ultimately defined by what is safe.

None of us intend to make a very good and reasonable expectation (safety) into an ultimate thing (safetyism). Yet that's the unavoidable result of catechizing ourselves with therapy speak, of habituating self-protection until it has thoroughly reshaped our affections. Tom and Heather's cycle of conflict had exacted a catastrophic toll on two of their most important relationships—with each other and with their church. In both, therapy speak deepened the ruts of self-protection in their hearts while allowing the ruts of compassion to slowly fill back in from disuse. Every trip down that road in which they didn't steer toward vulnerability only made safetyism easier to slip into the next time. Eventually, forgiveness became a burden too risky and too traumatizing to be considered at all.

The only way out of this grievance-fueled cycle is to start a new one of receiving and offering forgiveness, of grace-fueled repentance even when you have no idea if it will be received well, and of trusting because you've already entrusted yourselves to each other.[20] For anyone stuck in a cycle of conflict—romantic, ecclesial, or otherwise—that prospect probably feels about as safe as jumping from a fast-moving train. But it beats running out of track. One is doomed, the other only seemingly so.

Jesus knows what it's like to stare doom in the face—not in defiance or despair but in extraordinary compassion. He prayed, "Father, forgive them, they know not what they do" (Luke 23:34) for those who had just finished crucifying him and were, in that very moment, taking perverse pleasure in mocking him. The Son of God endured a harm so uniquely wicked and torturous that we had to invent a new word for it:

---

20. Like infidelity, unrepentant abuse is an aberration where one or more parties has functionally abandoned the covenant of marriage, and removing yourself from that situation is wisdom, not safetyism.

"excruciating," which means "from the cross." With his dying breath, Jesus proclaimed that what's truly sacred isn't our intuited self but our giving ourselves away. For "greater love has no one than this, that someone lay down his life for his friends" (John 15:13). Love spurned safety and absorbed catastrophic harm to save those consumed with saving themselves.

Christ's prayer from the cross is as strange, discomforting, and counterintuitive to us as it was to those who heard him utter it. Although it doesn't make any sense to us, that it made perfect sense to Jesus is why we can trust that he is ultimately safer than safetyism. His self-giving love, not our self-protecting intuition, is our map and compass for finding the true healing and deep community we need to thrive in a world that so eagerly crucified love incarnate. If we trust only ourselves for safety, we won't find it. If we entrust ourselves to Jesus, even imperfectly, we will find refuge in his broken but beloved body—the church.

Reflection Questions

1. Does church make sense to you? Why or why not? Read passages from Scripture, such as Acts 2:42–47, Colossians 3:12–17, or Hebrews 10:24–25. What does or doesn't make sense or sit well with you from those passages? Why?

2. How has "the belief that we, individually, are our only reliable source for truth and . . . identity" made belonging in a church more elusive? How might belonging *to* a church, and vulnerably entrusting yourself to others, change your experience? What are a few first steps you could take in that direction?

3. Have you ever used therapy speak to avoid facing a hard reality about yourself or God? How might an overemphasis on emotional safety be shaping your view of church? The next time you notice yourself using therapy speak to describe a spiritual reality, try using words and categories from Scripture. Notice where it changes how you see yourself and your attitude toward others.

3

Counterfeit Institutions

How Social Media Unmakes Disciples, Undermines Churches, and Unravels Society

The real problem of humanity is . . . we have Paleolithic emotions, medieval institutions, and godlike technology. And it is terrifically dangerous, and it is now approaching a point of crisis overall.

—Edward O. Wilson

Church Defeater 3: Counterfeit Institutions. Digital platforms that bypass gatekeepers, hijack incentives, and manipulate user behavior to extract and monetize our attention—at the cost of deforming individuals and unraveling society.

S tarting as early as 2014 or 2015, most pastors began noticing a subtle change in the Sunday morning vibe. The typical visitor walking through the front doors of a church went from expecting to be shaped and formed *by the church*, to expecting a church to be shaped and formed *by them*. We've gone from entrusting our formation to a church, to insisting a church conform to us. Our alignment with a church's theology is no longer as important as a church affirming our pre-existing cultural commitments, political allegiances, and social convictions—especially gender, sexuality, and sexual ethics. And while those are undoubtedly important issues, they still fall short of ultimate importance. We can't hope to fully experience resurrection life in the body of Christ if we aren't willing to relinquish our white-knuckled grasp on mere cultural issues. Before we even get to sacrificing real time or money in service of a church and love for our neighbor, this upside-down reversal of expectations can make the prospect of becoming a member of a church sound an awful lot like death.

And, to be clear, that's pretty accurate. We live in a world steeped in the implicit belief that we can be godlike and omniscient through technology, and church constrains us to finite limits. Choosing to embrace that diminishment will feel a lot like dying to ourselves unnecessarily. But dying to ourselves is the necessary cost of both becoming a disciple and living as one. It is the ABC's and A-to-Z of following the Lord of Life.

That process is unnatural and impossible to do on our own. And while all healthy institutions shape the character and virtue of its members to varying degrees, Jesus calls Christians to pick up our cross and follow him in a breadth and depth of faithfulness that no merely social institution can hope to facilitate. Not fully, anyway. Only when we entrust ourselves to a church and allow God to sanctify us *within* and *through* his people, can we find the supernatural help and spiritual formation we need to mature as disciples of Jesus.

This change in posture, from *entrusting* to *insisting*, is but one symptom of a well-documented trend called Main Character Syndrome

(MCS)—the tacit belief that we are the protagonist at the center of every story, and go about our day "as if [we're] the only person whose life matters, as if [we're] a player character among a gaggle of NPCs"[1] (or "Non-Player Characters"). And where we presume to be the essential protagonist, others become tangential to our story. We insist they play supporting roles and treat them like we do the virtual and discardable figures populating video games.

Filtered through MCS, we'll feel intentionally and unfairly targeted by sermon illustrations that hit a little too close to home. Offense gets amplified because we assume that we are the norm and that everyone who doesn't anticipate our unique experience *must* have intentionally excluded us. We'll be okay with some sacrifices, like giving generously, because austerity is an essential part of any hero's journey. Yet we'll insist on maintaining our own charitable portfolio and buck at the suggestion that God might obligate our generosity anywhere, never mind toward our church primarily. We can hardly make a name for ourselves if someone else determines how we chart our course, so we assert our autonomy and demote the bride of Christ to an ignorable NPC. Whatever aids us in our journey toward ever greater freedom.

You get my point.

MCS isn't malicious or personal. It's unlikely that we're even aware of this shift in assumption because it has slowly permeated throughout society, leaving us haunted by the nagging fear that if we're *all* "main characters," none of us are. We center ourselves to flip the script and ensure we never get relegated to being someone's NPC. A shift that subtle and pervasive can only be the fruit of very institution-like formation. In this case, it is social media functioning as a *counterfeit institution*.

Unlike the other four church defeaters, a counterfeit institution isn't itself a belief, but a digital medium that *shapes* belief through social interaction and incentives. Social media is upstream of MCS in much the same way a church is upstream of Christlikeness. In that sense, using

1. Katherine Alejandra Cross, "All the Feels: Therapeutic Language Is Proliferating on Social Media. No, That's Not a Good Thing.," *Wired Magazine*, n.d., https://apple.news/Ar0Yzs W03Sk2PPqtKc3cvhQ.

social media isn't unlike going to a church's worship service. As soon as you walk in the door (pull up the app), you're greeted and handed a bulletin (newsfeed) with announcements and upcoming events (ads and links). The order of service will include various interactive elements like singing songs steeped in shared meaning (memes), confessing sin (posting text or video), receiving assurance (likes and comments), sharing testimonies (retweets), and hearing God's Word preached (longer threads or articles). Whether the style is more modern (TikTok), contemporary (Instagram), or traditional (Facebook), every liturgy uses an overarching narrative (algorithms) to organize and communicate a coherent message (content). Also like a worship service, we don't merely consume social media, we *participate* in it. It's the addition of that "social" dimension that gives otherwise traditional or online media the institution-like power to form and shape users. That said, no imitation can ever replace the genuine article.

How Counterfeit Institutions Unmake Disciples

Tristan Harris, co-founder of the Center for Humane Technology, explains that any truly new technology reveals new resources that were always there but we didn't know existed. Once that resource is recognized, it becomes a new commodity, birthing a new market and economy around it. Social media revealed and commodified the previously unrecognized resource of human attention. Likewise, I am convinced that the sum total of our present digital revolution has revealed the previously unrecognized resource of *identity*.

Consisting of people instead of processors, genuine institutions are the sense-making communities and norms by which we organize ourselves in pursuit of common purpose(s). They are the original social technology, invented to give us protected social space needed to receive, affirm, and test out shared identity—to become by practicing who we are. As such, institutions are gardens and storehouses of wisdom, where humanity has preserved, cultivated, and passed on desirable qualities and virtues to subsequent generations. Though we give inordinate attention to national elections every four years, it is the remarkable, diverse ecosystem of mediating institutions that bestows a shared social identity, sustains society, and keeps us from killing each other between (and despite) those elections.

Though clad in a masterfully engineered digital interface designed to be as invisible as possible, social media manages a bait-and-switch that would have made Houdini proud. Like any counterfeiter, social media companies create a false perception of value to extract profit from those who use their fraudulent currency, product, or service. The better the counterfeit, the longer it takes to recognize you've been had and the more value that can be extracted from an economy (financial, political, social, or otherwise). Social media digitally counterfeits the formative social structure and dynamics of institutions, but then uses an algorithm to incentivize very different behaviors (engagement) for very different ends (profit rather than purpose).

As those behaviors become habituated, their incentives likewise reshape our affections. That whole process is jump-started by extracting the most valuable resource related to spiritual formation and discipleship: our attention.

Though we use different terms, Christians understand the formative relationship between attention, desire, and identity when we say things like "you are what you love." We give attention to what we desire, and we come to desire what we attend to. The more we give Jesus our attention—via God's Word, sacrament, and prayer—the more our desires will be shaped by what he loves (his bride and our neighbor). God doesn't command us to practice repentance and forgiveness merely because it's the right thing to do, but because habitually attending to what God desires (reconciliation) shapes our own. The more we attend to God's forgiveness, the more we want to give and receive forgiveness. The more we habituate that desire, the more God's limitless grace gives shape to our identity. Wash. Rinse. Repeat. Only within the body of Christ can we regularly receive the gospel's declaration of our true identity: God's broken-but-beloved.

The same pattern plays out when we attend to things other than grace. An Instagram reel exhorting us to cut toxic or negative people out of our lives may sound ridiculous the first time we watch it, but it'll start sounding more plausible as algorithms saturate our newsfeeds and consume our attention with pop psychology and soft narcissism—i.e. therapy speak. We like to think that we make judgments based on objective evaluation, but what we desire is formed more by habitual engagement than *in*formed by data. In other words, social media shapes our sense of self not with content but by the all the visible and invisible means through which we consume it.

Canadian philosopher Marshall McLuhan, a pioneer in media theory, captured this profound truth with his famous adage, "the medium is the message." The vehicle (medium) captivating our attention is at least as formative as the content (message) it delivers. A medium's content "is like the juicy piece of meat carried by the burglar to distract the watchdog of the mind." The short-form limitations of social media teaches us that truth requires neither context nor nuance. The "share" button is a digital gun to our heads filtering self-expression through threat of cancelation. The existence of photo filters implies a message: you need, and should always want, to be more beautiful. Social media further mediates desire by presenting us with a constant stream of online influencers whose primary "purpose is not to model the physical articles of clothing but the *desire to wear the clothes* . . . to make us want what they have. What you actually want is their face, their body, their withering stare—which don't come with the clothes."[2]

Because desire is mimetic—i.e., what we want is based on what we see others wanting—24/7 exposure to an infinite variety of idealized wants and dreams will overload and scatter our desire into a million different directions and our selves into a million potential identities. Algorithms are designed to deliver a customized experience of whatever we want, moment-by-moment, so they can deliver more no matter what the objects

---

2. Luke Burgis, "Mimetic Desire 101," Luke Burgis, accessed October 10, 2024, https://lukeburgis.com/mimetic-desire-101/.

of our desire may be and adapt no matter how quickly they change. High school is so difficult, in part because you're trying to figure out who you are by imitating the desires of those around you while simultaneously fitting in and standing out among a hundred peers who are all *doing the exact same thing*. Imagine having to navigate the same dynamic, but with tens of millions of peers across social media. It's a marvel that any teenager with a smartphone makes it past that gauntlet to graduation.

If McLuhan is right that every medium tells a story and participating in that medium shapes who we are, then immersing ourselves in algorithmic narratives will leave us feeling like we've been existentially drawn and quartered by our own desires. The result is a permanently liminal identity—a sense of self so liquid and malleable that any physical social environment meant to shape or stabilize us (e.g., a Christian worship service) feels increasingly alien, if not threatening.

There's a reason social media conflict feels so much like high school drama: both naturally provoke debilitating insecurity. One is simple immaturity, the other a weaponization of mimetic desire. As damaging as that sounds for individual users, it is even more compromising for institutions.

How Counterfeit Institutions Undermine the Church

As a digital platform, a counterfeit institution can't "embody" anything, so it relies on algorithms to shape the conduct of users. Whereas healthy institutions (the church chief among them) incentivize compromise and reconciliation, social media rewards conflict and polarization. The former grows by cultivating *in*tention between members but the latter profits by extracting *at*tention from users. Although they take the form of an incomprehensible equation, algorithms incentivize behavior not according to our better angels, but according to demons that most effectively capture our attention: fear, anger, disgust, and the unholy grail of all three combined—outrage.

If it seems like the world is falling apart, you're not wrong. Our awareness of the world's problems has never so vastly outpaced our ability to address them, but that gap will only stoke stress or anxiety if enough of our attention—and thus our experience of the world—becomes untethered from where we can make the most difference. Social media only amplifies that disconnect. The combination of interactive exchange and algorithmic incentives redirects our attention toward distant problems, overwhelming and depleting the agency of individual users. Once social media reached market saturation, algorithms gained unprecedented sway over public discourse by introducing a dangerous temptation new to most institutional leaders—audience capture. The more social media rewarded leaders and institutions tailored their messages for maximum approval and punished those who didn't, the more algorithmic incentives rewired institutions and reshaped institutional leaders over time.

In *A Time to Build*, Yuval Levin explains how that dynamic sows institutional distrust across every dimension of American life: "When we don't think of our institutions as *formative* but as *performative*—when the presidency and Congress are just stages for political performance art, when a university becomes a venue for vain virtue signaling, when journalism is indistinguishable from activism—they become harder to trust. They aren't really asking for our confidence, just for our *attention*" (emphasis added).[3] Pastors moonlighting as influencers and ministry leaders "leaving loud" (even if for valid reasons) are just a couple examples of how attention-seeking incentives can rewire us to see even our church as a performative platform rather than a formative institution.

To understand how that happens, let's delve a little more deeply into an institution that isn't quite so close to home.

Traditional media outlets were among the first to show signs of performative pressure. Before social media, journalists' primary consideration for personal and professional conduct was how it would reflect on the institution that employed them. They would be beholden to

---

3. Yuval Levin, *A Time to Build: From Family and Community to Congress and the Campus, How Recommitting to Our Institutions Can Revive the American Dream* (Basic Books, 2023).

standards as set by, for example, *The New York Times* or *ABC* or *CNN*. Their institutions, in turn, had a vested interest in supporting and developing the journalists who bore their name. It was a mutually beneficial arrangement of reciprocating trust, with institutions well represented and its journalists receiving a level of prestige and authority that their personal name rarely carried on their own (especially at the beginning of their careers). This didn't prevent all mistakes or failures, but generally speaking, institutional incentives were all aligned to foster both individual responsibility and institutional accountability—key elements for maintaining public trust as a reliable news source.

So what happens when those incentives are suddenly and subversively inverted, and we're able to make a name for ourselves more quickly and easily on our own, without institutions?

It has led to a world where many journalists have "found themselves following social media trends instead of reporting on events . . . [and] news outlets chased audiences in a splintered marketplace."[4] As *The New York Times* became rewired by counterfeit incentives, journalist Bari Weiss felt she had no choice but to conform to them or leave. In her July 2020 resignation letter, she said "Twitter has become its ultimate editor."[5] Where the fourth estate of journalism first made democracy possible, social media is sowing enough institutional distrust to make neither journalism nor democracy sustainable.

That's why few arguments are more likely to give me an aneurism than likening social media to the printing press. Sure, the inventions of both the horse saddle and rocket propulsion improved how quickly we could get from point A to point B, but only one allows you to escape earth's gravity. Like rocket propulsion, social media represents something fundamentally new and far more disruptive than the printing press. Unlike any other human invention, social media platforms combine bidirectional communication, unlimited user-generated content, and

---

4. Chris Stirewalt, "Llamas, Life Online, and Lessons Learned," *The Dispatch*, February 27, 2024, https://thedispatch.com/article/llamas-life-online-and-lessons-learned/.

5. Bari Weiss, "Dear A.G.," Bari Weiss, accessed September 30, 2024, https://www.bariweiss.com/resignation-letter.

algorithmic curation all on an infinitely scalable digital platform. In shockingly short order, Facebook attained a breadth and depth of reach that traditional media couldn't have imagined in their wildest dreams. They achieved the very impact Mark Zuckerberg envisioned in his last Founder's Letter before taking Facebook public in 2012: "We hope to rewire the way people spread and consume information. We think the world's information infrastructure should resemble the social graph—a network built from the bottom up or peer-to-peer, rather than the monolithic, top-down structure that has existed to date. . . . *We hope to change how people relate to their governments and social institutions.*"[6]

When a vision that ambitious comes from a company whose internal motto was "move fast and break things," we shouldn't be surprised that institutional trust is eroding faster than Superman is crippled by kryptonite. But even if Mark Zuckerburg isn't Lex Luthor with curly hair, vicious cycles are the inevitable fruit of incentivizing performance. Telling someone to "be better" in person won't help them become better, but we justify doing so online because we'll get a lot of likes and reposts. More vice does not virtue make, even when we insist it's for another's good. Quite the opposite.

In an essay aptly titled, "Outsourcing Virtue," L. M. Sacasas explains how this happens, writing that Americans have a perennial "technocratic impulse, an impulse that presumes that techno-bureaucratic structures and processes can eliminate the necessity for virtue."[7] We think that if we could just invent a perfect-enough device or pass a perfect-enough law or marry a perfect-enough spouse or land a perfect-enough job or find a perfect-enough church, we'll be able to resist attending to our vices without having to do the hard work of developing character. Being a good person is contingent on the world making it easy to become good.

6. Mark Zuckerberg, "Founder's Letter, 2012," Facebook, 2012, https://m.facebook.com/nt/screen/?params=%7B%22note_id%22%3A261129471966151%7D&path=%2Fnotes%2Fnote%2F&refsrc=deprecated&_rdr.

7. L. M. Sacasas, "Outsourcing Virtue," *The Point Magazine*, February 22, 2023, https://thepointmag.com/criticism/outsourcing-virtue/.

Social media platforms promise exactly that, if tacitly, but embedded in the code that delivers data to our eyeballs in 4k are "systems so imperfect that it turns out everyone will need to be extraordinarily good."[8] And "when we're unable to act with as much virtue as the system requires, there's an ever greater demand for systems that render virtue superfluous."[9] Hoping that others will be virtuous so we don't have to be, we weaponize whatever we deem necessary to enforce our sense of good upon others and insist they not respond in kind. And when, not if, they disappoint us, we double down on our insistence and feel justified in doing so. Chris Wetherell regrets inventing the "Retweet" function for Twitter because it injected nitrous into this vicious cycle, saying, "We might have just handed a 4-year-old a loaded weapon."[10]

If there is a better explanation for why our country is so divided, and why the church hasn't been the salt-and-light exception that it should be, I haven't found it. I wish social media were only a *church* defeater, but it is also an institutional defeater eroding *all* social ecosystems. Each platform conducts a kind of divide-and-conquer institutional piracy, dividing us by hijacking our shared incentives and sowing distrust. Individually and collectively, social media doesn't deliver us more deeply into good news that shapes our desires according to Christ's, but further into disordered desires that undermine both the church and our spiritual formation the same way counterfeit bills rob both a business and a customer: exploiting all participants in the system equally, invisibly, and at scale.

If unmaking disciples and undermining the institutional church weren't enough, counterfeit institutions unravel society at an individual level by distorting reality, disenchanting experience, and exploiting our most cherished relationships.

---

8. Sacasas, "Outsourcing Virtue."

9. Sacasas, "Outsourcing Virtue."

10. Alex Kantrowitz, "The Man Who Built the Retweet: "We Handed a Loaded Weapon to 4-Year-Olds," BuzzFeed News, July 23, 2019, https://www.buzzfeednews.com/article/alex kantrowitz/how-the-retweet-ruined-the-internet.

Counterfeit Institutions Unravel Society by Distorting Reality

Despite not being able to physically embody anything, counterfeit institutions are the digital architectural equivalent of a spiderweb. Highly conductive, an event at one end of its web will reverberate across connections to reach us almost instantaneously. We don't just read the news; we have countless disembodied perspectives injected straight into the palm of our hand. What could go wrong? To start, our grasp on political realities will be distorted when only 9% of users say that they often share political views or content online, and ". . . users with relatively moderate views are more reluctant to post about political or social issues."[11] Algorithms aside, anyone looking to social media for political content will, far more likely than not, have their perception shaped by the political extremes.

No matter how intentional our evaluation of the facts, every social media platform is its own plausibility structure, replete with its own value judgments that "shape the often-unnoticed background of our lives, framing the worlds in which certain arguments make sense and others don't, certain questions can be raised but others not, and certain propositions bear the burden of proof while others have the force of foundational assumptions."[12]

Recounting every way that framing happens is way beyond the scope of this book, but three are especially dominant in distorting our sense of what's true on a neurological level:

1. **Context Flattening:** There is only so much context that can be squeezed into a camera's field of view, and much less into a social

---

11. Colleen McClain, "70% of U.S. Social Media Users Never or Rarely Post or Share About Political, Social Issues," *Pew Research Center*, May 4, 2021, https://www.pewresearch .org/short-reads/2021/05/04/70-of-u-s-social-media-users-never-or-rarely-post-or-share-about -political-social-issues/; "Tech Poll," *The Center for Growth and Opportunity*, September 19, 2023, https://www.thecgo.org/research/tech-poll/.

12. L.M. Sacasas, "Technoculture and the Plausibility of Unbelief," The Hedgehog Review, Fall 2023, https://hedgehogreview.com/issues/markets-and-the-good/articles/technoculture-and -the-plausibility-of-unbelief.

media post. Trying to distill meaning into bite-sized chunks and deliver via an infinite-scrolling news feed invites our brains to fill in the gaps with our own context. Whether we intend it to or not, this subconsciously shapes our experiences and inflates the significance of our own perspective (which makes us less open to being shaped by the gospel or God's people).

2. **Information Oversaturation:** More information is not always good. Because we are not physiologically able to absorb the 24/7 bombardment of everything happening in the world, we struggle "to discern what is real in a sea of slant, fake, and fact."[13] To cope with the anxiety that stokes, our brains automatically switch to pattern recognition and (often arbitrary) dot-connecting to craft a narrative that makes sense of the data. Having technology's near-omniscience without God's omnipotence can make even skeptics susceptible to spin and conspiracy theories.

3. **Cognitive Off-Loading:** When we repeatedly access external information, our brains outsource knowledge and "only the gist of information (or its location) is retained, while learners often gain the illusion of having memorized that information. Furthermore, off-loading substantially increases the risk of memory manipulation, potentially posing a societal problem."[14] Like a hard drive with limited storage capacity, moment-by-moment access tells our brains that the information is safely stored elsewhere, so there's no need to retain it in our own wetware.[15] Similarly, if everyone always wears a name tag, why bother remembering names at all? Even if you want to, it takes more effort to stick because your brain is wired to prioritize retaining information it can't access

---

13. George Etheredge, Photo Caption, "'No One Believes Anything': Voters Worn Out by a Fog of Political News," *The New York Times*, November 18, 2019, C. M. S. Admin, "Willow Creek Repents?," *Christianity Today*, October 18, 2007, https://www.christianitytoday.com/2007/10/willow-creek-repents/.

14. Alexander Skulmowski, "The Cognitive Architecture of Digital Externalization," *Educational Psychology Review* 35, no. 101 (October 10, 2023): 101, https://doi.org/10.1007/s10648-023-09818-1.

15. Don't tell Skynet I said this, but we should be at least as worried about AI's content inflation and our subsequent loss in cognitive capacity for retention as we are sci-fi doomsday scenarios.

externally. The more off-loading we do, the more our memory storage and recall will atrophy.

Together, these contribute to what Patrick Miller calls internet brain. It's why we are so disoriented when we spend time in "a world where information is contextless, disjointed, and pell-mell—short bursts of uselessness designed for a culture with a deficit of attention, creating a growing inability to think well, reason thoroughly, and sift matters of importance from wasteful distraction."[16] If you're having trouble reading nonfiction books, studying or remembering Scripture, falling asleep without worrying about (insert global conflict you're powerless to change), it's because social media use reroutes and cements new neural pathways. Internet brain is the inevitable result of habituating longer and deeper online engagement.

I don't think it's a coincidence that many of the people in my own church who are most desperate for an easier way to cultivate Bible study, prayer, and stillness are also the most online due to remote work (especially data-intensive jobs like coding), social media use, or both. All this neurological conditioning influences our sense of what is real or true as potently as any traditional institution or church, except for over seven hours per day[17] rather than an hour or so per week. As of 2024, the average American "spends upwards of 40% of their waking hours on an internet-connected screen." Even though counterfeit institutions are digital, and therefore less potent than embodied participation in a church, they make up for it in sheer ease of access and immersion. How can we "take every thought captive" (2 Corinthians 10:5) with social media demanding our attention from our pockets 24/7? Not even the most inspiring sermon will stick with us as long as a viral news story, and that's especially true if both are experienced through a screen. Cognitive off-loading doesn't discriminate based on content, but by medium.

16. Patrick Miller, "Internet Brain," February 14, 2024, https://www.endeavorwithus.com/does-internet-cause-brain-damage.

17. "Alarming Average Screen Time Statistics (2024)," Exploding Topics, accessed October 11, 2024, https://explodingtopics.com/blog/screen-time-stats.

Social media may not be "real life," but how we engage—and how much we engage—on their digital stage will backfill and spill over into all of life. That doesn't just distort our view of objective reality, it also disenchants our experience thereof.

Counterfeit Institutions Unravel Society by Disenchanting Experience

In the two-time Emmy Award–winning Netflix documentary *The Social Dilemma*, Tristan Harris argues that social media is unlike any other technology: "We've moved away from having a tools-based technology environment to an *addiction-* and *manipulation-based* technology environment . . . [Social media] has its own goals, and it has its own means of pursuing them *by using your psychology against you*."[18] It's strangely appropriate that the tech industry is the only legal trade to refer to their customers as users. Social media is a behavioral and substance addiction masquerading as an app.

Dopamine is the feel-good hormone that induces feelings of pleasure, satisfaction, and motivation. Our bodies ordinarily release dopamine in response to social connection and affirmation. It's responsible for the relief you feel after processing work stress over coffee with a friend, and for motivating you to keep exercising on a regular basis (or so I hear). The dopamine cycle also influences our desires by rewarding us when we get what we want, but not if we always get what we want. There has to be a chance of *not* getting what we want. Anticipation, surprise, and novelty are all key ingredients.

If you're ever in a casino, try walking from the card tables to the slot machines. It is noticeably and eerily quiet by comparison, despite the buzzers and sounds emitted by the machines. No one talks to each other. Everyone just stares, zombie-like at the screen in front of them,

---

18. *The Social Dilemma*, directed by Jeff Orlowski-Yang, Documentary (Netflix, 2020), emphasis added.

deadpan and expressionless. There won't be any windows because you'll stay longer—and lose more money—by reducing the immanent frame to what's in front of you. The entire presentation is designed to ensure you lose track of time and space. Any gambling can be addictive, but no medium more closely parallels a smartphone's finely tuned promise of pleasure in order to extract value from users like a slot machine. Both are designed to deliver a cocktail of dopamine-inducing triggers like endless novelty, intermittent approval, and attention-breaking notifications. But only one of them can wave that tantalizing carrot-on-a-stick from our pockets. The phantom ring, or feeling your phone vibrate in your pocket even though it's on the other side of the room, is your dopamine-addicted brain reaching out for another hit.

It's no wonder Facebook executives don't let their children use what they actively market to their children's classmates. "They figured out what every junk peddler already knows: It's more profitable to get users locked in while they're young."[19] This hacking of our biochemistry and behavioral incentives is a defining feature, not a bug. More and more Silicon Valley whistleblowers are confirming that social media companies "want to dig down deeper into the brain stem and implant, inside of [us], an unconscious habit so that [we] are being programmed at a deeper level."[20]

As this dopamine doom loop carves out new neural pathways, we might notice that our in-person social interactions get harder. Hanging out loses its luster. Conversations feel saturated with a dense layer of "meh." That's because, like any drug, we build up a tolerance to dopamine over time, requiring more for the same pleasure and greater stimulus to trigger release. Dopamine tolerance makes messy, middle-school-dance awkwardness of in-person community not worth the effort. It's harder to pay attention, or even stay awake during a worship service. Small group

---

19. Georgia Wells, Jeff Horwitz, and Deepa Seetharaman, "Facebook Knows Instagram Is Toxic for Teen Girls, Company Documents Show," *The Wall Street Journal*, September 14, 2021, https://www.wsj.com/articles/facebook-knows-instagram-is-toxic-for-teen-girls-company-documents-show-11631620739.

20. Wells, Horwitz, and Seetharaman, "Facebook Knows."

discussions and Bible studies will feel numb and unsatisfying. We will favor connection that offers engagement without requiring us to wake up on time, show up anywhere, or give up anything—all of which are essential to meaningful participation in a local church. Responding to a notification is simply more pleasurable and less anxious than making up just one shallow reply to "hey, how's it going?"

In other words, social media disenchants what we would otherwise find beautiful at a neurological level. It physiologically saps our attention, agency, and emotional energy for community and still moments. Both lack sufficient stimuli to compete with a smartphone for our attention. Although God's presence isn't limited to what gives us synaptic pleasure, being still and knowing God becomes even harder to enjoy and, therefore, habituate. A social media–induced dopamine tolerance will make God feel distant, if not utterly absent. If for no other reason than this, social media is spiritually dangerous. It so utterly depletes us of our most valuable commodity—our loving attention—that nothing seems worth giving ourselves to. Even if reality is still objectively full of enchantment, social media leaves our subjective *experience* of reality thoroughly disenchanted.

Counterfeit Institutions Unravel Society by Exploiting Relationships

I have often hoped that social media will go the way of smoking: when we realize that constant use is unhealthy and addictive, it will fade into a niche hobby for those who enjoy it responsibly (e.g., the occasional cigar). But that analogy is limited. Smoking and social media are both addictive. But unlike quitting cigarettes, breaking our addiction to social media requires the equivalent of going without nicotine *and* oxygen.

Behavioral psychologist and author Jonathan Haidt's research on teen mental health underscores this social dynamic in what he calls a cohort effect: "Suppose that in 2015, a 12-year-old girl decided to quit all social media platforms. Would her mental health improve? Not necessarily. If all of her friends continued to spend 5 hours a day on the various platforms then she'd find it difficult to stay in touch with them. She'd be out of the loop and socially isolated. If the isolation effect is larger than the [dopamine] effect, then her mental health might even get worse."[21] This, Haidt says, creates a trap for teens and parents, simultaneously worsening the consequences of leaving and capitalizing on implicit pressure on all participants to engage. "Each girl might be worse off quitting Instagram even though all girls would be better off if everyone quit."[22]

Counterfeit institutions are so manipulative because they are a systemic problem requiring a systemic solution. Everyone within an interconnected social ecosystem must near-simultaneously reject the counterfeit and absorb its cost to be freed from it. But the more rewires our personal incentives, quitting will become even more costly.

A recent *New York Times* investigation with one of the most soul-chilling headlines ever published—"A marketplace of girl influencers managed by moms and stalked by men"—proves Haidt's thesis with a single quote, from the mother of a child influencer: "'I really don't want my child exploited on the internet . . . But she's been doing this so long now,' she said. 'Her numbers are so big. What do we do? Just stop it and walk away?'" Even our most cherished (and previously sacred) institutions like parenting and family can be compromised by counterfeits.

Despite lofty talk about contributing to the common good and connecting the world, social media platforms are not institutions. They are a product. No matter how much a platform is marketed as a digital sherpa for discovering what is true, good, and beautiful, they are in fact digital marketplaces where our attention is extracted, monetized, and sold to the highest bidder. When the product is free, *you're* the product.[23]

---

21. Jonathan Haidt, "Social Media Is a Major Cause of the Mental Illness Epidemic in Teen Girls. Here's the Evidence.: Journalists Should Stop Saying That the Evidence Is Just Correlational," *After Babel*, February 22, 2023, https://www.afterbabel.com/p/social-media -mental-illness-epidemic.

22. Haidt, "Social Media."

23. In Q3 2023, Facebook surpassed 3 billion monthly active users, or almost 40% of the world population.

An Unraveling Society Is Extremely Profitable

Considering how many hours we spend every week attending to internet outrage and concentration-breaking notifications, who of us wouldn't want or expect a church to conform to our (algorithmic) narrative? Now multiply that over years and decades, and for three *billion* active users (of Facebook alone). Very little collective action will happen with 40% of the world's population caught in a vicious cycle of perverse incentives and dopamine addiction. I don't care how cute those cat videos are. Our reality is too distorted, our experience too disenchanted, and our intimacy too threatened. It's a wonder we entrust ourselves to anyone anymore. Even if discipleship *was* possible apart from the body of Christ, immersion in that environment can unmake any disciple.

Social media companies profit most from existential problems going unresolved. We put a man on the moon but can't even agree whether a dress is blue and black or white and gold.

But virtual dumpster fires alone are insufficient fuel. As a fire needs oxygen, the attention extraction model relies on crises both real and imaginary to drive engagement. You have created truly perverse incentives when the world needs to keep burning in order to keep earning, when collective action poses an existential threat to shareholder value. Global warming. Christian Nationalism. Police shootings. Accusations of electoral fraud. Book banning. Flag burning. Volatile school board meetings. Drag queen story hours. The January 6th Capitol riots. While the printing press brought a whole lot of good into the world, it also caused a series of religious wars that lasted more than three hundred years and cost over ten million lives. So even if it were an apt comparison to social media, it shouldn't be a comforting one.

Nothing drives engagement more than the distrust or downfall of an institution. News both real and fake are all the same gasoline-soaked kindling to an inhuman algorithm designed to keep the dopamine doom loop going. But at least it's free, so it'll only cost you everything money can't buy. As counterfeit institutions propel us further into a vicious cycle and our search for transcendent meaning grows more desperate, we become an easy mark for the false promise of our next church defeater: (un)civil religions.

Reflection Questions

1. Start tracking your screen time. Is there a correlation between your mood or emotional energy and how much time you've spent on social media?
2. Are you likely to feel more "FOMO" (fear of missing out) because you missed viral content on your newsfeed or a churchwide announcement on Sunday morning? Which carries more personal meaning for you, and why?
3. Think about a friend you know in real life and on social media. Are they different online versus in person? Over time, would you say that their in-person presence became more like their online presence, or vice versa? What would they say if asked the same questions about you?

4

(Un)Civil Religions

How Making Enemies to Make Meaning Leaves Us Angry and Empty

The surest way to work up a crusade in favor of some good cause is to promise people they will have a chance of maltreating someone. To be able to destroy with good conscience, to be able to behave badly and call your bad behavior "righteous indignation"—this is the height of psychological luxury, the most delicious of moral treats.

—Aldous Huxley, *Crome Yellow*

Church Defeater 4: (Un)Civil Religions. Because political associations have become a primary source of identity and formation, we define ourselves by who we are against and trust performative politics to satisfy our existential emptiness.

Few people are likely to remember the name Karl Becker, but for a few weeks in October 2016 he was a bipartisan national hero. Millions of viewers were fed up with the circus masquerading as that year's second presidential debate, where then-candidates Donald Trump and Hillary Clinton spent almost 90 minutes trading schoolyard put-downs that would make even a seventh grader cringe. The question that Becker, who was sitting in the audience, had prepared and submitted to the debate's organizers was already screened and approved, but it was up to the moderators whether he'd have a chance to ask it. Thankfully, they saved the best for last.

During an interview in the days following the debate, the 49-year-old sales director said the primary motivation for his question was to inspire and set an example for his teenage children—18-year-old Darcy and 15-year-old Shane. As an undecided voter, he wrestled mightily with what his question would be but thought, "How about a question that would show some humanity, some compassion."[1] The twenty-six words he spoke into the mic were, by far, the most memorable of the evening: "My question to both of you is, regardless of the current rhetoric, would either of you name one positive thing that you respect in one another?"

I remember standing up from my couch, stunned and speechless, upon seeing the instantaneous nonverbal reaction the question elicited from each candidate. I'd never seen the fourth wall crumble so fast. With a mix of amusement and shame, Trump and Clinton looked like children caught with their hands in the cookie jar. Neither candidate was able to answer the question without getting in at least a minor jab (Trump) or contorting themselves to plug their candidacy one last time (Clinton). But that moment of civility, however brief, still felt as miraculous as Moses parting the Red Sea.

And then it was over—both the debate and our reprieve.

---

1. Colby Itkowitz, "Meet the Dad Who Made Trump and Clinton Play Nice at the Close of Sunday's Debate," *Washington Post*, October 10, 2016, https://www.washingtonpost.com/news/inspired-life/wp/2016/10/10/meet-the-dad-who-made-trump-and-clinton-play-nice-at-the-close-of-sundays-debate/.

Our church plant launched weekly worship three weeks later, just two Sundays before the 2016 presidential election. As you can imagine—and likely remember—that fall also marked a tipping point where "evangelical" went from a label describing shared spiritual beliefs to one increasingly associated with anti-establishment populism and the MAGA movement. My non-Christian neighbors weren't the only ones asking, "How could the same white evangelicals who condemned President Bill Clinton as morally disqualified for office now break so heavily for a playboy who paid off a porn star?" For most, it wasn't a rhetorical question either. It was sincere, and what most of them wanted to talk about long after the election. Whether that perception was accurate or how it had come to be was, for me, beside the point. The fact that it was the perception of most of our church's neighbors made planting a church in Boulder County—one of the most progressive[2] and the least churched[3] county in Colorado—even more difficult than it already was. Whether chicken or egg, the odds of our neighbors knowing or befriending a Christian of any political persuasion who might buck the Fox News stereotype or MSNBC caricature was practically nil.

To further complicate things, Christians who had moved from significantly more churched contexts may have gone through even greater disorientation. It's tough to go from being in the spiritual majority to a tiny minority no matter what your politics are. Millennials who grew up in evangelical circles believed their parents and pastors sincerely valued authenticity and integrity in their leaders, so they didn't understand what seemed like an overnight hypocrisy among many of their Trump-supporting family members. Many hid their light under a bushel and avoided sharing the gospel because they didn't know how to untangle their faith from what evangelicalism had become. Many who nevertheless tried to wear their faith on their sleeve at work or in their

---

2. 77% Democrat. "Boulder County, Colorado Detailed Profile—Houses, Real Estate, Cost of Living, Wages, Work, Agriculture, Ancestries, and More," accessed May 25, 2024, https://www.city-data.com/county/Boulder_County-CO.html.

3. Less than 9% evangelical. "Boulder County, Colorado Detailed Profile - Houses, Real Estate, Cost of Living, Wages, Work, Agriculture, Ancestries, and More," accessed May 25, 2024, https://www.city-data.com/county/Boulder_County-CO.html.

neighborhoods were quickly discouraged by the simmering disdain—and sometimes outright hostility—they encountered. Nobody was comfortable. That election scrambled social norms and had everyone walking on eggshells . . . for a little while at least.

Sadly, Becker's question seemed to be the high-water mark for civil discourse in the 2016 presidential election. Since then, we've devolved even further into "a nation of partisans decrying partisanship."[4] But as concerned as I am about the havoc that tribalism is wreaking on American political institutions, I'm far more concerned about how it is affecting our churches.

I can't remember the last time a first-time visitor to The Table asked me about a theological position our church holds. While I'm grateful that our views on non-essential[5] doctrines like infant baptism or pre-mil dispensationalism are no longer deal breakers, they are still more biblical as screening questions and more relevant than a pastor's personal opinions on immigration, economic policy, universal healthcare, or other prudential areas where Christians should be able to coexist in good faith disagreement. Like many pastors, I long for the days when I was asked about the problem of pain rather than problematic political positions.

But if American politics had only become more volatile and divisive, they wouldn't rise to the level of a church defeater. Upstream of our volatility is a loss of locally and socially derived meaning that, neglected for long enough, escalates into religious-like importance and urgency. In the introduction for Robert Nisbet's *The Quest for Community*, Ross Douthat named this underlying dynamic as early as 2010:

> But all that constraining tissue [within institutions] served a purpose. Man is a social being, and his desire for community will not be denied.

4. Jonah Goldberg, "Weak Parties, Weak Democracy," *Los Angeles Times*, accessed May 25, 2024, https://enewspaper.latimes.com/infinity/article_share.aspx ?guid =79 b98 3b9 -baa5 –47d0-b3b6–479e82bfe169.

5. To clarify, "non-essential" doesn't mean unimportant, simply that one's position on those issues are not essential for *salvation* as a Christian, nor should a stated difference thereof necessarily preclude involvement in a church.

The liberated individual is just as likely to become the alienated individual, the paranoid individual, the lonely and desperately seeking community individual. And if he can't find that community on a human scale, then he'll look for it on an inhuman scale in the total community of the totalizing state.[6]

(Un)civil religions are more than an erosion of civil discourse; they are an intensification of sociocultural conflict that makes politics ripe for being repurposed as a source of social and religious identity. Political contests now carry the weight of a crusade, with partisan disagreement charged with zeal not normally found outside an inquisition. It isn't enough to vote; we have to really *mean* it. Democracy depends on it, or something. Our rhetoric has escalated to reflect the supposedly higher stakes of every election, but I say "supposedly" because there's just a limit to how much or for how long we can keep caring. We can't psychologically live in a perpetual state of hypervigilance without frying our nervous system and everything blurring together. Not that it stops us from trying.

Since 2016, a whole cottage industry and publishing genre has materialized around the need to answer the question: "Why have our politics suddenly become so broken?" Potential answers include everything but the kitchen sink. While most hypotheses describe something real about our dysfunction, their solutions almost always focus on addressing symptoms rather than treating their underlying cause. Accounting for both, Jonah Goldberg's explanation traces a clear line back to widespread institutional breakdown: "The decline of strong independent institutions—religious, civic, and familial—has people searching for other outlets to find *a sense of meaning and belonging*. Identity politics, populism, and nationalism are filling that void. That's happened before, but when it did, the parties were there to filter, constrain and channel those passions in a healthy direction. The Potemkin parties can't, or won't, do that anymore" (emphasis added).[7]

---

6. Robert Nisbet, *The Quest for Community: A Study in the Ethics of Order and Freedom* (Regnery Gateway, 2010), ix.

7. Goldberg, "Weak Parties."

That sense of meaning and belonging is more than just co-located within institutions, it is wholly dependent on them.

From Religious to Political Association

Our first step down this postinstitutional road was a shift in where we derive everyday meaning: from *religious* to *political* association. This well-documented shift started before there was a Moral Majority or a modern social justice movement, but after reaching a tipping point early in the 2016 election season, it metastasized into full-blown civil unrest in 2020. All of it, and I mean *all* of it, is rooted in real grievance that gets amplified the more we use politics as a vehicle for creating our own meaning. But using politics in this way subjects our ultimate meaning—and, therefore, us—to the very roller coaster that "ultimate" meaning should be able to transcend. When political association becomes our primary—or worse—our *only* association, we're left with no choice but to keep upping the ante, resorting to more and more extreme forms of political activism. Not only for our sake, but for those with whom we most closely associate.

Meaning must be apprehended in community. Even the idea that we *can* create our own meaning is, ironically, an inherited assumption passed down from the same Romanticism that seeded our flight from institutions (see chapter 1). Without a critical mass of participation in that middle layer of society's connective tissue, individuals go without a firebreak from top-down political volatility, and politicians go without insulation from bottom-up majoritarian pressure. We all are tossed to and fro, subject to the biting winds of change and the tempting allure of populism.

It doesn't help that the combination of smartphones, the internet, and social media make our shift from religious to political association significantly easier. We now project onto the national stage the same expectations of transparency, access, and response time we rightly expect from our local government. Despite the coronavirus pandemic demonstrating how much influence state governments can have over everyday life, we still treat national elections as more important. The result is an inversion of the adage that "all politics is local." Now even the most hyperlocal issues are politicized according to national controversies. Electing a pro-life/pro-choice candidate to a school won't tip the scales in either direction. So why do we vote as if it does? Because we're in the midst of a perfect storm of postinstitutional incentives that penalize politicians who faithfully represent and mediate our interests while rewarding those who exploit our unfiltered desires and disappointments to stay in power.

And wow, do we have a lot of unfiltered desires and disappointments. We've become more aware than ever of our differences at the same time technology has enabled us to project our differences into the world. What could go wrong?

Even if we weren't drowning in 24/7 reminders of how different we are, it's natural to seek community among like-minded people. "Me too!" is a more satisfying and effortless connection than "Wait, really?" While that impulse isn't new, our gravitation toward homogeneity has taken on a desperate and militant tone, as if driven more by an urgent need for sociopolitical refuge than natural cultural affinity. Whether intentionally or not, and largely supercharged by the post-pandemic normalization of remote work, we are in the midst of a "Great Sort" along partisan lines. Many families still move across the country to take a new job, but more and more are uprooting to live where their political views are the overwhelming majority. "Of the nation's total 3,143 counties, the number of super landslide counties—where a presidential candidate won at least 80% of the vote—has jumped from 6% in 2004 to 22% in 2020."[8] While our constitutional freedom of association at least includes the freedom to move to another county or state, the sheer scale and political filtering of our self-sorting makes that a bigger deal than it seems at first blush.

An assistant professor of political science at the University of Pennsylvania, Michele Margolis, documented this shift early and predicted in a 2018 book based on her research that, "As partisans become

---

8. John Burnett, "Americans Are Fleeing to Places Where Political Views Match Their Own," *NPR*, February 18, 2022, https://www.npr.org/2022/02/18/1081295373/the-big-sort-americans-move-to-areas-political-alignment.

even less likely to interact with politically dissimilar people . . . the political biases and partisan hostility that currently exist in American politics will continue to grow."[9] David French calls this dynamic the "Law of Group Polarization," which says, "When like-minded people gather, they tend to grow more extreme . . . sometimes more extreme than the most extreme member."[10] Our politics will only more closely imitate social media drama as we geographically sort ourselves, and our in-person social lives, according to the same algorithms.

The conventional understanding of the relationship between politics and religion is that our political positions are downstream of our religious convictions. But Margolis shows that if the opposite were true—that if our religious identities were downstream of our political partisanship—the results and data would be utterly identical. That means the Law of Group Polarization affects more than our political views. Inasmuch as we lack an institutional anchor (e.g., deep involvement in a church that resists partisan polarization) it will also backfill and shape our religious identity.

Consider the implications for church involvement: if the most common reason people stop going to church is moving to a new place[11] and we're now willing to move across the country to be around people who share our politics, then the risk of church shoppers becoming church *droppers* increases exponentially. And if we're willing to uproot our lives to be surrounded by more politically like-minded people, we likely won't hesitate to apply the same political filter in our search for a church home. With Main Character Syndrome (chapter 3) layered on top of our political self-sorting, churches are facing the lose-lose choice of either caving to partisan expectations or losing any opportunity to disciple across the aisle.

Whenever we gather based on shared political affinity, we risk

9. Michele F. Margolis, *From Politics to the Pews: How Partisanship and the Political Environment Shape Religious Identity* (University of Chicago Press, 2018), 6.

10. David French, *Divided We Fall: America's Secession Threat and How to Restore Our Nation* (St. Martin's Press, 2020), 89.

11. Jim Davis and Michael Graham with Ryan P. Burge, *The Great Dechurching: Who's Leaving, Why Are They Going, and What Will It Take to Bring Them Back?* (Zondervan, 2023).

growing more politically extreme in both our views and fervor, making us less hospitable toward those who don't share them. But there's also an upside to the Law of Group Polarization: when our gathering is centered on the gospel, we grow more extreme in our graciousness, more secure in Christ, and, thus, more hospitable to all, regardless of their politics. However we sort ourselves, every community will grow more extreme in their shared affinity and more secure in their shared identity over time. It is a church's identity in Christ and shared affinity in the gospel that makes political diversity possible and non-polarizing.

Anxious Anti-Visions

Like most pastors across the country trying to hold their church together in the midst of a global pandemic, subsequent lockdowns, impossible decisions of whether to mask or not, social unrest in the wake of George Floyd's murder, and mounting election anxiety on top of all the usual shepherding crises, 2020 was the worst decade of my life. Or at least, it felt that way.

In a near-perfect case study in the cliché that "the road to hell is paved with good intentions," I made the brilliant—and by that, I mean *terrible*—decision to preach a sermon series on a Christian view of politics, dubbed "Citizens in Exile." During lockdowns. Over live stream. More on my regrets in a moment.

In each sermon I took the time to define terms, distinguish between considerations of what is moral/immoral versus what is wise/ unwise, and otherwise laid a foundation for public theology. Reactions were . . . varied. On the one hand, I received a lot of positive feedback from those who would likely describe themselves as politically homeless or moderate. For them, the sermon series provided much-needed clarity and principles that helped them navigate the political chaos. But about halfway through the series, the hemorrhaging began. Several families left our church in the last few weeks before the election. Two of them left just a day apart in the week following my sermon on Joshua 5:13–15.

One left because they perceived "an increasing collectivist mentality and political liberalism from the pulpit," and the other because they detected a "political agenda [that] would make sexual minorities feel unwelcome." Both sought reassurance that Jesus was on their respective side yet heard me say the opposite in my preaching that Christians should focus more on asking whether *we* are on *his* side.

I learned many lessons that fall, but two are especially instructive here.

First, I had no idea how much the anxiety of that season was affecting all of us—myself included—and I severely underestimated the difference that in-person versus live streamed worship services would have on that anxiety. McLuhan's "the medium is the message" applies to more than social media. Physiologically speaking, being in another's physical presence is a powerful way to release accumulated anxiety. Virtual connection exacerbates anxiety because screens can't replicate all the nonverbal social cues our brains subconsciously process in sending and receiving communication. Not being able to meet in-person was at least as influential in families leaving as any content I communicated in a sermon.

Second, I never thought I'd describe catching bullets from all sides as a gift but, in a strange way, it was. When you strip away the sociological jargon, negative polarization is essentially a phenomenon of human empathy. Receiving criticism or anger from one political end of the spectrum makes it easier to empathize, identify, and eventually associate with those they attack on the opposite end of the spectrum. No one is immune to that temptation and its subsequent distortions, but they are a *lot* easier to resist when you're getting friendly fire from every direction simultaneously. If for no other reason, political diversity is a gift to congregations and the pastors charged with shepherding them.

Don't get me wrong, friendly fire *isn't*. Anti-visions just aren't nearly as seductive when everyone is shooting at you and no side seems safe.

An anti-vision is a motivating "why" defined by what you are against. That's not just another way of describing run-of-the-mill polarization. It's one thing to grow more extreme in your view of something you are *for* (e.g., universal healthcare or religious liberty), even if what you are for conflicts with what someone else is for. That's just life, and unavoidable in a democracy—by design. It's another thing to grow more extreme according to what you are *against* (e.g., forcing nuns to pay for healthcare that includes contraception or risk losing their tax-exempt status[12]). Where positive visions require persuading those who disagree, anti-visions make it much easier to demonize them.

I'm sure there are exceptions, but most of us embracing political anti-visions don't do so because we want or intend to demonize anyone. That's merely a by-product of reducing huge, complex problems down to a narrow, more manageable focus for our effort. When all we have are simplistic explanations for what ails us, we can't fathom why anyone would stand in the way of equally simplistic solutions. Those who do must, therefore, be evil. They must be stopped. Eventually, stopping them overrides even our own self-interest.

Of course, nothing rewards our anti-visions more than social media. There's always someone wrong on the internet. Someone who needs demonizing. Anti-visions are catnip to algorithms designed to make real-world political differences even less tolerable. They automate our digital sorting, at scale and without our asking them to, into ever-more niche and atomized associations according to our political identities and anti-visions. Nothing will more quickly saw off the branch upon which we are so precariously perched than allowing this digital manipulation—or the anti-visions fueling it—to keep us from participating in institutions.

It's helpful to think of institutions as society's dialysis machines. They make individuals and communities of every size healthier and more adaptive by filtering toxic anxiety out of our systems (political or otherwise). They provide localized meaning to anchor us whether our candidate wins the national election or not. It's just harder to stay angry at someone if you know you'll have to look them in the eye every Sunday. Healthy social and spiritual institutions channel our disappointment and frustration toward constructive opportunities to solve the collective problems that most immediately (and locally) affect us. Simple

---

12. *Little Sisters of the Poor Saints Peter and Paul Home v. Pennsylvania*, No. 19–431 (US Supreme Court, July 8, 2020).

embodiment can be a guardrail that provides a surprising degree of accountability in all our relationships.

Anti-visions simply don't have near the sway over us when we pour ourselves into healthy institutions. They don't get a foothold in our hearts. Without church anchoring us to a transcendent source of meaning greater than what we can self-create, political toxins will continue to accumulate and pressure will continue to build until it all breaks down or boils over.

Just as our shift in association accelerates negative polarization, anti-visions inject partisan politics with steroids. Combined, those two dynamics all but guarantee the culture wars will continue. Fixing or even mitigating polarization is far from simple, but the first step is. We either embrace the only institution uniquely equipped to inoculate anti-vision with transcendent grace (the body of Christ), or something *will* replace the church's role in our lives and the everyday meaning it provides.

But there is still one more ingredient fueling our (un)civil religions, and the ingredient isn't just polarizing us—it may also be radicalizing us.

Kayfabe, Chaos, and Too Many Elites

American civic life has, to our shame, become more of a performative feedback loop than the give-and-take mediation needed to solve the complex problems of a diverse society. But that doesn't mean we don't accomplish anything. Political performances aren't a totally empty exercise. They represent something in the same way that both politicians and professional wrestlers represent something.

Yes, you read that right: professional wrestlers.

Even though I've never watched more than a minute or two of professional wrestling in my entire life (and then, only by accident), almost all of us have followed politics closely enough that we don't have to. According to the Cambridge Dictionary, kayfabe is the practice of "trying to make people believe that (professional) wrestlers are particular characters, when in fact they are only pretending to be those characters."

Each wrestler's persona represents qualities, whether virtues or vices, that their respective fans identify with and cheer on. When your favorite wrestler wins a match, it's a win for you too. This is true in every sport but, at risk of pointing out the obvious, *professional wrestling isn't a sport*. It's a performance more akin to Broadway than baseball. Winning in professional wrestling doesn't necessarily draw more fans. Rather, whoever draws the most fans wins the championship title. It's kayfabe all the way down.

Electoral incentives are likewise infected with kayfabe—i.e., fandom—not character, leadership, or policy as the only dimension of competition. As a result, our politics are about solving problems the same way professional wrestling is about winning.

So, what exactly is the point of kayfabe politics? Why do we invest so much time and energy into something we know won't deliver much in the way of tangible outcomes? Quite simply, because that's not what we hope to get from politics anymore. Both professional wrestlers and partisan performers are mascots representing real people locked in a visceral competition for a very specific dimension of meaning. And because dimension is so upstream of our polarization, it has been subjected to even more disruption than presidential politics. That is, *social status*.

To understand why people spread hostile political rumors and conspiracy theories, a group of political scientists and researchers conducted several studies wherein participants were given hypothetical stories and asked whether they would share them online. If so, they were then asked what motivated them to do so. To the surprise of researchers, the reasons were not exclusively to weaken the opponents of their preferred political party or candidate. Nor did their reasons fall along expected partisan lines drawn by polarization. Rather, they stumbled on a social pattern within the American public they call a "need for chaos," which is "a mindset to gain status by disrupting the established order."[13] For these respondents, disruption isn't motivated by altruism (e.g., reducing

13. Michael Bang Petersen, Mathias Osmundsen, and Kevin Arceneaux, "The 'Need for Chaos' and Motivations to Share Hostile Political Rumors," *American Political Science Review* 117, no. 4 (November 2023): 1486–1505, https://doi.org/10.1017/S0003055422001447.

economic inequality or unemployment), but by out-group animosity and retribution against elites who've failed "to accord them the respect that they feel they personally deserve."[14] In other words, we're empty and stuck, but maybe we'll feel better if we make them pay. Consequences be damned.

Remarkably, this need for chaos is thoroughly bipartisan. "A desire to 'burn it all down' may emerge from multiple pathways shaped by current societal cleavages, yet for different reasons."[15] This anti-systemic impulse is greatest among Black males and white males, but its fuel isn't limited to any single political persuasion, socioeconomic class, race, or gender: "Increased inequality intensifies status competitions across the entire status hierarchy . . . and can induce even those who are objectively well off to feel that they are losing ground as others pass them."[16] This doesn't mean we don't have real, concrete problems that need solving, but that one reason we might talk about solving problems a lot more than we solve them is that we're using real issues and policies as totems for deeper (yet no less real) existential angst. In other words, this need for chaos is the inevitable symptom of discarding the churches and institutions we once trusted to confer social status and infuse everyday life with meaning.

We've all experienced this angst at one point or another. We know the feeling of spinning our wheels despite following life's formula and doing everything right, when you just can't get ahead no matter how hard you try or how many hours you work. But when that goes on long enough, it can seem like the only way to get a break is to break the system. Whether because we've abandoned local institutions or because they no longer exist (a critical problem for many rural and urban areas) national politics might be the only arena where many of us can work out our loss, grief, and, yes, anger with even the slimmest hope of validation.

---

14. Petersen, Osmundsen, and Arceneaux, "Need for Chaos."

15. Petersen, Osmundsen, and Arceneaux, "Need for Chaos."

16. While the study's authors point out the similarities between the need for chaos in Black males (due to historically low social status) and white males (due to perceived loss of status), they don't address the potential underlying causes or significance of men being overwhelmingly more likely than women to experience status frustration. Petersen, Osmundsen, and Arceneaux, "Need for Chaos."

That's the most anyone can expect of a system too broken to provide relief. Besides, there's something poetic in using politicians in much the same way they use us. So we put our hope in paper tigers, not necessarily because we think they will affect tangible change but because they offer us a way, if vicariously, to claw back meaning and ease our sense of drowning through their electoral victory. Like professional wrestlers, we elect kayfabe politicians to be our avatars, fighting tooth and nail for the meaning and social status we've been unfairly denied.

Politicians further stoke and leverage our fear with pugilistic slogans like "take our country back" or "democracy is on the ballot" (even though democracy *is* the ballot) or "drain the swamp." Again, they aren't asking for our vote so they can enact policies that better our lives or the lives of our neighbors, but so we don't feel so empty or worthless when they win. When we thus elevate politics as our ultimate source of meaning and identity, it becomes a civil religion. We treat voting like a sacrament—a sign and seal that imparts our blessing and authority upon a ~~wrestler~~ candidate to ~~smash our opponent's face with a metal folding chair~~ raise our social status with an electoral victory. When they win, *we* win. And really, *everybody* wins when privileged insiders and establishment elites lose their seat at the table. They didn't earn it anyway.

Every society needs prophetic outsiders to hold insiders accountable. But when everyone is an outsider, nobody is. A society or institution composed only of outsiders is no different than one filled with insiders. Neither are capable of building or repairing much of anything. Trust least of all. Like it or not, we need both. And so despite my hyperbole, we should neither condemn nor commend populism too quickly because, if nothing else, it tells us something isn't working for a large part of society. Something is misaligned at a systemic level.

In 2010, Peter Turchin claimed that we were in the midst of a critical period of social disintegration that would culminate in a full-blown political crisis in or around 2020. His prediction was met with understandable skepticism at the time, but the 2020 election cycle and the Capitol riots on January 6, 2021, made him one of the most sought-after interviews for several months thereafter. His 2023 book—ominously titled *End*

Times—names three main factors making our politics so volatile, but what he calls "elite overproduction"[17] is especially helpful here.

Here's his argument in short: Imagine society as a game of musical chairs where participants are elites and the empty chairs represent available positions of influence. In a society with healthy elite production, someone will always be disappointed and not reach the position (chair) they hoped for. But that disappointment is spread out over time. It's sustainable. Even though a chair is removed along with a player each round, their odds of landing a chair are still pretty good because there's never more than one elite than available chairs.

Unlike the traditional game, elite overproduction is the equivalent of *keeping* chair-less participants in the game while also *adding* a new player. Every. Single. Round. The first still only results with a single loser, but the usual number of losers is doubled in round two, tripled in round three, etc. The ratio of players (elites) to chairs (positions) grows disproportionately. That isn't sustainable. The longer the game is played, the more disappointed players there are and the more fiercely they compete. Resentment increases exponentially among recurring losers because, even though they technically still have a chance, they know their odds of winning will only diminish with each round. We've been playing this latter version of musical chairs for several decades.

Except we're not talking about a circle of empty chairs. We're talking about our core social infrastructure. In a society that promises the American Dream—upward mobility and social status for anyone able and willing to work for it—elite overproduction guarantees widespread disenfranchisement. We use words like "disestablishmentarianism," and not ironically. We start to bend the rules and stand guard over an empty chair. We jostle and jockey for position. We might even throw an elbow or two if it means protecting our chances of landing an elite position. Besides, everybody else is. But eventually, what Turchin calls "misery immersion" and frustration reaches a boiling point, and we start breaking

---

17. Turchin defines elites as those who are in the top 10% of a given society, which has the most economic, social, cultural, and political power. Peter Turchin, *End Times: Elites, Counter-Elites, and the Path of Political Disintegration* (Penguin Press, 2023).

the rules. We do whatever it takes and justify our activism because we don't trust others to play by the rules anymore either. After all, if liberal or conservative establishment elites are using their power to keep a stranglehold on opportunity for them and theirs, then we have a moral imperative to fight back. Maybe even to take up arms. We take on the sacred duty of breaking up the circle of chairs (institutions) to restart the game (society) so people like us have a chance of winning. All too quickly, culture wars can reach escape velocity and escalate into a full-blown secular crusade for (insert righteous cause here).

Like fact-checking on social media, my sermon series on politics was well-intentioned but ultimately misguided. Beneath our crises of division is, ultimately, a crisis of meaning. MAGA populism resonates so strongly with rural communities and the working class for the same reason progressive activism resonates with minority communities and young adults: Anti-vision is a powerful rally cry for anyone who feels like they're losing ground, can't get ahead, or both. It's possible, probable even, that they're all right about it too. That frustration is rooted in something real, even if the solution is tragically performative. But the longer we go without relief from real stress, the more kayfabe politics slide toward nihilism, and then it's not even about winning anymore. That ship has sailed, and with the American Dream on board. Now, political anti-visions are primarily about *not losing anymore*, and measured by the enjoyment we get out of seeing our opponents get a taste of their own medicine.

Our system of government is designed to force us to compromise. Anti-vision, and the nihilism it inevitably produces, is what John Adams feared when he wrote, "Our constitution was made only for a moral and religious people. It is wholly inadequate to the government of any other."[18] He almost certainly had the French Revolution's unrestrained violence in mind when he penned those words in 1798, so he understood how dangerous and tempting nihilism can be to a defeated spirit. The more

---

18. John Adams, "Letter from John Adams to Massachusetts Militia," October 11, 1798, https://www.johnadamsacademy.org/apps/pages/index.jsp?uREC_ID=2003858&type=d&p REC_ID=2094472.

we tacitly embrace (un)civil religions, the more readily we'll believe that "elections aren't for eliminating problems, they're for eliminating our 'enemies.'"[19] Having political opponents won't be enough. We'll start making meaning by making enemies and pulling the chair out from under them by any means necessary. And for some who become sufficiently radicalized by anti-vision, the collateral damage done to the institutions along the way will be a feature, not a bug.[20]

Our Antidote to Anti-Vision

(Un)civil religions are not so much the result of our politics infecting our faith or our conflating the two—though that may also be true—so much as we are using partisan politics to fill the void of status and meaning that institutions used to fill—the church first and foremost. Without immersion in politically and socioeconomically diverse tidepools, we will be ground down by wave after wave of (social media–delivered) reminders that we're being left in the dust of someone, somewhere who is sitting comfortably in a chair they didn't earn. All this leads to the birth of not just *one* (un)civil religion, but as many as we have enemies or causes we can blame for keeping us from a more meaningful life. Getting stuck in that feedback loop would wear anyone down, and tempt us to shed norms, break constraints, and tear down any institution we suspect is holding us back.

That's why satisfying our need for chaos in political arenas is, at its root, a behavior of despair. Knowing that makes it so much clearer, even understandable, why partisan differences might determine our commitment to a church, or any church at all. How could you coexist with someone whose politics perpetuate the system responsible for your loss

19. Jonah Goldberg, "Democracy Is Not on the Ballot," *The Dispatch*, November 4, 2022, https://thedispatch.com/newsletter/gfile/democracy-is-not-on-the-ballot/.

20. "Accelerationist ideologies" are those that intentionally provoke dysfunction in order to hurry the collapse of a society or institution that no longer works for them, all in the hope of picking up the pieces and rebuilding social structures to benefit them. For more, see Elizabeth Neumann, *Kingdom of Rage: The Rise of Christian Extremism and the Path Back to Peace* (Worthy, 2024).

of status, prestige, or any possibility thereof? How could you commune with a member of the conservative/progressive elite who doesn't deserve the power they wield? I certainly wouldn't feel safe among those who vote against my worth, but that's only a risk if we put our hope in electoral victory to provide the justification Christ already won on the cross. Simply being aware that our political volatility is a symptom of profound spiritual need is a powerful first step in demoting the primacy of political association in favor of a transformative relationship with church.

The good news is that, rather than making meaning by making enemies, Jesus chose instead to die for them—for *us*—in love. Neither his teaching nor his example allows any exception to loving our enemies. That includes the person or people who God brought to mind as you read, *especially* if you believe they're guilty of this church defeater. Jesus calls you to love them as he loves you. Not to pity or dismiss them, nor to forgive and forget them. The point of understanding the systemic roots of (un)civil religions isn't to have more cause for condemning or canceling our political opponents. My hope, rather, is that familiarizing ourselves with root causes will validate how truly difficult this is, bleed off some of the anxiety contributing to our hypervigilance, and resuscitate Christlike consideration of each other. There's no other way to break out of our vicious cycle.

Even if it doesn't seem true in our day-to-day, in Christ we've already won what matters most. Jesus already defeated sin and death. Ultimate meaning is found in and through Jesus making friends out of his enemies. His victory is already ours, the spoils of which are a life fuller of meaning, more rich with vindication than any or all political outcomes in our favor—past, present, and future. We have only to live into that more true reality by trusting him to provide for our social, economic, and political futures, and entrusting ourselves to his church. There is, of course, more to loving our enemies as ourselves, but we can't hope to accomplish any of it apart from all-in and meaning-full involvement in the local church.

Reflection Questions

1. For yourself (not others), how would you know if you were deriving more everyday meaning from political outcomes than the finished work of Christ? Who could you ask to tell you honestly if you already were? What makes them trustworthy?

2. On a scale of one to ten, how much does the American Dream (however you define it) motivate you? On a scale of one to ten, how close are you to achieving the American Dream? Consider the difference in those two numbers. How much do they shape your politics? How do they color your view of church?

3. Think of someone in your life who you think most exemplifies this church defeater. How would you approach a conversation about politics with them now versus before reading this chapter? What questions would you ask to better understand (not convince) them? What's stopping you from initiating that conversation?

5

Virtuous Victimhood

How Justifying Coercion and Weaponizing Compassion Incite Vicious Competition

Our chief desire is not to honor and help victims, but to become them. Where virtue was once the cultivation of a great heart, nowadays we seek to demonstrate a thin skin.

—Glen Scrivener, *The Air We Breathe*

Church Defeater 5: Virtuous Victimhood. Because compassion is one of few remaining grounds for moral authority in a secular society, we position ourselves and identify as victims to deflect criticism, silence disagreement, and compete for social status.

Nothing has so comprehensively reshaped or fundamentally transformed any society, before or since, like the compassionate movement of justice and mercy that took root in the Roman Empire as the gospel permeated every dimension of society. Roman culture did not value compassion as a laudable virtue to be celebrated but as a dangerous vice and weakness to be stamped out. "The starving deserved no sympathy. Beggars were best rounded up and deported. Pity risked undermining a wise man's self-control. Only fellow citizens of good character who, through no fault of their own, had fallen on evil days might conceivably merit assistance."[1] Strength was its own moral authority. Mercy was anathema, a capitulation to weakness and selfishness that threatened the empire's strength and stability.

And yet, within just a few centuries, this society that valorized power and scorned the weak was turned upside down by a suffering Savior who didn't even have the dignity to fight back. The average Roman citizen could not have imagined their empire being transformed by a "revolution that has, at its molten heart, the image of God dead on a cross."[2]

As the gospel spread across the face of the Roman Empire, Trinitarian societies were established in the wake. These outposts, not of a worldly empire but of an otherworldly kingdom, incubated and shaped generations of Christians. Dozens, then hundreds, and eventually thousands of these countercultural communities helped believers live out the implications of their faith in every sphere of life. Their love for God and neighbor demonstrated a very different kind of power—one not accumulated through conquest but "made perfect in weakness" (2 Corinthians 12:9). Over time, these small communities became indispensable to everyone around them, growing and maturing into the culture-shaping institutions on which the Modern West was built. Though the gospel

---

1. Tom Holland, *Dominion: How the Christian Revolution Remade the World* (Basic Books, 2021), 58.
2. Holland, *Dominion*.

sparked compassion everywhere it spread, that spark would have flickered and died without churches to keep the fire.

Western society is in the midst of another revolution—one that redefines power and moral authority but employs very different means and ends.

While the "software" of society has been on a noticeably post-Christian cultural trajectory for decades, the more post-Christian our institutional "hardware" becomes, the more the hard-won fruit of the early church is withering. As individualism continues driving deeper wedges between us and the "formative structures of our social lives,"[3] we lose the unique capacity of institutions to steward power equitably. Once "compassion is divorced from the Christian story,"[4] we lose compassion's distinctly cruciform shape, making it susceptible to being co-opted by other cultural narratives or purposes. Combined, we seem to almost be returning to pre-Christian Rome's values and attitudes toward power, but with one exception: we now justify coercive use of power in the name of weakness rather than strength, and for those we believe are most worthy of compassion—ourselves first and foremost.

Our final church defeater, virtuous victimhood, is Christian compassion that's been severed from its roots and grafted onto secular definitions of power that make it socially acceptable, and often beneficial to coerce anyone with more relative power. This surprisingly coherent set of post-Christian beliefs and postinstitutional incentives still clings to vestiges of Christian compassion for moral authority, not to appeal to our better angels, but to force desired outcomes without having to win anyone over to our side. As effective as that may be in the short-term, it has a huge long-term blind spot: the less we believe persuasion is possible, the more we resort to coercion; yet the more we rely on coercion, the less we bother trying to persuade. This slope is as perilous as it is slippery. Without persuasion, coercion is the only tool

3. Daniel E. Burns, "Our Post-Pandemic Institutions: A Conversation with Yuval Levin," *American Enterprise Institute*, May 3, 2021, https://www.aei.org/articles/our-post-pandemic-institutions-a-conversation-with-yuval-levin/.

4. Glen Scrivener, *The Air We Breathe* (London: The Good Book Company, 2022).

virtuous victimhood has left. And if all you have is a hammer, everyone will start looking like a nail.

The engine driving this vicious cycle is a profoundly cynical, zero-sum approach to power that replaces trust as our currency for relationship. The more power you have, the less trust you deserve. The institutions designed to steward power are trusted least of all. The potential for harm is just too high to let our guard down or let anyone in, much less risk being complicit in systemic injustice. Even if we are part of a local church, viewing institutions so cynically keeps Christ's body at arm's length—in perpetuity.

Like the other four, this church defeater is rarely, if ever, consciously adopted. To the degree virtuous victimhood describes us, it is because we're like foster children who can't help but feel angry and insecure after being uprooted from our family. It is a reactive adaptation and coping mechanism for being uprooted from institutions and living in a state of perpetual instability. In a post-Christian society that no longer trusts institutions to steward power, virtuous victimhood becomes our default and last resort for getting the attention or help we need. And, like foster children, it is a self-reinforcing habit that becomes harder to break the longer we stay in the system.

The Push and Pull of Disintermediation

We can debate how quickly or effectively a given church or institution mediates social conflict, but doing so peacefully is impossible without them. Power that isn't stewarded by groups of stakeholders can quickly and easily be wielded coercively by individuals. That is never truer than when frustration with an institution is used to justify consolidating power in a single person.

Sometimes mediating interests, needs, and dreams is very inter-personal and efficient, but most of the time it feels unnecessarily impersonal and convoluted to the extreme. No institution looks at the local DMV as a paragon of technocratic efficiency. But what feels like agonizing slowness is often by design: to give stakeholders reasonable notice and opportunity to understand, process, and decide how to exercise their voice and/or agency. As an example even less exciting than the DMV, the Book of Church Order governing churches in my denomination, the Presbyterian Church in America (PCA), requires at least one week's notice and a quorum (1/4 or 1/6 of communing members, depending on the church's size) to call a congregational meeting. A vote to leave the denomination requires at least a thirty-day notice to ensure such a significant decision is only made on the other side of a robust shepherding process (persuasion), and not by ramming a vote through (coercion). Even a right decision made too quickly can cut stakeholders out of the process or push them to act against their interest. Slow, incremental change is often more inclusive and just. Institutions are the only way to give everyone opportunity to participate in decisions affecting more than a few dozen people. For that reason alone, we should "defend due process and institutions even if we find them cumbersome and conflictual."[5]

If the world seemed to explode between the summer of 2020 and early 2021, this is why. We suddenly became aware of serious and systemic social problems at the same time our incentives for solving them through persuasion were replaced with incentives for coercion. After months of being disconnected from mediating institutions, we stopped trying to arbitrate our differences, settled for airing our grievances online, and baptized it as "making a difference." Social media disintermediates by luring users out of institutions with the promise of less vulnerable mediation. Citizens can instead participate in society via "passive . . . acts of affirmation and peer pressure"[6]—or pull and push coercion, respectively.

Andy Crouch observes that, without institutions to steward power, we default to wielding power through either violence or beauty.[7]

5. N. T. Wright and Michael F. Bird, *Jesus and the Powers: Christian Political Witness in an Age of Totalitarian Terror and Dysfunctional Democracies* (Zondervan Reflective, 2024), 169.

6. Burns, "Post-Pandemic Institutions."

7. Brad Edwards and John Houmes, hosts, PostEverything, season 1, episode 32, "How Christians Are Formed by Power with Andy Crouch," 1 hr. 17 min., April 10, 2024, https://

Embedded in the design of counterfeit institutions are corresponding levers of social pressure (via viral outrage) and popularity (via viral affirmation). However we label them, mediation is reduced to two forms of coercive power—push (offensive and direct) and pull (defensive and indirect). Neither are governed by process or require persuasion.

Frustrated that the city denied your building permit? No problem. Anyone who can sufficiently frame themselves as a victim and their plight as egregious can stoke enough outrage (violence) or sympathy (beauty) to bend the city to their will. What we call cancel culture is simply disintermediated power being exercised at scale.

Most revolutions start with the genuinely good intention of fixing something broken about society, yet none conclude without at least some unintended consequences—some much worse than others. Likewise, disintermediation is often a well-meaning attempt to fix real problems but frequently ends up solving it for some stakeholders, quickly and efficiently, by cutting other stakeholders out of the process and redistributing the consequences onto them—often without their awareness or consent.

For example, a network of city-based Facebook groups called "Are We Dating The Same Guy" (AWDTSG) began with a truly good and noble vision: "to make courtship safer."[8] That vision has borne significant fruit: "Countless women say they have called off potentially dangerous dates, left a cheating partner or verified their concerns about a man because of what they've read."[9] Who wouldn't celebrate that? But there's a trade-off: with 3.5 million members across 200 groups, confidentiality is practically impossible. There's no guarantee that accusations won't get back to the accused. "Women speak of being confronted by the very men they warned others about,"[10] exacerbating their traumatic experience.

---

podcasts.apple.com/us/podcast/how-christians-are-formed-by-power-with-andy-crouch/id16 76174977?i=1000652004394.

8. Brittany Shammas and Marisa Iati, "Are We Dating the Same Guy? Facebook Groups Offer Intel but Upend Lives.," *The Washington Post*, March 2, 2024, https://www.washington post.com/technology/2024/03/02/dating-same-guy-facebook-groups/.

9. Shammas and Iati, "Dating the Same Guy."

10. Shammas and Iati, "Dating the Same Guy."

As far as unintended consequences go, that's pretty significant for the women AWDTSG is trying to help, but it's not hard to see how it likely prevents countless other women from enduring similar trauma.

Unfortunately, there are other significant trade-offs.

Even if nine out of ten posts describe legitimate abuse or assault, no digital moderator or user is able to discern between a genuine victim and a jilted ex. Not online. A merely painful (but non-abusive) breakup would leave any of us raw and tempted to exaggerate in our anger, and with similar result. An accusation doesn't have to be false to do catastrophic damage to someone's reputation or career, and using what amounts to trustless mediation all but guarantees it. The exes of several group members recently filed a defamation lawsuit against Facebook and its parent company, Meta, for "being questioned by employers, losing relationships and spiraling emotionally over accusations they insist are untrue."[11] Even if false accusations are rare, the most conservative estimate could easily number in the tens of thousands when scaled up to 3.5 million users.

The question isn't whether there is a problem but whether we mediate relationships through trust-building process and persuasion or we disintermediate risk using online push and pull coercion to redistribute the problem. "Unlike when families or colleagues used to play matchmaker, which added a layer of accountability, many couples now meet online. And it can be a dangerous free-for-all."[12] AWDTSG was started in good faith to address a real and urgent need. But trading the risk of one coercion (assault) for another (defamation) doesn't solve anything. Both can ruin lives. I know that for many, that trade-off is worth it, but coercion motivated by compassion is still coercive and perpetuates injustice.

So . . . you know . . . why *not* take my life into my own hands and write a whole chapter about how virtuous victimhood has injected self-righteous jet fuel into our tribalism and turned us all into secular legalists? If this chapter were a high school senior, it would be voted most likely to get me canceled.

---

11. Shammas and Iati, "Dating the Same Guy."
12. Shammas and Iati, "Dating the Same Guy."

Or am I just positioning myself as a potential victim to cut off criticism before it starts?

Weaponizing Compassion to Coerce

Even if we can't put our finger on why, we intuit that power has become a scarce resource. Without mediating institutions, we need some way of getting large groups of people to act in our interests. Virtuous victimhood provides moral authority by reframing pull and push coercion as bare minimum acts of compassion. There are multiple ways to leverage that authority, but all of them rely on one or both of the following distortions of compassion: "Victims are inherently virtuous" (pull), and "power differentials are inherently harmful" (push). Each contain a kernel of truth, but both become coercive through what they share in common: "inherently."

Pulling Compassion: "Victims Are Inherently Virtuous"

In a chilling episode of NPR's *Hidden Brain* podcast, host Shankar Vedantam explored "the strange psychology of wanting to seem worse off than we really are."[13] He interviewed Harvard Psychologist, Jillian Jordan, on a peer-reviewed study she conducted measuring the perceived moral character of someone who was the victim of a crime—or, the "virtuous victim effect."[14] Volunteer participants were divided into two groups, each of which were given a fictional scenario involving a college student named Sarah. In the first scenario (the neutral condition), Sarah lends her iPad to a classmate, Gabrielle, to look something up, after which she and Sarah's other friends leave Sarah's dorm room to go out. It ends there, but the second scenario (the victim condition) picks up where the first scenario left off to explain that Sarah also left her dorm room and, while away, Gabrielle returns, breaks into her dorm room,

---

13. Shankar Vedantam, host, Hidden Brain, "Crying Wolf," April 10, 2023, 56 min., https://podcasts.apple.com/us/podcast/crying-wolf/id1028908750?i=1000608260467.

14. Jillian J. Jordan and Maryam Kouchaki, "Virtuous Victims," *Science Advances* 7, no. 42 (October 13, 2021), https://doi.org/10.1126/sciadv.abg5902.

and steals Sarah's iPad. After hearing their respective scenarios, participants were then asked whether they thought Sarah was a good person. Because Sarah's behavior and actions were identical in both scenarios, there shouldn't have been any statistically significant difference between how the two groups perceived her moral character or virtue. But there was. Across seventeen experiments and 9,676 volunteers, participants consistently viewed hypothetical characters with a victim condition "to be a more moral and a more trustworthy person than [those with] the neutral condition."[15]

Jordan's study shows how "victim narratives are an increasingly prevalent staple of contemporary discourse," as well as how they "may shape the policy and legal responses that follow wrongdoing toward victims, the ways that victims are treated by members of their social networks, the decisions that victims make about whether to share their stories with others, and the ways that society frames and evaluates moral debates surrounding allegations of victimization."[16] Importantly, the study explicitly calls for future research to answer the natural question of how their "results relate to victim blaming" or excusing perpetrators' behavior. But the key takeaway in all of Jordan's findings is a deep-seated ideological commitment that subconsciously ascribes both *moral authority* and *unique insight* to victims.

Few events in recent history are more tragic than the 2018 mass shooting at Stoneman Douglas High School in Parkland, Florida, that killed seventeen people and injured seventeen others. It is good and right to have compassion for every victim, without exception. So when one of the student survivors, David Hogg, began advocating for gun control policies that he believed could have prevented it, compassion compelled the country to listen and take him seriously. Again, rightfully so.

But as policy experts began weighing in, good faith disagreement with some of Hogg's proposals sparked an uproar. They were, critics said, "attacking a child who was speaking up only because he and his

---

15. Vedantam, "Crying Wolf," emphasis added.
16. Jordan and Kouchaki, "Virtuous Victims."

classmates had been attacked already."[17] This important national conversation was complicated further when bad faith commentators like Alex Jones started spreading conspiracy theories and claiming the whole thing was staged. A hoax. Nothing excuses the ad hominem waged against Hogg. It was merciless and vile. Those contributing to it deserve as much of our contempt as victims deserve our compassion. But even more grievous than grifting off murdered teenagers was how the actual problem got lost (and disintermediated) in the process. That moment of relatively unified public opinion could have catalyzed meaningful compromise and bipartisan legislation. Instead, we've squandered the opportunity and still don't have a solution.

The outrage over good faith criticism and bad faith disinformation had something in common. Both shared the ideological premise that victims have both moral authority and unique insight rendering them above reproach, not because they have demonstrated integrity in their response to suffering, but because their perspective is *inherently* sanctified merely for having suffered a horrible experience. Counterintuitively, Jones accepted the premise of those who were outraged by his behavior. If no one can question Hogg's unique insight and moral authority as a victim, then the only way to effect change is to attack the source of that insight and authority—his status as a victim.

Please don't hear what I'm not saying. This isn't victim-blaming, nor is coercive abuse or personal attack ever justified. Many good and important victim advocacy organizations are birthed in the wake of tragedy. We need such projects. But like nearly all modern attempts at collective action, they are hampered by the very problem I'm describing. Alex Jones is a caricature, but his example helps us see where virtuous victimhood pollutes the air we breathe, suffocating our ability to learn from tragedies or prevent them in the future. Surviving a mass shooting gave David Hogg a lasting appreciation and passion for gun control, and that's something, but it's not everything. Alone, his experience didn't

---

17. Molly Roberts, "Can We Criticize the Parkland Kids?," *The Herald News*, March 1, 2018, https://www.heraldnews.com/story/opinion/2018/03/01/can-we-criticize-parkland-kids/13988927007/.

give him any wisdom or insight to navigate any of the practical, legal, or political realities that make gun violence one of the most challenging social problems in a generation. If we are serious about preventing another Parkland, we would be foolish to cut ourselves off from *any* perspective that might aid our effort. So why do we? I think we are, collectively, too addicted to self-righteousness and too disintermediated to care for longer than a news cycle or two. Numbed out by wave after wave of digital distraction, Christ-less compassion gives us permission to play the martyr, the zealot, or both.

Most tragic of all is how "pulling compassion" accomplishes the opposite of what it intends—it sets victims up for being defined by their experience by cutting them off from a powerful means of grace. For if victims are *inherently* above reproach, Christ's insistence that we forgive and love our enemies will seem like a cruel and unjust burden too heavy for victims to bear. While forgiveness will always go against the grain in this age, forgiveness isn't only grace for perpetrators, it's also a gift meant to free victims from wounds that might otherwise redefine them. Virtuous victimhood alienates victims from where true healing is most ordinarily found and experienced because it denies any *need* for the mediating institution wherein forgiveness is regularly given and received—the church.

Pushing Compassion: "Power Differentials Are Inherently Harmful"

How do you relate to someone you don't trust? It's not an easy question to answer for several reasons. It will largely depend on the nature of your relationship with them, and especially the scope of the other person's authority. If you don't trust a fast-food worker, you might ask them to repeat your order back to you or confirm they gave you everything before leaving the drive-through window. If you don't trust your doctor, you might get a second opinion—which you might do even if you *do* trust them. When we trust someone, we are giving them power over us according to the scope and nature of their authority. The difference in the cost of a cheeseburger and your future health requires very different levels of trust and authority and, therefore, corresponding time and rigor spent in their training. So while you might trust your doctor to give you all the fast food you ordered, you probably shouldn't trust the teenager leaning out the drive-through window to operate on your heart. It's not personal, it's wisdom. Trusting the wrong authority can have disastrous consequences.

The inverse is also true. Distrusting a fast-food worker to give you all the food you ordered bears relatively little consequence. But when Steve Jobs was diagnosed with pancreatic cancer, "he believed in the power of his diet and 'magical thinking' to heal himself" more than the expertise of his oncologist or surgeon.[18] The fact that Jobs came to regret his decision shortly before he died demonstrates that distrusting the right authority can be just as disastrous as mistrusting the wrong authority.

But what happens when distrust of authority is more than a misplaced wariness or skepticism? What happens when our distrust is the result of believing an imbalance of power in any relationship is inherently harmful? To start, we will categorically view those with less power as victims who can do no wrong and those with more power as oppressors who can't do anything right.

It was this ideological justification that fueled the nationwide campus protests in the months following Hamas's terrorist attack on Israel on October 7, 2023. A now-infamous poster published by the National Students for Justice in Palestine featured the image of a Hamas paraglider—many of which descended on a pro-peace (and largely pro-*Palestinian*) music festival and slaughtered hundreds of innocent civilians. Since then, and whether they were Israeli citizens or not, Jewish students on American college and university campuses have been harassed and threatened, fearing for their own safety.

Rank anti-Semitism may explain some of the abuse targeting American Jews, but it doesn't even remotely explain the widespread celebration of terrorists as freedom fighters. Neither does mere

18. Jeannine Mancini, "Steve Jobs Followed an Extreme Diet Consisting of Certain Fruits and Vegetables and Fasting for Days—When Diagnosed with Pancreatic Cancer, He Declined Treatment Not Wanting to Be 'Violated In That Way' but Later Regretted the Decision," *Yahoo Finance*, January 29, 2024, https://finance.yahoo.com/news/steve-jobs-followed-extreme-diet -220010824.html.

anti-Semitism explain how a nation resurrected from the ashes of the Holocaust and formed by refugees returning to their ancestral homeland could be categorized as "colonial oppressors." The only unfying principle that makes sense of all the above is disturbingly simplistic: Because Israel is more powerful than Hamas—economically, politically, and especially militarily—Hamas can do no wrong and Israel can't do anything right.

This oppressor-vs-oppressed narrative has so thoroughly infected Western politics and diplomacy that Hamas, in blatant violation of international law yet without any meaningful consequences, has had free rein to locate command posts in civilian hospitals,[19] stage highly explosive munitions in elementary school basements, and fire on evacuating civilians[20] who refuse to be their human shields. In contrast, when the Israel Defense Forces (IDF) have intel showing Hamas leaders within a civilian building, their standard operating procedure is to employ a tactic called roof knocking. Before leveling a building, the IDF drop a non-explosive or low-yield munition to warn civilians and give them a ten- to fifteen-minute window to evacuate. International law doesn't require it, and not even the US Military holds itself to such a high standard. Where Hamas treats civilians as valid military targets, the IDF gives their military targets time to escape to preserve civilian life. Who is more virtuous: those with less power or those who wield power more compassionately?

I know we're talking about a conflict spanning several decades, if not centuries. The relationship between Israel and Palestine is *extremely* complicated, more than any handful of sentences could ever fully or fairly represent. That's my point. I'm not insinuating that Israel is blameless or that Gazan civilians get what's coming to them. The contrast illustrates how the oppressor-versus-oppressed narrative does gross injustice to the complexity of the conflict and catastrophically misleads outside

---

19. Melissa Koenig, "Viral Video Appears to Show Hamas Firing on Civilians Fleeing Gaza Hospital," *New York Post*, November 10, 2023, https://nypost.com/2023/11/10/news/video-reports-to-show-hamas-firing-on-civilians-fleeing-childrens-hospital/.

20. Yuval Barnea, "Who Killed a Group of Civilians Fleeing to the South of Gaza?," *The Jerusalem Post*, November 4, 2023, https://www.jpost.com/arab-israeli-conflict/gaza-news/article-771632.

observers. Moralizing power differentials upstream cuts off the ability to evaluate or address harmful use of power downstream. That unrealistic moral simplicity is why it's so attractive. The world is just easier to navigate if all we need to know is that "punching up" is inherently righteous and "punching down" is inherently evil. Call me crazy, but the direction of our punching seems less important than how hard we're punching or why. It certainly shouldn't be the only moral consideration.

Power differentials are real and an unavoidable part of every relationship. It's good to be aware of them. Parents blind to how much influence they have over their children can lead to both abuse (over-application of power) and neglect (under-application of power). But merely having more power than someone else isn't unjust, using power unjustly is. It is not authoritarian to insist my young sons don't play in the street. Special occasions notwithstanding, giving them the power to eat ice cream before dinner isn't good for them. What matters more is whether parents steward their power for their children's formative good (intent) and how wisely they do so (impact). Where authority is mutually accepted and wisely exercised between two or more people, trust is deepened and relationships flourish.

Whether we have less power or more in a relationship, the belief that power differentials are inherently harmful makes power, and not trust, the currency for relationship. Over time, this implicit bias imparts a hyper-vigilant posture. Trusting anyone with more power becomes dangerous and immoral when it might only be uncomfortable, scary, or unwise.

I have lost count of how many people have come through The Table who have never personally experienced spiritual abuse, yet are riddled with anxiety over the mere possibility of it happening. In contrast and almost without exception, those who *have* endured abuse are the least anxious. Most of them describe finding significant rest and healing in our congregation. We never set out to be that kind of church. It just happened, and it's been one of the happiest accidents in all my ministry as a pastor. So it took me a long time to understand why those who have never directly experienced church hurt or suffered under a narcissistic leader seem convinced that it is inevitable. It was only after I started asking questions about how they viewed me as a person versus as a pastor that

I started putting it together. As a person, sure, they felt safe and at least relatively comfortable. But as a pastor in a position of authority, I could never demonstrate enough safety or earn enough trust. How wisely, or for whose good, I stewarded that power was irrelevant.

Unfortunately, someone who sees power differentials as inherently harmful rarely stay in a church for very long. Many eventually stop going altogether because virtuous victimhood precludes the one thing that can assuage their anxiety: trust. Those who have experienced spiritual abuse aren't nearly so reticent to trust because they can't afford *not* to. Healing is impossible without trust. Frankly, it takes a whole lot of privilege to make power a viable currency for relationship. Yet once that transaction is made, submitting to any spiritual or moral authority other than our own, be they peer or pastor, will be as repulsive as compassion was to pre-Christian Rome.

Whether via bottom-up pressure or a self-imposed "do no harm" bias of our own, pastors can fall into the same trap. I did—for my first several years in ministry. It is a mark of wisdom and maturity to be aware of the power imbalance between sheep and shepherd. That ought to humble us, but not paralyze us. We can't be so fearful of our authority's potential to amplify hurt that we pad truth with so many qualifiers that we dampen the Holy Spirit's conviction. If truth without love is abuse, love without truth is neglect. Neither are shepherding.

The Competitive Victimhood Treadmill

As virtuous victimhood permeates American culture, it dangerously reshapes fundamental social incentives and creates a perilous self-perpetuating feedback loop. Opportunities for compassion become a competition for status—by both positive and negative association. If someone in our tribe is unjustly maligned, we can gain social standing by signaling our identification with them (positive association). But if someone who isn't in our tribe is canceled or mistreated, we also can't risk losing face by defending them (negative association). We can't just call balls and strikes anymore because the rules were changed and now depend on what team is up to bat.

And the only thing more American than baseball is a down-and-out underdog. Americans love underdogs, so we have to make sure we're the underdog in every situation. We can't allow any shift in narrative that might give our already overpowered bullies/oppressors/persecutors/haters a foothold. Narrative is all-important because postinstitutional power is primarily measured by influence. We care little about position or title anymore. Instead, we believe that if we can shape the perceptions of enough people, we can shape reality according to our interests. We now primarily attain and maintain power by weaving narratives that provoke or coerce compassion. But that power comes at a cost: we're also a whole lot more likely to trust or distrust "facts" based on whether it supports our narrative. We might even justify spreading falsehood if it serves a good (our) cause. Needless to say, this environment is ripe for manipulation.

In the same *Hidden Brain* podcast episode I mentioned earlier, entitled "Crying Wolf," Shankar Vedantam also interviewed psychologist Karl Aquino, who found a surprising correlation between "people who self-identified themselves as victims" and another scale measuring what's referred to as the "dark triad" of personality traits:

> *Machiavellianism*, [which is] whether you're willing to immorally manipulate others to get what you want. *Narcissism* . . . a grandiose belief about yourself. You think you're superior to others. And then *subclinical psychopathy*, which is not the psychopathy that you associate with a serial killer, but really more of [an] . . . emotional shallowness or lack of remorse when you do bad things. (emphasis added)[21]

That correlation doesn't mean everyone claiming a false or exaggerated victim status is pathological. What it does mean is that we shouldn't uncritically believe anyone merely *because* they claim victim status.

---

21. Vedantam, "Crying Wolf." For the full study, see Ekin Ok et al., "Signaling Virtuous Victimhood as Indicators of Dark Triad Personalities," *Journal of Personality and Social Psychology* 120, no. 6 (June 2021): 1634–61, https://doi.org/10.1037/pspp0000329.

Online platforms like GoFundMe can absolutely raise awareness and money for victims, but there is no mechanism for evaluating whose needs are greater. The only thing social media platforms are designed to measure is which expression of need resonates with more people. And any social ecosystem that relies on frictionless communication and privileges victimhood identities without accountability is catastrophically vulnerable to bad actors "[using] these signals for personal gain."[22] Harm and abuse is inevitable whenever falsely claiming or exaggerating victimhood is as easy as putting on a uniform.[23]

Where Jesus "humbled himself by becoming obedient to the point of death, even death on a cross" (Philippians 2:8) to impute his righteous status to sinners, virtuous victimhood does the exact opposite—it appropriates the status of victims to be seen as righteous. Manipulating undeserved compassion from others by flaunting challenges that don't exist or claiming a victimhood greater than we've experienced[24] isn't just dishonest and potentially dangerous. It makes a mockery of the same gospel that sparked Rome's compassionate revolution.

Even if you don't think such manipulation is as pervasive as I am describing, it is undeniable that it's easier than ever to gain influence by framing ourselves as victims and broadcasting our plight to everyone who will listen. It might even be wise to do so pre-emptively because, if we don't, someone else will beat us to the punch. Or, at least, that's the hypervigilant rationale of both woke progressivism and right-wing nationalism. For if we're not numbered among the unjustly persecuted then we are naïve at best and likely an oppressor ourselves. Zero-sum power is as uncompromising as it is merciless. We have no choice, it seems, but to participate in the "Oppression Olympics"—a never-ending competition to out-perform

---

22. Vedantam, "Crying Wolf."

23. I'm alluding to the post-9/11 "stolen valor" phenomenon where civilians falsely appropriate veterans' social status by (often incorrectly and absurdly) wearing military uniforms, rank, and/or medals. The online videos veterans recorded to document people caught in the act are more awkward than a Michael Bay–directed sequel of *Napoleon Dynamite and about* as funny. "What Is 'Stolen Valor?,'" Stars and Stripes, accessed October 17, 2024, https://www.stripes.com/veterans/what-is-stolen-valor-1.107359.

24. Vedantam, "Crying Wolf." For the full study, see Ok et al., "Signaling Virtuous Victimhood as Indicators of Dark Triad Personalities."

and out-(virtue)signal our victimhood to ensure no one else gains the social clout or influence to threaten our standing.

Could there be a more tragically hopeless way of relating to each other? Or of seeing the world? More than making us cynical, competitive victimhood ropes us into a self-perpetuating cycle that nourishes a truly hopeless view of reality. The stories we tell shape how we perceive ourselves. Maybe not at first, but constantly broadcasting ourselves as victims will backfill into our hearts. Emphasizing our defeats over our victories slowly inculcates a cognitive distortion called catastrophizing—we assume people are acting out of the worst possible motive and jump to the worst possible conclusion in every situation. Everything wrong in the world becomes totalizing data points supporting our cynical narrative, reinforcing our despair. And because we have to focus on brokenness and injustice in the name of compassion for our tribe, whatever good we do find in the world or among our enemies can't be trusted. It is an exception at best. Everywhere competitive victimhood infects our social incentives, catastrophizing will be the self-reinforcing fruit.

If "the strange psychology of wanting to seem worse off than we really are"[25] stopped there, that would be bad enough to warrant our concern. But it also makes it harder for victims to transcend or heal from a traumatic experience.

Most Christians know that every human being has an inherent dignity because we are made in God's image. But the *imago Dei* also reflects God's creative power in the form of a universal human agency intrinsic to our nature. Victims of especially evil acts describe feeling helpless or paralyzed because victimization is more than suffering a painful experience, it is also the dehumanizing experience of having your personal agency stolen from you. It's why victims of sexual assault and advocacy organizations use language of empowerment. Recovering one's agency in the wake of trauma is a real and visceral need in the healing process. To be overpowered by a person or circumstance is to have a very good power (agency) temporarily stolen, and that theft can leave us feeling

---

25. Vedantam, "Crying Wolf."

bereft of dignity for long after we've recovered our agency. Agency almost always lags behind dignity. Victim-based identities impede that healing because compassion may impart dignity, comfort, and support for facing our pain, but compassion alone can't offer a hopeful vision or freedom from our wounds. Virtuous victimhood can't provide any of that.

The gospel can. A crucified Savior offers victims compassion, but a *resurrected* Savior offers us victory. In Christ, we have a dignity that transcends victimhood. So much of victimhood culture is a pendulum swing from spiritual pragmatism that rightly prioritized the cross's victory over sin but often underemphasized (impractical) compassion for victims. Unsurprisingly, we now face the opposite error, and risk offering victims an equally lopsided gospel. We must be careful to start at the cross, but we can't stop there. Post-Christian compassion—which doesn't also help victims recover agency or gain victory over trauma—is admittedly easier and requires less investment. Victory that rushes to the empty tomb without dwelling in the shadow of the cross and compassion that never moves beyond the crucifixion are both highly susceptible to being co-opted for performance.

I know I'm painting a bleak picture, but without the resurrection's hope of restored dignity *and* agency, the crucifixion is meaningless—and Rome was right. If seeing yourself as a perpetual victim is the only way you feel seen and empowered, it's likely you're battling a relentless cycle of anxiety, cynicism, and loneliness. Perhaps daily. Even if you can bring yourself to trust a church, hope won't penetrate more than skin deep.

You can still experience a foretaste of resurrection victory, but not without first releasing your white-knuckled grip on virtuous victimhood. You have to let Jesus take your place on the cross.

Getting Off the Treadmill and Into Church

If you're asking yourself, "What does Christlike compassion even look like?" or, "If it's this easy to fall into the trap of competitive victimhood,

how do I even begin to avoid it?" There are few examples more powerful, more compassionate, or more worthy of emulation than that of
Dr. Martin Luther King Jr. His leadership was not powerful *despite* his
refusal to respond to coercion with violence, but *because* he didn't. He
refused to play that game or according to those incentives. Neither did his
activism ultimately rely on the African American community's legitimate
status as victims for moral authority.[26] His dream took oppression seriously and transcended it. When Dr. King described riots as "the language
of the unheard,"[27] he meant it descriptively, as an understandable but still
unacceptable response to oppression. He never intended his movement to
excuse or justify the widespread destruction of property in the summer
following George Floyd's murder, but he also wouldn't have had any less
compassion for those rioting. Grace isn't zero-sum.

If anything, it is compassion that likely would have motivated him to
stand in the way, pleading as ardently for peace as he did when standing
up to those who resisted giving Black Americans the dignity and agency
the rest of us enjoyed. His dream included everyone. For "injustice anywhere is a threat to justice everywhere. We are caught in an inescapable
network of mutuality, tied in a single garment of destiny. Whatever
affects one directly, affects all indirectly."[28] Dr. King's example didn't
weaponize compassion; it held up a mirror to the injustice of a society
hypocritically proclaiming "justice for all" while living in apathetic
acceptance of justice for some.

Christlike compassion doesn't give oppressors the excuse to gloss

---

26. "My personal trials have also taught me the value of unmerited suffering. As my suf-
ferings mounted I soon realized that there were two ways that I could respond to my situation:
either to react with bitterness or seek to transform the suffering into a creative force. I decided to
follow the latter course... to see my personal ordeals as an opportunity to transform myself and
heal the people involved in the tragic situation which now obtains"; "'Suffering and Faith' | The
Martin Luther King, Jr. Research and Education Institute," accessed December 3, 2024, https://
kinginstitute.stanford.edu/king-papers/documents/suffering-and-faith.

27. Ryan Taylor, "MLK Jr. The Other America Speech | Transcripts," Rev, accessed October
17, 2024, https://www.rev.com/blog/transcripts/the-other-america-speech-transcript-martin
-luther-king-jr.

28. Martin Luther King Jr., "Letter from a Birmingham Jail [King, Jr.]," *African Studies
Center–University of Pennsylvania,* April 16, 1963, https://www.africa.upenn.edu/Articles_Gen
/Letter_Birmingham.html.

over injustice, but neither does it give the oppressed inherent freedom
to return it in kind. Without mercy, forgiveness, and, yes, love for our
enemy, virtuous victimhood is a recipe for distrust and contempt. It was
precisely virtuous victimhood's zero-sum view of power and human
flourishing that Dr. King rejected in his "I Have a Dream" speech: "We
must not allow our creative protest to degenerate into physical violence.
Again and again, we must rise to the majestic heights of meeting physical
force with soul force. The marvelous new militancy which has engulfed
the Negro community must not lead us to a distrust of all white people,
for many of our white brothers, as evidenced by their presence here today,
have come to realize that their destiny is tied up with our destiny."[29]

Now, as then, a crucified and resurrected Christ offers transcendent
hope. Jesus will always be the greater victim, and it was the sin of the
oppressed and oppressor alike that put him there. Yet by grace, he went
willingly, so we can know he also doesn't hold that against us. But if we
identify with Christ and allow our destiny to be tied up with his, then
his resurrection victory is ours and we have the power to transcend any
experience of suffering. In Christ, we are freed to humbly come along-
side victims in their plight and extend compassion without needing to
appropriate their experience or status. Christ became a victim to make
us victors. What greater compassion is there?

Jesus is the only way to reverse the cycle of virtuous victimhood,
and identifying with him means our destiny is also tied up with those
for whom he died to save—the church. So if you really, truly want
to fight injustice, fight the oppressive hegemony of competing victim
narratives that keep us outraged, isolated, and fearful of each other.
Resist lazy dependence on political saviors who attain and keep power
by stoking our distrust in each other and, therefore, the church. Build
institutions instead of burning them down. Go to church. Trust in
mercy. Repent of injustice. Go *back* to church. "Love one another with
brotherly affection. Outdo one another in showing honor" (Romans

---

29. "Read Martin Luther King Jr.'s 'I Have a Dream' Speech in Its Entirety," *NPR*, January 16,
2023, https://www.npr.org/2010/01/18/122701268/i-have-a-dream-speech-in-its-entirety.

12:10). Keep going back to church—*every* Sunday. "Act justly . . . love mercy . . . [and] walk humbly with your God" (Micah 6:8 NIV) every week in between. Invite your neighbor to church, welcome them to tie up their destiny in Christ and his body as you have. Jesus won't be caught dead (or alive) anywhere else. Nothing could further social and spiritual justice more than compassionately inviting our neighbors into the broken-but-beloved bride for whom Christ died and rose to make new.

If it worked for pre-Christian Rome, the post-Christian West is very fertile soil . . .

Reflection Questions

1. If two spouses only ever confess each other's sin, they're stuck in a cycle of competitive victimhood. How would you advise them? How can they break their stalemate?

2. When has a desire for validation or recognition tempted you to frame yourself as worse off than you really are? Did it work? Did anyone reach out to offer other kinds of help?

3. Read Micah 6:8 and, with open hands, ask Jesus to show you where he wants you to grow in acting justly, loving mercy, and walking humbly with the Lord. Then ask him to give you genuine compassion for those you deem least deserving.

Bonus Questions

1. Now that we've covered all five church defeaters, do you see any connections between the first four and virtuous victimhood? Where might there be overlap with the sacred self (e.g., adopting therapy speak to gain social status) or (un)civil religions (e.g., using anti-vision to justify coercive use of power)? Where do you see the "oppression Olympics" unfold on social media or in kayfabe politics?

2. Take some time to consider how someone might use one or more church defeaters as "brick and mortar" to make a name for themselves. How do they try to achieve their dignity, value, and worth? What motivates them? Are they happy or discontent? How do they respond to difficult circumstances?

PART 2

The Body and Bride of Christ

It was not easier in the first century than it was in the 20th to come together and stay together in genuine Christian community. There were no fewer distractions and no fewer temptations towards selfish, aloof individualism, protective of one's privacy. Yet the early church was a gathering of people who rejoiced to be together consistently, to eat, share, and serve together . . . The familial bond uniting believers to one another is of most importance to the identity of Christ's church and to our identity as individual members. Delight over belonging to the family of God evokes a joyful eagerness to be with and share with new siblings.

—Dennis Johnson

Gordy wasn't a member of our church, but his daughter and her family are, and even though I hadn't had more than a handful of conversations with him, I was always struck by his kindness and sincerity. Where some people merely pay attention when you're talking, Gordy listened with his whole body. He smiled a *lot*. "Beaming" wouldn't be an overstatement. He even smiled after our Christmas Eve service, when he told me he was diagnosed with pancreatic cancer earlier that day. "Merry Christmas!" he said. "I have Jesus—what more could I ask for?" He passed away eighty-four days later.

Funerals and memorials are among the few communal rituals where we process pain, sorrow, and loss in public. And because no family is without relational tension or conflict, funerals are also where family dysfunction can come out sideways. You often hear it simmering beneath the surface of eulogies that include a disclaimer, conceding the brokenness everyone knows about but never talks about.

"She wasn't exactly the ideal mom, but . . ."

"We all know he liked his whiskey, but . . ."

"We didn't always see eye to eye, but . . ."

I've been to my share of funerals as a pastor, but Gordy's memorial may be the first I've been to where the overwhelming theme was *redemption*. I listened, slack-jawed, to testimonies from his two sons and daughter about a hard-fought kindness that went even deeper than I had imagined. How Gordy's relationship with Jesus motivated him to be the kind of on-the-floor dad he wished he'd had himself. Tender moments of care, affirmation, acceptance, and belovedness were made more potent because he gave them despite his own deep pain and alienation.

Because of the transformation Jesus wrought in the life of one man, their family was made better and more beautiful than it could have been *without* the brokenness. That requires a tragically rare depth of devotion—not just of one family member to another but of each member to their family as a whole. Though he was already at the side of his Savior, Gordy's life nevertheless testified to an essential element of the gospel's truth, goodness, and beauty: that redemption only comes *through* brokenness, not by sweeping it under the rug or succumbing to it as inevitable.

Not all families are so extraordinarily blessed as Gordy's, but there is one where even greater redemption can be ordinarily found. In the family of God, Jesus leaves his fingerprints everywhere sin has left a scar.

As a pastor, I am often painfully aware that church might be the one place where family dysfunction comes out sideways more often than at funerals. Babel isn't only a cautionary tale of individualism's implications for individuals. As I've written elsewhere, it is also "a full-throated theological condemnation of institutions fundamentally compromised by rank self-interest."[1] Like many of you reading this, I know firsthand the harm done when spiritual authority is wielded not by shepherds for the good of Christ's sheep, but by wolves in sheep's clothing for their own good.

Thankfully, Scripture doesn't shirk from the personal and social brokenness caused by sin,[2] but neither does it accept that sin's corrupting influence on institutions renders the body of Christ broken beyond repair. If it did, sin would prove more powerful than God's redemption and refuge.

So *how* then do we live in that fallen world? We know there's no getting out of this life alive, but is it possible to thrive between here and there? Despite everything, the body and bride of Christ is God's resounding answer.

At the end of the day, if God rescued us by submitting himself to our most cruel instrument of torture and execution, he can surely redeem and restore us through a vehicle of our hurt and disappointment. I am not advocating that anyone naively subject themselves to spiritual abuse. God doesn't call us to blind faith. We will live with the need to "be wise as serpents and innocent as doves" (Matthew 10:16) for as long as churches are made up of fallen human beings, but it is in that tension that redemption is ordinarily found. Otherwise, none of us would be allowed through the front doors.

That said, while it would be a truly wonderful start for anyone who is *de*churched to *re*church, it also isn't enough to just go back to church. Those of us already in church have some serious work ahead of us. We

---

1. Brad Edwards and Chris Martin, "Social Media Fosters Distrust in Institutions. But We Can't Live Without Them.," *The Gospel Coalition*, March 25, 2022, https://www.thegospel coalition.org/article/social-media-distrust-institutions/.

2. For example, Ananias and Sapphira (Acts 5:1–11) looking to make a name for themselves by taking advantage of the Jerusalem church in her infancy should be a startling and humbling warning for every Christian.

have to "do church" in a way that is more Christian than post-Christian and, yes, more institutional than individualistic. Deconstructing the false promises of church defeaters is only the first step in finding a true and better sanctuary. Now that we better understand the cultural miasma that has been dulling our spiritual senses, we need the expulsive power of Christ's affection for his people to break through anew.

We need to fall back in love with the bride of Christ.

If there is a bright spot in everything we've covered so far, it's that we're starting to wake up that need due to how unsustainable our current postinstitutional trajectory is. Derek Thompson, an agnostic who has "spent most of [his] life thinking about the decline of faith in America in mostly positive terms," wrote in *The Atlantic* that perhaps he was at least partly mistaken: "Maybe religion, for all of its faults, works a bit like a retaining wall to hold back the destabilizing pressure of American hyperindividualism, which threatens to swell and spill over in its absence."[3]

He's not the only secular thinker to question their long-held skepticism. Justin Brierley has been documenting a remarkable groundswell of similar sentiment among those who've most ardently opposed the church—especially on political grounds—the "New Atheists."[4] Longtime atheist, author, and speaker Ayaan Hirsi Ali announced her embrace of church and subsequent conversion to Christianity in November 2023.[5] She wrote that her journey began with a growing, unavoidable realization that our post-Christian society is a "cut flower, and cut flowers die."[6] Severed from the roots of faith, we are wilting into sociopolitical warfare, "but we have the remnants, the symbols of western

---

3. Derek Thompson, "The True Cost of the Churchgoing Bust," *The Atlantic*, April 3, 2024, https://www.theatlantic.com/ideas/archive/2024/04/america-religion-decline-non-affiliated/677951/.

4. Justin Brierley, *The Surprising Rebirth of Belief in God: Why New Atheism Grew Old and Secular Thinkers Are Considering Christianity Again* (Tyndale Elevate, 2023).

5. Ayaan Hirsi Ali, "Why I Am Now a Christian," *Unherd*, November 11, 2023, https://unherd.com/2023/11/why-i-am-now-a-christian/.

6. Alliance for Responsible Citizenship, "*What Is the West?—Panel*," October 30, 2023, 49 min., 30 sec., https://www.arcforum.com/videos/v/https/youtube/wtzq-zf1qg4?categoryId=65f1b6dd1ce7524140689af2.

heritage, and their seeds. All we have to do, those of us who inherited it, is to go and see them, grow them, nurture them, water them."[7]

In truth, we have something even better than the remnants, symbols, and seeds of western heritage. We have the gospel—"The power of God for salvation to everyone who believes" (Romans 1:16)—and God's people for its soil. Thus, what follows is vision for seeing both our relationship to church and God without individualism obscuring our view. Part 2 outlines five reasons for church, and why the body of Christ is God's gift to those who wonder whether thriving is possible in an age that seems so inhospitable. They aren't the only reasons, not by a long shot. I leave out a lot of true things that could be said of church, the Church, and local churches. Instead, we'll focus on why the church is the true and better refuge, to which neither individualism nor its defeaters can compare.

---

7. Alliance for Responsible Citizenship, "Panel."

6

A People Named Glory

How God Bestows Identity and Significance to the Church

"The glory that you have given me I have given to them, that they may be one even as we are one."

—Jesus (John 17:22)

The promise of glory is the promise, almost incredible and only possible by the work of Christ, that . . . [we] shall please God. To please God . . . to be a real ingredient in the divine happiness . . . to be loved by God, not merely pitied, but delighted in as an artist delights in his work or a father in a son—it seems impossible, a weight or burden of glory which our thoughts can hardly sustain. But so it is.

—C. S. Lewis

I have an unusual interest in the subject of names, mostly because I *really* don't like mine.

My given name, Bradley, means "broad meadow" and originates from Old English and Anglo-Saxon dialects. What could be more vanilla, indistinct, and unnoticeable than something defined primarily by its lack of noticeable features (e.g., mountains, forests, or streams)?

Yes, I'm exaggerating, but it gets far worse by association. Second only to Chad, my name might be Hollywood's favorite for characters behaving with the special kind of jackassery and cluelessness we have dubbed a bro. Whether by fraternity membership or temperament, Brad is almost always a foil to the protagonist but too lame to be a true bad guy. I suppose my name *could* foreshadow a fall to the dark side, as if losing too many games of beer pong made one a Sith Lord. But even then, it would require a renaming because there's just a limit to the significance Bradley can impart to an evil space-wizard in a galactic western. You'll never see a character with gravitas named Brad.[1]

I so disliked my name that the summer before starting eighth grade at a new school, I briefly considered going by a new nickname. It was, of course, a *terrible* idea, and I'm glad I never went through with it.

From the absolute beginning, names are a massive theme in Scripture, as is humanity's wrestling with identity. Likely penned by Moses at some point while Israel was wandering in the wilderness, the first five books of the Christian Bible are the origin story of God's people—Israel. But long before God delivered Israel from slavery in Egypt, Genesis was already being passed down and circulated through oral tradition for several generations. That preservation alone shows the vital role Genesis played in the life of God's people. It was their existential anchor, the source of Israel's identity and how they knew they were a distinct people named Israel in the first place.

If you were a young Israelite growing up under Pharoah's heavy yoke, you'd have all kinds of huge questions: If we're not originally from here, where are we from? Who is this Elohim, and why do we worship him instead of the Egyptian gods? How did we come to be slaves, and how do we endure this life without despairing? Is it even *possible* to thrive when

---

1. Lt. Bradley Bradshaw from *Top Gun: Maverick, played by actor Miles Teller,* gets close, but I'd argue he's still a caricature for three reasons: (a) his initial scenes portray him as a jokester like his dad, (b) his call sign ("Rooster") only reinforces that levity, and (c) the repetition in his first and last name is an awkward verbal foil to Pete "Maverick" Mitchell trying to get his attention on the carrier deck (twice). So, yes, I sometimes overthink things.

we are just barely keeping our heads above water? And perhaps most importantly: Will we ever be free to worship our God, or are we destined to forever suffer the indignity and dishonor of building monuments to someone else's gods?

In other words, Israel had a whole lot of questions, all revolving around their collective identity: *Who are we?*

Genesis provides a series of surprisingly comprehensive answers in the form of a multigenerational story punctuated with the biographies of several key figures. Each episode is preserved and woven together using the profoundly emblematic names of those key figures.

Adam ("soil/earth") was created out of the dust of the earth. The builders of Babel (which sounds very similar and forms a pun with the Hebrew word for "to mix up" or "confuse"[2]) tried to make a name for themselves but were left as scattered and confused as their name implied. God told Abram ("father") that he would make his name great and bring forth a great nation from him and his wife, Sarai ("my princess/woman of strength"). When they scoffed at God's seemingly absurd promise that they would conceive children at Abram's ripe young age of ninety-nine, God doubled down. He changed Abram's name to Abraham ("father of multitudes") and Sarai's name to Sarah ("*the* princess/woman of strength"), and he told them to name their yet-unconceived heir Isaac ("he laughs"). After so long of a wait, Abraham and Sarah would already remember that God delivered on his promise despite their doubts every time they looked upon their son's shining face. But Isaac's name was more than a reminder of God's faithfulness, it made him an heir of the promise.

Other names in Genesis can be a little less . . . optimistic. Isaac's son, Jacob (which sounds like "heel" but means "to supplant") steals his brother's birthright and tricks his near-death and blind father to bless him instead of his brother, Esau ("hairy"). Unfortunately, bending

---

2. "The narrator parodies Akkadian *bab-ilu*, meaning "gate of god," with its Hebrew phonological equivalent *babel*, meaning "confusion."" Bruce K. Waltke, *Genesis: A Commentary* (Grand Rapids, Mich: Zondervan, 2001), p181.

the rules to make a name for himself was a consistent pattern in Jacob's life. And yet, despite all the broken hearts and relationships lying in the wake of Jacob's vain pursuit of glory, God physically appears and wrestles with him one night from dusk till dawn. So when Jacob refuses to let go of God unless God blesses him first, God renames him "Israel" because he had "striven with God and with men, and [had] prevailed" (Genesis 32:28).

As if to make sure we fully appreciated Jacob's redemption, Hebrew words for Esau's "birthright" (*bekorah*) and God's "blessing" (*berakah*) are anagrams of each other.[3] Jacob extracting his *birthright* from man was ultimately foolish, leaving him empty and alone to face the consequences. But Israel's new name wasn't just a reminder that the *blessing* he longed for can only come from God, it proclaimed him the heir of God's promise to Abraham. Israel's birthright is God himself.

Imagine how comforting such a story might be to a people struggling to believe God could or would deliver on his promise—and deliver them from bondage. From beginning to end, the book of Genesis assures Israel that they were not a mistake, an accident, or a failure to launch (even when they behaved like it). Their collective name was more than a reminder, it made them heirs of the promise. Genesis is a dramatic account of God's habitual faithfulness across many generations, no matter the odds or obstacles (including their obstinance). Israel's enslavement, then, was *despite* and not a *result of* who they were to God. Their hope was not in taking matters into their own hands and thus repeating Jacob's mistakes, but to live as a transformed Jacob—as Israel—and to trust that God would bring about the reality he promised. God would make good on Israel's name because their very existence as a people fulfilled the name God gave to Abraham.

---

3. Each word becomes the other when you reverse the inner and outer letters. This clever play on words "invites the listening community to marvel rather than to explain. The reality of blessing is not simply the result of human ingenuity. Nor is it a matter of good luck." Walter Brueggemann, *Genesis: In Bible Commentary for Teaching and Preaching*, Interpretation, a Bible Commentary for Teaching and Preaching (Atlanta: John Knox Press, 1982).

The Modern Identity Crisis

Unlike pre-Exodus Israel, we are truly blessed to live in a democracy and the freest society in world history. And yet our quest for (and questioning of) identity may be even more desperate. Our impulse for self-discovery isn't new. If anything, it's a defining feature of Western history and the culture we've grown up in. Whether we would have chosen them or not, we've inherited a set of assumptions about our individual identity—particularly, that identity is something we discover or achieve for ourselves.

It certainly doesn't help that, culturally speaking, we use the word "identity" as what's called an "empty signifier"—a visual or linguistic symbol that can mean whatever we choose to fill it with. Brands do this all the time: so long as there are no negative associations with the word or image, naming a product or app with an empty signifier (e.g., Zillow, Tumblr, Uber, or Venmo) can reach a much larger market.[4] Yet we can take this too far. When Elon Musk rebranded Twitter, he maybe didn't anticipate that a brand so empty of meaning (X) might invite everyone to continue referring to his product as Twitter like nothing ever happened. Likewise, once enough of us use identity for little more than a subjective, catch-all vehicle to attach adjectives describing our roles, relationships, ethnicities, sexual orientations, or political affiliations, our self-worth becomes equally impossible to pin down and, therefore, empty.

Initially, a blank-slate identity sounds enticing. We're full of potential and free to define our "selves" for ourselves. But that potential can become surprisingly burdensome, if not tyrannical. Choosing the wrong college major can be paralyzing—what if you're wrong? What if you spend all that time and money on a degree you end up hating or never use? What if you can't hack it? Thankfully, we can't stay paralyzed forever. The practical constraints of time and/or money will eventually force us to commit to something or drop out. Not so with our identity.

---

4. Alex Blumberg and Lisa Chow, hosts, StartUp, season 1, episode 5, "Gimlet 5: How To Name Your Company," Gimlet Media, October 13, 2014, 22 min., 45 sec., https://gimletmedia .com:443/shows/startup/emhw6d.

In a culture that celebrates self-definition and rewards self-discovery, we can technically remain undefined forever. Yet while our options may seem limitless, we aren't. We are finite creatures, mere reflections of an infinite Creator. Living otherwise, even within a culture conspiring to sustain the illusion, is a recipe for emptiness.

We're right about one thing: The moment we say yes to one identity, we limit ourselves and say no to every other option. We're certainly less free—but what if that's okay? What if some freedoms are limiting, and some limitations are freeing?

Self-definition affords more options, but anyone who has eaten at a Golden Corral knows that having more options isn't always better. Submitting to the predetermined menu of a culinary school-trained chef guarantees a meal more physically and existentially satisfying than any buffet.

Constant redefinition risks more than temporary indigestion. If we put on and take off identities like a child playing with colorful stickers, we will be likewise unsettled when they lose their stickiness. Liquid identities are insecure and malleable, susceptible to both outside influence and self-deception. Eventually, neither Bruce Wayne nor Batman know who is real and who is the mask.

Individualism promises a secure, bespoke identity of our own making. We're taught by almost everything around us that we must be self-made, that it's not just possible but a moral imperative to become who we imagine ourselves to be. And it's all a lie. No matter how much we self-optimize and no matter how many opportunities we have for self-expression, we can't change our nature. As image bearers, we are made to receive our identity through relationship. Trying to self-create in denial of that reality or muster it up from within ourselves is how we got here.

I had a hunch even in eighth grade that rebranding myself with a new nickname couldn't give me what I was looking for. I know now that I would have been left with the feeling that the Bible describes as meaningless or "vapor"—the literal meaning of the word translated as "vanity" in the book of Ecclesiastes. Its author, Solomon, knew all too well that making a name for ourselves, competing for honor, and achieving our own significance are all ultimately "chasing after the wind" (Ecclesiastes 1:14 NIV), and leave us even more glory-empty than when we started.

Being honest about that frustrated fruitlessness helps us recognize what's really driving our search for identity: a hunger for significance that lasts, that's worth giving ourselves to. We long for the weight of glory.

Beauty and the Weight of Glory

In our frustratingly rare and fleeting encounters with significance, we're left reeling. We suddenly become weak-kneed amateur poets grasping for words to capture the ineffable. Like Adam first encountering Eve, discovering a sense of completion we didn't know we lacked can also spark our spontaneous eruption in song. We're always surprised when we encounter significance. Despite spending most of our lives searching and grasping for it, we never see it coming. It's sneaky like that.

Every year, thousands of people pack up and move to Colorado so they can live within a short drive of the Rocky Mountains. Why? Because we all "do not want merely to see beauty . . . We want something else which can hardly be put into words—to be united with the beauty we see, to pass into it, to receive it into ourselves, to bathe in it, to become part of it."[5] We revel in the surprising comfort in feeling small before magnificent beauty.

So we chase it, empty signifier in hand, hoping to cork that wonder-full lightning in a bottle. Man is endlessly inventive in our attempts to capture and contain significance—through conquest, exploration, higher learning, romance, social progress, vocational success, or scientific advancement just to name a few. There are infinite ways to make a name for ourselves. Identity is our container of choice even if, like a dog looking at a finger rather than the direction his owner is pointing, we often confuse the sign (identity) with the thing signified (glory).

Part of that confusion comes from being taught that seeking glory is at least vain, and likely selfish and immoral. But the Bible's use of the

---

5. Lewis, *Weight of Glory*.

word "glory" means far more than the cheap or commercial caricatures we so often associate with it (e.g., celebrity, fame, or influence). And, much like Jacob's relationship with birthright and blessing, whether our pursuit of glory is vain or fleeting depends on where we seek it.

In both the Old and New Testaments, "glory" is typically positive and reference what is objectively good and worthy of honor. To have glory means to have great significance or worth. In the Old Testament, the primary Hebrew word translated as "glory," *kavod*, can mean to honor, respect, or magnify, or to have special distinction. When used in reference to God (see Isaiah 6:3), it implies a magnificence closely related to his holiness and worthy of (even demanding) our worship. "Holiness is God's hidden glory: glory is God's all-present holiness."[6] In the New Testament, the Greek word for glory, *doxa*, has a lot of overlap with the Greek word for honor, *time'*. They're often used in parallel to describe different facets of the same thing—i.e., "all honor and glory"—but *time'* is more often used as a verb to describe a relationship (as in "Joe honored Hannah"). When "glory" has a relational trajectory or is attached to a person, it conveys significance at the level of one's essence. To say a person "is so-and-so's glory" is exactly how we use the word "identity" today—as a source of dignity, value, and worth.

Sometimes we just want to go skiing, and sometimes we want to be *the kind of person* who skis. There's a big difference between merely (if thoroughly) enjoying one of God's gifts and expecting it to offer more than temporal significance. With the latter posture, we are making an identity out of it. Maybe even an idol.

When we are in a relationship of reciprocal significance with God, we exist as he designed us to live, and so we experience his shalom. For example, Psalm 89:17 says that the Lord is "the glory of their strength; by your favor our horn is exalted." "Favor" means to honor or bless, and the word for "exalted" is the same as "glorified." Together, they depict a flourishing feedback loop of glory between God and his people. Our

---

6. J. Alec Motyer, *The Prophecy of Isaiah: An Introduction Commentary*, 9/15/93 edition (Downers Grove: IVP Academic, 1993), p77.

experience of that glory bestowed is more than just some generic value that we can find anywhere in the world, it is the status and soul-deep sense that *we are worthwhile*. This "weight of glory" (2 Corinthians 4:17), is uniquely experienced through our Creator and Redeemer's pleasure in us. Longing for that isn't bad or selfish at all; it's where our greatest good is found.

We can't contain that glory, no one can. But we were made to refract it.

Refracted Glory

Several years ago, I had the opportunity to view *The Four Holy Gospels*, a collection of four stunningly beautiful paintings created by internationally renowned artist and author Makoto Fujimura. He utilizes the techniques and materials of Japanese Nihonga in a modern abstract style that you must see in person to fully appreciate. Nihonga uses crushed precious stones mixed with glue for pigment, and layer after layer of the purest gold and silver leaf to create depth and space greater than its two-dimensional surface could contain.

The Four Holy Gospels were a small window into the beauty that the Apostle John might have glimpsed when he described the New Jerusalem in Revelation 21 as a city of "pure gold, like clear glass" (v. 18). The surface of each painting had a translucent, glass-like quality. But they didn't reflect light, so much as they absorbed, reshaped, and refracted light back into the world in a tint more beautiful for having been altered. It was unsettling. Seeing them in person, I now appreciate just a little of what Fujimura wrote regarding his experience studying Nihonga many years prior: "The weight of beauty I saw in the materials began to crush my heart. I could not justify the use of extravagance if I found my heart unable to contain their glory."[7]

There is a glory too great for words to do justice, and none of us have a big enough "'shelf' on which to place that beauty inside [our] heart[s]."[8] For man to be made in the image of God is to uniquely *refract* his glory in

---

7. Makoto Fujimura, *River Grace* (Poiema Press, 2007).
8. Makoto Fujimura, *Refractions: A Journey of Faith, Art, and Culture* (NavPress, 2009).

creation, not to merely reflect it, nor to emanate it from within ourselves. Our dignity, value, and worth does not come from what we make of ourselves individually but from the One who made us collectively. God set Adam apart as a uniquely special creation by breathing his spirit into him, but it is only when God gives him Eve ("life") that they are, together, declared as created "in the image of God" (Genesis 1:27).[9]

It was trying to achieve an authority and significance of their own that got our first parents kicked out of the garden of Eden and made God's glory so elusive for the rest of us. Now it is now far easier to sense glory's absence: "our longing to be reunited with something in the universe from which we now feel cut off, to be on the inside of some door which we have always seen from the outside . . . is no mere neurotic fancy, but the truest index of our real situation."[10]

We can't ignore that emptiness any more than we can ignore the instinct to inhale. But if making a name for ourselves is vanity and "chasing after the wind," how in the world do we find or experience the significance we're supposedly made for? For starters, we must stop searching and start receiving, because glory can only ever be *given* by another. We don't find it so much as we are encountered by it.

The Unique Gift of God's Loving Gaze

Think about the best gift you've ever received. What makes it so significant to you? Is it the most expensive or most fun gift you've ever received? To be blunt, I highly doubt it. Personal quirks notwithstanding, the gifts we cherish most convey a sense that we are both *especially worthwhile to*, and *deeply known by*, their giver. An expensive gift can communicate general worth to a recipient, but not necessarily. Gifts that don't also flow out of deep, relational knowing say a lot more about the giver's ability to pay for the gift than whether they believe the recipient is worth the cost.

---

9. See also Genesis 2:18–23.
10. Lewis, *Weight of Glory*.

Christianity is utterly unique among all the world's religions and belief systems in that we believe God multiplies his glory by bestowing it. God is the original, uncreated gift-giver. Whether we give him credit or not, we are awestruck by natural beauty because it testifies to the existence of One who both created a beautiful cosmos and designed our hearts to *apprehend* its beauty. Giving gifts is who he is, and receiving them is who he made us to be.

God freed Israel from Egyptian slavery as a pure, unadulterated gift. He made that much explicitly clear: "It was not because you were more in number than any other people that the LORD set his love on you and chose you, for you were the fewest of all peoples, but it is *because the LORD loves you and is keeping the oath that he swore to your fathers*, that the LORD has brought you out with a mighty hand and redeemed you from the house of slavery" (Deuteronomy 7:7–8, emphasis added). God loves his people because he chooses to love his people, and he keeps his promises because he has promised to keep them. That's it. Period. Full stop. The end. If he had any other motivation outside himself, he couldn't be more than the second Most High God and his love couldn't be more than kinda-sorta steadfast. Thankfully, we are made in his image and not the other way around.

If you can believe it, God's gift-giving goes deeper still. Deuteronomy 7 also says, "For you are a people holy to the LORD your God. The LORD your God has chosen you to be a people for his treasured possession, out of all the peoples who are on the face of the earth" (v. 6). But don't read what God's not saying. Resist the temptation of reading "treasured possession" as a synonym for "favorite toy." God chose Israel to be his people in the way we might say "so-and-so are my people." It is a statement of relational fondness and familiarity, of identifying with Israel as family. To God, Israel is priceless.

Just sit with that for a moment. What could be a more pure expression of being *especially worthwhile* and *deeply known*? What could be more loving than your Creator telling you that, despite rejecting him and his gifts, *you* are still the greatest gift he could ever give to himself? This gift comes from and is given to the One who spoke creation into existence. With infinite options available or creatable, God chose the same incandescently foolish people who, mere days after being delivered from generational slavery, spat in God's face and gave him the middle finger. That may be a shocking way to frame it, but that's functionally what Israel did when they worshiped a golden calf while the glory of the Lord was still *visibly present* on Mount Sinai. The idea that Israel could be especially worthwhile to *anyone* boggles the mind. That we, the church, are God's treasured "people for his own possession" (1 Peter 2:9) should leave us dumbstruck and speechless with awe. Indeed, that the Lord would so condescend to be Israel's God makes him a gift-giver worthy of all our reverence and worship. That he came and died for his enemies demands it.

Imagine the difference it would make in our church shopping if we viewed God's people through his eyes. We'd be far more likely to choose a church based on their grasp of God's scandalous love and how it fueled, if imperfectly, their faithfulness to love God and neighbor. At the bare minimum, we'd have a much harder time treating God's treasured possession like a spiritual nonprofit. We simply underestimate how much using a metaphor of consumption ("church shopping") in lieu of Scripture's metaphor of marital commitment ("Christ's Bride") undermines our ability to treasure God's priceless possession as he does.

Our problem, however, goes deeper than the influence of first-world consumerism. As Western individualists, we live in a "guilt/innocence" culture that ascribes value based on individual achievement and rights. Shame and honor cultures (e.g., the ancient Near East, modern Middle East, and East Asia) ascribe value by collective association and responsibility. Neither are right or wrong. Both are cultural reflections of something universally true. We need both dimensions to be fully human. But because most Americans are culturally unfamiliar with shame and honor dynamics, we miss much of how Scripture invites us to receive identity, glory, and worth in Christ. We're spiritually starving for something that's good and readily available, but many of us give up and settle for what neither satisfies nor nourishes because we can't read the menu. We're completely unaware that glory is literally staring us in the face. And by that, I mean God's face shining upon and gazing into ours.

God uses this very language in the first and only time in all of Scripture where he explicitly commands priests (and pastors) to use a particular script for blessing his people:

The LORD spoke to Moses, saying, "Speak to Aaron and his sons, saying, Thus you shall bless the people of Israel: you shall say to them,

> The LORD bless you and keep you;
> the LORD *make his face to shine upon you* and be gracious to you;
> the LORD *lift up his countenance upon you* and give you peace.
> (Numbers 6:22–26, emphasis added)

Christian philosopher Esther Meek argues that God's shining face does more than impart blessing. Like an infant who becomes self-aware upon seeing the love reflected in their mother's face, the identity and significance we long for is found beneath our God's loving gaze: "To the gifting of the mother's present, delighted face of love, the child responds in rapture and delight. Mother is a being like me, with me, but other than me. In that beauty-filled, love-brimming face, a face that was looking for us before we were looking for her, is the gift of an intimate welcome home to belong in this world."[11] For our Heavenly Father to direct his glory-imparting gaze upon us is "an incomprehensible miracle."[12] Having his utmost regard "shapes [our] whole being and involvement with"[13] reality itself precisely because the "fundamental unit of existence and identity" is found within "the gaze of the loving other."[14]

That, my friends, is a glory-full encounter so significant that we won't just *feel* worthwhile. Inasmuch as his spoken word brought creation into existence, the gaze of our loving Creator *makes* us worthwhile. That's more

---

11. Esther Lightcap Meek, "Recovering Our Love of the Real," *Comment Magazine*, October 31, 2023, https://comment.org/recovering-our-love-of-the-real/. Meek explores this concept further in *Loving to Know: Covenant Epistemology* (Cascade Books, 2011).

12. Meek, "Recovering Our Love."

13. Meek, "Recovering Our Love."

14. Esther Lightcap Meek, "The Mother's Smile: Integrative Beauty," *Theopolis Institute*, March 5, 2019, https://theopolisinstitute.com/the-mothers-smile-integrative-beauty/.

than a reminder of who we are to him, it makes us fully and finally alive. Such is the redemptive power of being named God's treasured possession.

Abiding in his gaze is how we apprehend the full, lasting glory of that identity.

The End of Our Search for Identity

Think about the last time you met someone new. You probably introduced yourself by telling them your given name, and your last name if in a professional context. In doing so, you told them how you are unique as an individual (i.e., Brad, who isn't Dwayne, Jehosephat or, God forbid, Chad[15]). As Westerners, we generally understand ourselves by how we are different from others around us.

In a more collectivist culture, you likely wouldn't be asked what you do for a living and maybe not even your first name until after sharing where you're from, how many children you have, other people or (if in a professional setting) organizations you are affiliated with, and (*gasp*) what religion you belong to. For individualists, you are the sum of your *distinctives*—your personality, beliefs, skills, attributes, accomplishments, etc. For collectivists, you are the sum of your *relationships*—the communities, groups, and traditions you belong to. In other words, your *family* name matters a whole lot more than your *given* name.

Before Ancestry.com (or the internet) was a thing, my grandfather did a deep dive on my family's genealogy and wrote a book about it called *The Edwardes Legacy* (the "es" is the original Welsh spelling). He did his research the old-fashioned way, traveling to different parts of the country and, eventually, the Royal Library in London hunting down birth certificates, marriage licenses, and census records. I didn't know the book existed until my second semester of seminary, when my dad pulled out a copy from a box buried in his garage to prove a claim that I was still in shock and disbelief from hearing: that I was directly related to the "fire

---

15. My sincerest apologies to every Chad reading this.

and brimstone preacher," Jonathan Edwards. (My dad still loves referring to him as a "smoke and limestone preacher" just to irk me.)

If American culture was even a little more collectivist, I might have benefited from that association. But because we're so steeped in individualism, it has brought me little more than a few fleeting oohs and ahhs from particularly nerdy pastors. But that doesn't mean it's worthless. To the contrary, I learned that almost every generation between Jonathan Edwards and me were Christians, and half of them were also pastors. That discovery filled Edwards with a significance that more than made up for whatever dishonor I might have incurred by association as a Bradley.

In the verse immediately following the Aaronic Blessing, God says that the priests proclaiming this benediction "shall ... *put [his] name upon* the people of Israel" and therefore, God "will bless them" (Numbers 6:27, emphasis added). When God puts his Name-above-all-names upon his people, he more-than-symbolically and really, truly confers his glory—and all the authority and presence that entails. This miraculous gift affects powerful redefinition. God's name doesn't just describe Israel as his "treasured possession," it *makes* them so. God so completely co-locates his name and his blessing with his people, that he is practically indistinguishable apart from them. To know Israel is to know God. No Edwards can't compete with that, Jonathan or otherwise.

In that light, consider the words of Immanuel ("God with us") in the Great Commission:

> And Jesus came and said to them, "All *authority* in heaven and on earth has been given to me. Go therefore and make disciples of all nations, baptizing them *in the name* of the Father and of the Son and of the Holy Spirit, teaching them to observe all that I have commanded you. And behold, *I am with you always*, to the end of the age." (Matthew 28:18–20, emphasis added)

As individualists eager to achieve our dignity, value, and worth, we read Christ's declarations ("All authority ... I am with you") through the filter of the imperatives ("Go ... make"), as if Jesus's authority and presence are mere, if powerful, tools for making disciples both new and ongoing. And truly, Jesus's charge would be utterly impossible apart from Christ's authority and presence to fuel it! However, that is an incomplete understanding of the connection. Jesus absolutely prescribes the Great Commission is absolutely Christ's prescription for growing his church through evangelism and discipleship. But first and foremost, the Great Commission is a benediction—Jesus signing and sealing his name upon his once-for-all delivered people. It is the new Aaronic Blessing of a New Covenant with a new Israel—the church.

Why is that distinction such a big deal? Because the great name and great nation God promised Abraham were never two separate or distinct gifts, but two sides of the same blessing—each incomprehensible without the other. Having a name outside or apart from the nation of Israel would have been harder for someone living in the ancient Near East to comprehend than Wi-Fi or cloud storage. Likewise, discipleship that doesn't include the church as a good and necessary element in shaping Christian identity or refracting God's glory falls woefully short of making disciples in Jesus's great name. It is individualism, and not Scripture, that makes us think we can experience anything like an identity outside or apart from the church. I'm not saying that; Jesus did.

"But Brad," you might be thinking to yourself, "that's why we have the *universal* church. Even if we aren't part of a particular, local church, we are still *spiritual* members of the body and bride of Christ!" That is technically but only partially true, in the same way that decaf coffee is technically coffee, but it's missing the best part. Identity without glory is even less satisfying than coffee without caffeine.

To be blunt, elevating the spiritual realm and devaluing the material world is not biblical Christianity, but a major tenant of Gnosticism. But even if it weren't, every attempt to rely on our spiritual connection to the universal church without a meaningful attachment to a local church eventually devolves into the same individualistic search for self—just one overlaid with a Christian-ish veneer. We prefer to keep all our options open, or at least make it easy to cut out whatever (or whoever) we think is stopping us from achieving a worthwhile identity as we define it. Frankly, that's even more consumeristic and artificial than a concert followed by a TED Talk. Matter *matters* to God. If it didn't, God wouldn't have promised Israel a land of milk and honey, baptism wouldn't need water, we could take Communion with Guinness and donuts, and Easter wouldn't be more than a day off work.

If you really, truly value the universal body of Christ, then you will be hungrier to experience it in the midst of the corporately gathered church, not less. For it is uniquely there that the glory of God is particularly present in our being "surrounded by so great [*doxa*] a cloud of witnesses" (Hebrews 12:1) and our union with Christ is both spiritually and physically embodied.

The Context for Our Identity in Christ

We need church because, "Abstracted from the life of the church the biblical narrative loses its heart and soul."[16] It is only our being found within a people named Glory, under Jesus's loving gaze for his bride, that we can be regularly pulled from our navel-gazing to be satisfied by God's own glory. I can't think of any better summary than Richard Lints's:

> *The church is the context for our identity*, but in a time when the church sits lightly on the minds and hearts of many Christians in the West it is not a surprise that Christian identity has become so fragile. What is it that holds our identity together in and through the church? The presence of the risen Lord in the preaching of the Word and the celebration of the sacraments through which the Spirit has so chosen to make this presence manifest. This presence is intimately rooted in the history of redemption and it is that story which the church continually rehearses in its worship. *It is the story of the church that is the larger story of any individual Christian.*[17] (emphasis added)

---

16. Richard Lints, *Identity and Idolatry: The Image of God and Its Inversion*, New Studies in Biblical Theology, vol. 36 (InterVarsity Press, 2015), 170.

17. Lints, *Identity and Idolatry*, 166.

If the Great Commission is Jesus blessing and establishing his church by putting his name, authority, presence, and glory upon his people, then baptism is much more than a public declaration of our newfound faith. When we are baptized *into* the name of the Trinity (perfect, divine harmony of unity and diversity) we are baptized into where God's glory manifestly dwells until Jesus returns—the church.

Baptism itself isn't the identity or glory we long for—Jesus is—but it is our entrance into union with him. To insist that union is merely spiritual and individual and not also physical and collective, will slowly smother and suffocate Christian identity. Baptism is the sign and seal of our having moved out from under the covenants of glory-empty nations and into the great name and nation God promised Abraham way back in Genesis 12. In church, our individual*ity* is redeemed and our individual*ism* obliterated. We are no longer our own, in (the name of) Christ Jesus. Amen.

Reflection Questions

1. What is the greatest gift you've ever received (besides Jesus)? How did it communicate your significance to the one who gave it to you? How did it demonstrate a deep relational knowing?

2. When have you experienced beauty in the way C. S. Lewis or Makoto Fujimura described—a weight of meaning so significant that it makes you acutely aware of your smallness? Was it unsettling? Do you expect such an encounter within the bride of Christ? Why or why not?

3. Why does this chapter *not* feel like good news to you? Does receiving a great name from within God's people seem lesser than achieving it yourself? If so, why? How you answer that question will likely point to how you are most tempted to make a name for yourself (e.g., Jacob by striving and supplanting).

7

A Greenhouse for Exiles

How Church Integrates Life and Cultivates Faith

The God who formed the earth and made it . . . did not create it to be
a wasteland, but formed it to be inhabited.

—Isaiah 45:18 CSB

It is difficult to imagine the world in the year A.D. 2000 . . . In such a
dehumanized society the fellowship of the local church will become
increasingly important, whose members meet one another, and talk
and listen to one another in person rather than on screen. In this
human context of mutual love the speaking and hearing of the Word
of God is also likely to become more necessary for the preservation of
our humanness, not less.

—John Stott, in 1982

Many of us sympathize more than we'd like to admit with the seeds
that "fell on rocky ground" that Jesus describes in the Parable of
the Sower in Matthew 13:1–23. We feel rootless and scorched. Even if
we don't trace it back to anything specifically spiritual, our mounting

cultural exhaustion is provoking a growing spiritual reexamination from some very surprising places.

Staff writer at *The Atlantic* Derek Thompson wrote, "Maybe religion, for all of its faults, works a bit like a retaining wall to hold back the destabilizing pressure of American hyper-individualism, which threatens to swell and spill over in its absence."[1] For the rest of the article he argues that church affiliation, rather than distracting us or taking time from what really matters, is essential to the formation of happy humans and responsible citizens. Remarkably, Thompson is not a Christian. Yet he nevertheless recognizes Christianity's historical influence on society, as well as society's urgent need to rechurch.

According to a January 2024 study from Pew, churchgoing Christians are 10% more likely to volunteer in a civic organization, 12% more likely to vote, and 9% less likely to feel lonely in the last seven days than those who say their religious views are "nothing in particular" (a.k.a. the Nones).[2] We are, as Thompson puts it, already in the midst of "a great rewiring of our social relations,"[3] and our disconnection from the historic vehicles of our formation is leaving us—individually and collectively— with less of the resilience, wisdom, and maturity needed to thrive right when we need it most.

Whether we're "cut flowers" doomed to die, as Ayaan Hirsi Ali described post-Christian society, or rootless seed, we feel our environment growing more inhospitable to human flourishing.[4] We sense that life may not be sustainable for long without some kind of greenhouse—a sanctuary for nourishing and deepening roots.

---

1. Derek Thompson, "The True Cost of the Churchgoing Bust," *The Atlantic*, April 3, 2024, https://www.theatlantic.com/ideas/archive/2024/04/america-religion-decline-non-affiliated/677951/.

2. Gregory Smith et al., "Are 'Nones' Less Involved in Civic Life than People Who Identify with a Religion?," *Pew Research Center*, January 24, 2024, https://www.pewresearch.org/religion/2024/01/24/are-nones-less-involved-in-civic-life-than-people-who-identify-with-a-religion/.

3. Thompson, "Churchgoing Bust."

4. Alliance for Responsible Citizenship, "*What Is the West–Panel*," October 30, 2023, 49 min., 30 sec., https://www.arcforum.com/videos/v/https/youtube/wtzq-zf1qg4?categoryId=65f1b6dd1ce7524140689af2.

Surviving a Life in Exile

Have you ever wondered how your grandparents managed to do it all? Maybe you struggle to work your nine-to-five, spend meaningful time with your kids, stay healthy and physically active, afford a mortgage, build your résumé, visit extended family, disciple your kids, stay connected with friends, have a social life, pursue a hobby or even touch grass, take a vacation (with or without kids), go to church regularly, serve in church, give to charity, save for retirement (or your kids' college tuitions), etc. Maybe that list put you on the edge of a mild panic attack. If it feels like life since high school or college has been a series of bait-and-switch experiences leaving you more unsure of how to navigate life and thrive in this world, you're not crazy. It isn't just because everything is more expensive. Though it is. Have you *seen* the price of avocado toast these days?

Ordinary life seems to require more of us. It requires a shift in perspective not unlike what happens when we travel to another country. Ordinary aspects of life that we can normally do on autopilot—e.g., taking public transportation or running to the grocery store—require significantly more effort and intention in unfamiliar places. Simply going out to eat is a lot harder when you don't speak the language, can't read the menu, and need to make sure the ice is made with bottled water. Each step takes separate exertions of time, effort, and attention requiring more resilience, maturity, and wisdom than we're used to. That can be challenging but fun when we're aware of cultural differences, when we know to expect that the familiar will feel foreign. That's part of what makes a vacation refreshing.

But having that foreign experience without choosing it or knowing what to expect isn't a vacation, it's exile. And exile is no walk in the park. We may not have been geographically carted off to a foreign land like Israel was to Babylon, but we have been culturally relocated from what's familiar to an utterly foreign land. Our exile lacks only a change in scenery.

Labeling that experience "exile" might sound hyperbolic, but even that is understandable. Our cultural uprooting has been a slow-boiling crisis, facilitated more by emerging "technologies [that] have reordered our inner consciousness"[5] than the coercion of a foreign nation. Regardless, that bait-and-switch is no less disorienting. It still leaves us with a vague sense that life is fragmenting, and community is wilting under the pressure.

So, how did we get here? How did "home" become more alienating than welcoming, more scattered than whole?

The Dis-Integrated Fruit of Exile

The evolution of our relationship with physical fitness is both a helpful illustration and an example of all the feeds into to our sociocultural exile. The Ancient Greeks built the first gymnasiums so athletes could train with peers and receive coaching from retired competitors before entering the public arena, much like modern colleges or professional sports teams make available for their players. But unless you were training for an Olympic, collegiate, or similar competition, most Greeks would only set foot in a gym as an audience member. Human beings naturally got more than enough exercise. Everyday life required it. That ceased to be the norm as the Industrial Age gave way to the Information Age and factory workers became desk jockeys. Exercise began *dis-integrating* from work. Everyday life no longer required it. But because we still needed exercise for a minimum level of physical health, that dis-integration created new demand. Thus, in the 1970s, the physical fitness industry as we know it was born.[6] More recently, the post pandemic normalization of remote work made Peloton a household name and the overnight king of the industry's newest evolutionary stage, "connected fitness"—the many digital tools used to connect fitness equipment and activities for home use. No gym membership required. How convenient is that?

---

5. Lints, *Identity*, 160.
6. Cedric X. Bryant, "The Evolution of Fitness Trends," *US News & World Report*, December 28, 2020, https://health.usnews.com/health-news/blogs/eat-run/articles/the-evolution-of-fitness-trends.

Yes, a desk job is a whole lot safer and better paying than a factory, and remote work can be an incredible gift of flexibility—especially for working parents—but there's still a trade-off. Devoting focused time and effort toward one's physical fitness is no longer the niche need of amateur and professional athletes, but a historically new necessity for surviving a digital economy long enough to retire.

The Information Age comes with very direct trade-offs for our social and emotional health especially. As technology provides ever more efficient solutions for mundane tasks, the more everyday life is dis-integrated from organic community. Rather than deepen our social lives, hyper-connectivity dis-integrates individual friendships. We're stretched so thin and our social muscles are so atrophied that it requires herculean effort and intention to initiate any connection not mediated by our phones.

The indirect trade-offs are harder to see but no less consequential. In 2004 Google was already being used for two hundred million searches per day,[7] but it hadn't yet become our kneejerk default medium for learning new information. YouTube wouldn't be launched for another year, and internet-capable phones didn't start going mainstream until after Steve Jobs announced Apple's first iPhone in 2007. But it wasn't until sometime in 2013[8] that smartphones became affordable enough that a majority of Americans owned one.[9] It's now easier to Google a question of theology than ask your pastor, but that isn't what's most concerning. What keeps me up at night are the natural opportunities for community we've lost along the way.

Until only a dozen or so years ago, if we had a life problem we needed help with (e.g., fixing a lamp, filing taxes, or navigating drama at work),

---

7. Mark Hall and William L. Hosch, "Google," *Encyclopaedia Britannica*, accessed May 25, 2024, https://www.britannica.com/money/Google-Inc.

8. "How Many Americans Have Smartphones (2013–2024)," Oberlo, accessed May 25, 2024, https://www.oberlo.com/statistics/how-many-americans-have-smartphones.

9. Not coincidentally, this was right in the middle of an eight-year period that saw smartphones "exponentially driving digital media usage" until 2016, when smartphone ownership reached market saturation at 80% and growth in media usage started tapering off. See Will Sullivan, "Trends on Tuesday: Smartphone Ownership Reaching Saturation, Fueling Media Consumption," *Digital.gov*, April 26, 2016, https://digital.gov/2016/04/26/trends-on-tuesday -smartphone-ownership-reaching-saturation-fueling-media-consumption/.

we'd typically call a friend or family member who had greater experience or wisdom. But now, with YouTube at our fingertips, that's rarely our first impulse. We only want to "bother" friends or family if our problem is too specific or niche to find the solution online. Hypothetically, that efficiency affords us more time for the things that matter most, for phone calls with loved ones to be more about catching up than changing oil. In reality, it has done more to frustrate deep community than all of our political polarization and culture warring combined.

Asking someone for help is about more than getting answers or gaining knowledge. It jump-starts a process that deepens relationship and strengthens bonds with everyone you rely on.

For example, if you ask a couple of friends for parenting advice, they'd probably give you a lot more than the information you went looking for. They'd probably follow up a few days later to see how you're doing. They might offer to schedule a few playdates, or even watch the kids next Friday night so you and your spouse can have an overdue date night to get a break, reconnect, and remember why you married each other in the first place. Or so I've heard.

Even though you reached out for straightforward (if perhaps urgent) answers, you *couldn't* get those answers without walking through an integrated process that provided relational support and wisdom. It matured your perspective in ways you weren't looking for. There just isn't an app for that. And unlike an app, it never required separate effort or intention. It just did, naturally.

Between 2010 and 2015, in what Jonathan Haidt calls the Great Rewiring,[10] smartphones injected our dis-integration with more nitrous than a late sequel of *The Fast and the Furious*. The convenience of being able to access the sum total of human knowledge as quickly and easily as reaching into our pockets makes social interaction as optional as the garage made waving to our neighbors optional. Even if Haidt's thesis was wrong (it's not) and smartphones don't have a negative neurological

---

10. Jonathan Haidt, *The Anxious Generation: How the Great Rewiring of Childhood Is Causing an Epidemic of Mental Illness* (Penguin Press, 2024).

impact on our mental health (they do), the atrophying of our social and relational muscles would be more than enough to explain our loneliness epidemic.

So if it seems harder than ever to start, maintain, and deepen friendships, you're not crazy. If church community seems shallower or requires significantly more effort to cultivate, it does. Given a choice, few of us would pick the pot of boiling water. Yet here we are. And here we will likely remain until the trade-offs get too uncomfortable to be worth the convenience. But if we don't want to wait that long, we do have a far more humanizing alternative.

Church Unbundled

Whether it's your mechanic, a caterer, or an online retailer, almost everyone will offer you a discount for purchasing more of their products or services. The more you "bundle" in an order, the more you save. Similarly, institutions form and shape us by bundling dimensions of life that are essential to social health and happiness: community, ritual, meaning, and purpose. Unbundling them may offer more options and flexibility to customize, but at a greater overall cost to our limited capacity. This is the core of dis-integration. Ultimately, no matter how hard we try to pick up the pieces of our formation and reassemble them into our own personal greenhouse, it can only ever contribute to nostalgia for our institutional home. Technology can't return us from exile.

At no time did we feel the effects of unbundling more vividly than during the coronavirus pandemic. When our church wasn't able to meet due to pandemic lockdowns (March 2020–September 2021), I couldn't believe how much I had taken in-person worship for granted as an essential vehicle for shepherding. Livestreaming disembodies community and dis-integrates worship from any opportunity to hear the tone in someone's voice, notice someone's slumped shoulders across the room, or be organically available to people without them having to call or email for help. As the pastor of an unbundled congregation, I went over seventeen months without that gut-level nudging of the Holy Spirit urging me to ask if someone was really, *truly* as okay as they replied over text the previous week.

Without the ability to shepherd naturally, by virtue of us all just *showing up* on Sunday morning, I had to create a system for checking in with every individual family. No matter how much I optimized or streamlined each step of that process, it required extraordinary amounts of additional time, attention, and initiative to do artificially what happened naturally every Sunday morning. I hated every soul-sucking minute of it. And, to be completely honest, I did a terrible job. I was too slow to understand the pastoral implications of our digital exile, and because I was buckling under the same stress everyone else was experiencing, too many families fell through the cracks in my shepherding. Including my own.

The pandemic gave us all an acute, concentrated experience of our digital age's past and present dis-integration of life, and a stark preview of how much harder it could still get in the future. I was born in the mid-1980s, so I had an analog childhood to compare and contrast to a digital adulthood. Those born since the mid-1990s became the first generation to grow up with digital media as the default medium for consuming information. Those born since 2000 are the first generation to grow up with social media–equipped smartphones as the default vehicle for making and maintaining social connections. My children, along with everyone else born since 2015, will be the first to grow up with Artificial Intelligence having dis-integrated God-only-knows what we don't realize we're taking for granted. Each of the above phases in our digital revolution have ushered in a corresponding leap in convenience, but all of them come at the cost of dis-integrating life and formation from the greenhouses designed to cultivate them. It turns out we just can't dis-integrate life any more than we can unbundle spiritual formation from church.

The question isn't *whether* we will be formed by someone or something, but by whom and where we will be formed. If we are shaped by Jesus within his church, he will grow in us the resilience, maturity, and wisdom we need to thrive in exile. But if we're expecting our church to produce that fruit in us without fully integrating our lives into the life of the church, the false promises of Babel have shaped us more than we realize. We aren't abiding in the True Vine if we aren't devoting our whole selves to the body of Christ. It's a miracle we bear any fruit at all.

Spiritual Formation for Exiles

In Acts 2, shortly after a resurrected Jesus ascends to heaven, he sends the Holy Spirit to fulfill his promise—to be with his disciples until the end of the age and empower them to make disciples of all the nations. While we often marvel at the supernatural moment when blue flames rested upon each believer and they "began to speak in other tongues" (v. 4), Pentecost is much more than a miraculous event. It was a profound turning point in redemptive history:

> The Spirit's coming marked the reversal of the centrifugal momentum of proud humanity's dispersion from Babel. God now gathers scattered exiles from earth's ends and reforges them into his new international family, united not by coercion (as Rome attempted), but by his spirit of grace, and not for human fame, but for God's glory.[11]

Pentecost is an intentional and explicit juxtaposition between the ages, between the Tower of Babel (Genesis 11) and the New Jerusalem (Revelation 21), with a steeple bridging the gap. Exiles are no longer doomed to division and scattered across the face of the earth. The Greek word translated as both 'assembly' and 'church,' *ekklesia*, is the perfect name for this fledgling community because it is formed by combining the words for "to call" and "out of/from." At Pentecost, God *calls* "devout men *from* every nation under heaven" (v. 5) to gather and live as the "great nation" he promised Abraham in Genesis 12:1. Where the Fall is

---

11. Dennis E. Johnson, *The Message of Acts in the History of Redemption* (P&R Publishing, *1997*), 73.

the source of all entropy, this Spirit-bound *ekklesia* is entropy's foil. An oasis for the nations. Dis-integrated image bearers are welcomed and re-integrated within her walls. We are freed from needing to make a name for ourselves because, in Christ, we have been given a Name above all names.

Thus, the church is born. The gates of hell don't stand a chance.

I don't mean to ruin the moment, but if I had a dollar for every time I heard someone say, "We need to get back to the methods and practices of the early church," I'd never need to fundraise for ministry again. That doesn't mean I don't sympathize with that longing. Of course I do. Who wouldn't want to see the fruit Luke described growing among the church in Jerusalem in the wake of Pentecost?

> And they devoted themselves to the apostles' teaching and the fellow-ship, to the breaking of bread and the prayers. And awe came upon every soul, and many wonders and signs were being done through the apostles. And all who believed were together and had all things in common. And they were selling their possessions and belongings and distributing the proceeds to all, as any had need. And day by day, attending the temple together and breaking bread in their homes, they received their food with glad and generous hearts, praising God and having favor with all the people. And the Lord added to their number day by day those who were being saved. (Acts 2:42–47)

Now *that* is a fruitful, integrated life together! I want awe to come upon the souls of the congregation I pastor and the city where I live. Even if the "wonders and signs" were historically unique to that apostolic moment, being together and having "all things in common" sounds like an unfathomably refreshing church experience. Having "glad and generous hearts, praising God and having favor with all the people" is a dream we all aspire to, yet sometimes doubt whether it is still possible in such a cynical and negatively polarized world. It's understandable that we'd want to recover the beautiful and simple practices of verse 42: "the apostles' teaching and the fellowship, to the breaking of bread and the prayers." In every way, *yes and amen!*

So what's the problem then?

The problem is we read Acts 2:42 with the same intuitional assumption that we can dis-integrate community, ritual, meaning, and purpose without consequence.[12] Through individualism's filter, we interpret verse 42 as if it says, "And everyone received a balanced spiritual diet of biblical teaching, community support, communion with God, and regular quiet time spent in prayer." And as long as we are getting those four things, we can expect to grow more resilient, wise, and mature.

Except verse 42 doesn't say anything of the sort.

Rather, it says, "They [all, together] devoted themselves [fully, together] to *the* apostles' teaching [singular], *the* fellowship [singular], to *the* breaking of bread [singular] and *the* prayers [singular]." Luke's list isn't a description of four individual practices. It isn't a list at all. It describes a spiritual ecosystem with four life-giving dimensions. Or maybe a prism made of four indivisible facets. Whatever metaphor we use, the early church was absolutely not a spiritual buffet from which individual believers picked dis-integrated ingredients. "Awe" is not on the other side of a balanced spiritual diet. That's individualism talking. Instead, what Luke is describing is individuals called out from every tribe, tongue, and nation to become part of God's "great nation" (Genesis 12).

What Luke actually says is that these reborn exiles devoted themselves (plural) to the spiritual greenhouse (singular) God "assembled" to cultivate a fourfold integrated life together in Christ: gathering for worship (the fellowship) to receive the preaching of God's Word (the apostles' teaching), take the Lord's Supper together (the breaking of bread), and actively depend on him (the prayers). Those are not individual, personal practices. They are the substance and shape of the body of Christ, and that difference matters greatly. Dis-integrate any one of them and you lose what all four of them describe; you lose what makes church, church.

---

12. Although it isn't quite a clean, one-to-one equivalency, I'd argue that Burton's four sociological dimensions of religious identity roughly correspond to the four dimensions of church life in Acts 2:42. Tara Isabella Burton, *Strange Rites: New Religions for a Godless World* (PublicAffairs, 2020).

Reintegrating Life in God's Household

Perhaps the most important word in Acts 2:42 is the verb "devoted" (προσκαρτερέω or *proskartereō*). It means to diligently persist, associate closely, and serve personally. Or to abide even. Luke is calling us to commit ourselves to something far greater and, yes, far more costly than dis-integrated involvement or spiritual consumerism: membership.

A few weeks after Jason took our church's membership class, he asked to grab coffee to process some follow-up questions. He'd been attending The Table for a year or two by then and had previously shared enough of his story that I was eager to hear how everything was hitting him. Although he grew up in a healthy evangelical church in the Denver suburbs and attended a Christian college, he'd still been deeply wrestling with faith and doubt for the previous few years. As you can imagine, he especially appreciated the text-in Q&A we do at the end of every sermon. There aren't many spaces *anywhere* with that kind of room to breathe, so simply *inviting* questions gave him freedom to wrestle with doubt without fear of being judged or condemned for it.

I can't remember if he used the word "deconstruction" back then, but it applied to much of his experience trying to untangle Christianity from the modernist standards of certainty that hang thick in Western air. For someone as genuinely inquisitive (and legitimately brilliant) as he is, that atmosphere stoked a lot of cognitive dissonance and spiritual anxiety. To his credit, he refused to avoid uncomfortable questions or accept easy answers to resolving his discomfort. The membership process was no exception.

When we met up for coffee, Jason explained that he wanted to become a member, but he still wasn't convinced that Scripture was God's Word or that the Jesus it depicted was real. He understood what he was asking. That in becoming a member of a church, he was opting into a depth of shepherding, spiritual formation, and shared responsibility that needed a common theological foundation. Without shared beliefs regarding Word (the apostles' teaching) and sacrament (the breaking of the bread), we're not operating off the same definitions of community (the fellowship) or faith (the prayers). In fact, Jason intuitively understood and appreciated the church's formative role better than many *members* I've known over the years. Ironically, it was exactly his honest engagement with doubt, the genuineness of his search for faith, and the difficulty he's had in working it out on his own that made him even more aware of his need for a spiritual greenhouse than most.

I found our conversation so personally refreshing because the only thing I have heard more often than "we need to return to the early church" is "church membership isn't in the Bible." When I do, I point out that in both principle and literal meaning, Paul describes Christians as "members" in both 1 Corinthians 12:12–14 and Ephesians 2:19–22. In the latter, he says that we "are no longer strangers and aliens" (nor exiles), but instead "fellow citizens with the saints and *members of the household of God*" (emphasis added). If anything, that implies a significantly higher standard and expectation than most modern definitions of membership.

The Greek word for "household" is *oikos* and is where we get the word "economy." A household is at least a family, but also more. Like all institutions, an oikos is ideally a generative community where members are devoted to their collective good. That doesn't happen naturally, at least not in a world marred by sin and death. We need the structure, order, and intentionality that a household provides; otherwise we will always prioritize self-interest over self-sacrifice. But that order and structure is more than a matter of practicality or logistics. Households also inculcate trust and assurance that all individual members benefit, together, as the collective good is furthered.

Paul borrows the concept and language of a familiar institution ("household") while speaking to Gentile Christians because it was the closest analog of what Jewish Christians already understood as covenant community—the family "of redeemed sinners bound to their Lord and to one another in the bond of love known as the covenant of grace."[13]

---

13. David McKay, "Covenant Community," *Ligonier*, October 1, 2006, https://www.ligonier.org/learn/articles/covenant-community.

The gospel declares our spiritual union in Christ, and "members one of another" (Ephesians 4:25), but we most fully embody that spiritual reality in time and space by devoting our whole selves to the body of Christ. In other words, as members of a particular covenant community. Only then can we hope to see the natural and supernatural cultivation of the incredible fruit Luke lists in Acts 2:43–47.

Discipleship is, of course, more than going to church every Sunday, but it cannot possibly mean anything *less*. Gathering to praise and worship God doesn't guarantee fruitfulness, but if everything is an outflow from that spiritual spring, we're wise to sink our roots deeply and *fully* beside its waters. Doing so partially or shallowly, or while looking over our shoulder for better options, merely sips at living water and can't quench our thirst. If we've learned nothing else over the last several decades, it is that a dis-integrated devotion to the body of Christ results in anemic discipleship at best. Piling amputated limbs on a stainless-steel table isn't a "person." Neither can piling up dis-integrated commitments be considered devotion to the body of Christ.

Jesus invites us to experience resurrection life by devoting our whole selves to our church as fully as he devoted himself to us—"To the point of death, even death on a cross" (Philippians 2:8). We can't claim to be taking up our cross or following Christ if we aren't fully devoting ourselves to the bride he died to save. Not with a straight face, anyway.

That doesn't mean we must do it perfectly from day one. Right after Paul explains that the gospel makes a household out of former exiles, he reassures them that deepening that devoting themselves is a cooperative process with God. In Christ Jesus, the church, "being joined together, *grows* into a holy temple in the Lord. In him [we] also *are being built together* into a dwelling place for God by the Spirit" (Ephesians 2:21–22, emphasis added). In and through Christ's Body, God takes the mustard seed of imperfect faith and grows it into a life-giving shade tree. A refuge for the world. No greenhouse is more hospitable to exiles. No technology, no gadget, and no other intelligence—natural or artificial—can make formation more convenient or less costly. Again, there isn't an app for that.

We revisited that conversation a little over three years later. Time spent in our spiritual greenhouse didn't bring Jason much in the way of certainty, but he found something better. Even though he hadn't formally become a member, he spent the previous three years devoting himself to The Table in every other way. I could tell it made a difference too. His restless, sometimes even anxious, curiosity was replaced by a more mature and patient inquisitiveness. He didn't credit a come-to-Jesus moment or a dramatic conversion story. Instead, he shared a quite unexciting story of ordinary, day-to-date commitment to The Table that demoted certainty and, slowly, cultivated deeper faith in Christ. Not long after that he and his wife said yes to those vows and became full covenant members of The Table.

When I asked him what changed since our conversation over coffee, he said he realized that part of his problem was deconstructing without questioning whether certainty was even the standard he should be aiming for. So he started asking fundamental questions like, "Will reading books and listening to podcasts ever move me closer to God?" Slowly but surely, hope replaced certainty. Not just the passive *feeling* that comes from trusting Jesus, but hope as an active *posture* taken on faith: "Somehow hope is more potent when you're not certain of an outcome, when you *have* to hope for it and move in that direction anyway." Curious, I asked how he came to see hope and faith so differently than before. He listed a few things like participating in liturgy, receiving Communion, and having rich conversations with people about faith, but "at the end of the day, we just became a lot more rooted at The Table."

And God gave the growth.

Cultivating Faith in God's Garden

Whether you struggle to share the gospel with your neighbor, sacrificially love your spouse, pass the faith onto your children, or "love the LORD your God with all your heart and with all your soul and with all your might" (Deuteronomy 6:5), covenant membership is the A-to-Z of reintegrating life and cultivating faith in Christ. Paul says we can hope for and pursue that growth even within a profoundly flawed and imperfect spiritual greenhouse:

> I planted, Apollos watered, but *God* gave the growth. So neither he who plants nor he who waters is anything, but *only God* who gives the growth. He who plants and he who waters are one, and each will receive his wages according to his labor. For we are God's fellow workers. You are God's field, God's building. (1 Corinthians 3:6–9, emphasis added)

When God created Adam and Eve, he put them in a garden. Not a jungle, a meadow, or some other untamed environment. A garden. Gardens are both organic and ordered ecosystems. Paul understood that when congregations err in the *organic* direction ("field"), community is too much like a jungle. We expend so much energy fighting for sunlight and nutrients that we don't have anything left for deepening roots or bearing fruit. A church built on the relational happenstance, preferences, or desires of its members won't survive its first harsh winter. When churches err on the side of *ordered* ("building"), you get the perfectly manicured (and boring) gardens of Versailles—plants forced into shapes contrary to their nature. There's nothing to harvest from this garden because fruit is just too inconvenient and messy to deal with, so the fruit-bearing genes have been bred out of every species. Cultivation isn't for the plant's good but for the sake of appearances.

Thankfully, neither ecosystem is what Paul had in mind. Rather, the church is more of an English-style garden,[14] positively teeming and bursting at the seams with all manner of life. It may look wild and untamed up close, but its abundance is not the result of neglect or entropy as it may first appear. This garden is the marriage of form and function, splashing

---

14. I am shamelessly stealing this analogy from Jonah Goldberg, who shamelessly stole it from Friedrich Hayek, who first used it as a metaphor for how free markets cultivate economic growth. It turns out that what's true of a dynamic in one *"oikos"* is often universally true across all institutions. Institutions are consistent like that.

color across a monochrome landscape. The harvest is plenty, with enough bounty to share with our neighbors. Nothing is zero-sum. Likeness and difference thrive as part of a mutually dependent, generative whole. You might still see the occasional dandelion, but it'll stick out like a sore thumb and be uprooted long before it can do any lasting harm. None of that weeding and watering and fertilizing and pruning and waiting (especially the waiting) is in vain because *God gives the growth*.

God wants so much more for exiles than a dis-integrated way of life. He wants us to experience the teeming abundance of a life devoted to generative gospel community. We don't have to choose between the dog-eat-dog jungle of radical individualism or being rigidly forced into a Versailles-like conformity unnatural to our design. We can be redeemed and our life reintegrated within this teeming, institutional ecosystem wherein Jesus cultivates apprentice gardeners (disciples) out of potted plants (exiles).

It may be only coincidence, but when Mary Magdalene first encountered Jesus outside the empty tomb, she initially thought he was just "the gardener" (John 20:15). She wasn't entirely mistaken either. If God gives the growth, then the church isn't just a greenhouse for cut flowers. The Divine Gardener is in the business of resurrection. In and through his greenhouse, he brings dead and wilting flowers to life, roots them in fertile soil, and cultivates life-giving faith.

Reflection Questions

1. Does the description of contemporary life as "exile without the change in scenery" resonate with you? Where do you feel the greatest need for resilience, wisdom, and maturity in a post-Christian world? Describe your answers with a Christian or non-Christian friend and ask them the same questions.

2. How has the church been a greenhouse for your spiritual growth—in guiding, nourishing, and pruning your faith? How does a dis-integrated life challenge or threaten that growth?

3. The first question of the Heidelberg Catechism is based on 1 Corinthians 6:19–20. It asks, "What is your only comfort in life and in death?" and answers, "That I am not my own, but belong— body and soul, in life and in death—to my faithful Savior, Jesus Christ." How might devoting yourself to a local church bring you greater comfort? Whether you're a member or not, how could you adopt a more covenantal posture?

8

An Embodied Narrative

How We Inhabit and Participate in the Drama of Redemption

"If your eye is healthy, your whole body will be full of light, but if your eye is bad, your whole body will be full of darkness. If then the light in you is darkness, how great is the darkness!"

—Jesus (Matthew 6:22–23)

The narrative of Scripture is not simply a story of ancient events. . . . It interprets our present identity through which we see ourselves and our world . . . [and] stories require a community to provide them with living plausibility.

—Richard Lints

Kevin and I had become fast friends over a couple years. I've rarely met someone who cares as genuinely and deeply for people. A passionate humanist, he's the kind of guy who never has to say that he'll be there for you when it matters because he's so consistently there for you when it doesn't. He came to several launch team meetings when our church was still a twinkle in our eyes and hadn't started meeting for worship yet. And despite being very confident in his atheism, he still threw himself into everything and became a valued part of our fledgling community.

As a culinary school-trained chef he loved our theological vision of hospitality and loving our neighbors as ourselves. But it wasn't necessarily the vision that drew him in. He was used to Christians talking about loving their neighbors, but (as he put it) "mostly to pat themselves on the back whether they do it or not." He took love very seriously because his story and his experience had taught him that the root of all our dysfunction was a critical lack of love (no argument there!). What resonated with him wasn't that our people were more naturally hospitable than other Christians, it was that we genuinely believed he had something to teach us about hospitality. We needed him.

Planting a church with hospitality in its DNA would be radically humbling for anyone. But at the time, we also failed to see how our hospitality was already shaped by the same individualist metanarrative we were hoping to confront with the true story of the gospel. Not fully appreciating how individualism had shaped our respective stories made an already humbling endeavor feel impossible at times. Even before we could name it, we could feel when hospitality became a way to achieve our dignity, value, and worth—*through* loving our neighbors.

To state the obvious, no, that's not a very hospitable motive. We were essentially using our neighbors, but thankfully God used us anyway. At the very least, that tension made it even easier for us to genuinely believe we could learn from Kevin, which left him equal parts intrigued and bewildered. "None of you make any sense to me," he told me after one of our launch team meetings. Our genuine sincerity in welcoming him despite seeing the world through a completely different lens provoked a growing conflict between two narratives. One told a story of unceasing performance, and the other a promise of grace.

A few months before we launched The Table, Kevin took my wife and me up on the invitation to join us for a worship service at another church in the area. The sermon was on hope and the New Jerusalem in Revelation 21–22. It was the kind of flourishing vision I expected to resonate with Kevin, so I was surprised when he seemed agitated, and even a little angry when we sat down to process his thoughts over lunch. "It's just so typical. The world is burning down around us and what does he preach? A fantasy that God will just wave his magic wand and make it all better someday. Instead of telling them to *do* something about brokenness, he enabled everyone in that room to keep their head in the sand and wait for a messiah to do it for them."

Let's be honest. Who of us hasn't felt that way at times? Silicon Valley gurus and political candidates alike suffer from messianic delusions of grandeur, promising to solve all our problems with one wave of a magic wand. "There's an app for that" isn't just a pithy slogan, it's a five-word short story articulating a utopian vision for a fully optimized and frictionless life. With so many unreliable narrators in the world, I couldn't blame Kevin for thinking the preacher was just another in a long line of grifting charlatans. To him, Jesus's promise to make all things new is a religious spin on the same old story.

How We Make Sense of the World

We make sense of reality and express the meaning we make from our experiences by telling stories. The previous sentence was a micronarrative. Questions are requests for tales true and tall. How was your day? Where are you from? Should we go to church this week? What is the airspeed velocity of an unladen swallow? Questions alone can tell us something (e.g., whether one has seen the movie *Monty Python and the Holy Grail*), and every answer is a value-saturated interpretation of the world—as it is, was, or might be. And especially how the world *should* be.

It's no coincidence that the science fiction genre of books, film, and television exploded in popularity during the civil rights era. We needed fresh narratives for exploring deeper truths and the lies obscuring them (e.g., race and racism). Shows like *Star Trek* gave us sense-making opportunity at a safer emotional distance (i.e., alien races). Science fiction narratives may not be accurate in the sense of having happened, historically speaking, but that doesn't mean they aren't telling a true story. In 1968, only a year after the Supreme Court legalized interracial marriage in *Loving v. Virginia*, *Star Trek* asked and answered an equally important question, "Should interracial marriage be socially accepted?" with a story. In one of the first interracial kisses ever broadcast on television, William Shatner (as Captain Kirk) locked lips with Nichelle Nichols (as Nyota Uhura).

Stories don't just express our perspective on reality, they also shape our experience of reality the more we participate in them. In other words, stories are also scripts. We don't opt into most scripts, but we live in a world that has, and their narrative shapes how we live in subtle yet powerful ways. Lexus doesn't just sell you cars, it celebrates consumerism's metanarrative and declares you deserve one wrapped in a red bow on Christmas morning. Lilly (the pharmaceutical company that produces Cialis) doesn't just sell you a pill, it retells the story of perpetual youth, pleasure, and the virile masculine identity you long to recover. You don't have to buy anything to be shaped by a script, you just have to live in a culture that has.

All of culture expresses and reflects a larger story and meaning of life that we functionally (if not explicitly) believe—they are what we make of the world.

What story does our parenting tell about what is true, good, and beautiful? Is it a story of love and grace, or of performance and merit? Would our kids tell a different story?

What story does our calendar tell about what is true, good, and beautiful? Is it a story of freedom and rest, or of drivenness and anxiety? Would our friends and neighbors agree?

What story does our financial spending tell about what is true, good, and beautiful? Is it a story of generosity and wisdom, or of short-term satisfaction and consumerism? Which narrative better reconciles our bank account with God's account of how things *should* be?

Stories have the power to move the horizon on what is possible and shape our moral imaginations. Excellently told stories normalize the perspective they're told from. Jesus's parables are powerful because of the truths they communicate, but also because of the form they take.

Narrative bypasses all kinds of objections and emotional barriers to inject truth straight into our bones. C. S. Lewis beautifully articulated this relationship between story and truth: "I believe in Christianity as I believe that the sun has risen: not only because I see it, but because by it I see everything else."[1]

Overexposure to Artificial Narratives

Stories, like light, are not all created equal. Narratives can warm and comfort like natural light streaming through a glass pane in a greenhouse, or they can expose with the cold artificial glare found in every gas station bathroom. As modernity multiplies artificial sources of light, we blind ourselves to a sky filled horizon-to-horizon with the Milky Way. We miss out on all the majesty, awe, and wonder it evokes. Likewise, we are bombarded with so much content through so many perspectives that we lose sight of the truest story of all—and the goodness and beauty it illuminates. Smartphones, like streetlamps, promise to push back discomforting darkness and reveal our path a few million light-emitting diodes (LED) at a time, but overexposure to so many unreliable narrators only obscures. Too much light is as blinding as not enough.

Our information spaces are already so cluttered with alternative facts, fake news, and spin doctors that you can't throw a rock without hitting a conspiracy theory. And we're about to find out what happens when a society that no longer values revelation or reason is flooded with more AI-generated propaganda and deep fakes than we can possibly filter out. It's still possible to see by the light of the Christian story, but C. S. Lewis never had to squint past so many hot takes.

We can't help but tell stories to apprehend reality. That is a right and good impulse for image bearers. However, the longer we endure artificial light pollution, the more we'll be tempted to become our own sources

---

1. "Reflections: Christianity Makes Sense of the World," *C. S. Lewis Institute* (blog), accessed October 25, 2024, https://www.cslewisinstitute.org/resources/reflections-december-2013/.

of light. Why? Because the metanarrative of individualism proclaims that *we* are our only reliable narrators—that the only way to make sense of a washed-out world is to cut through the glare and narrate with even brighter luminosity.

If that sounds counterproductive, that's because it is. Individualism over-exposes our sense-making impulse until it devolves into a highly editorialized and subjective denial of reality we summarize as "speaking our truth." Originally, that phrase meant something akin to "sharing our perspective," but the more we've relied on it as a script, the emphasis on "our" truth inverted healthy sense-making. Now when we speak our truth, we do so to edit reality to fit our narrative. We elect ourselves as reality's sacrosanct narrators and remake the world in our own image.

This is the ultimate implication of individualism's narrative. Without a greater story, we can't help but sacralize our perspectives and canonize our narratives. But no matter how much we insist otherwise, we aren't reliable narrators. Flashlights are no more capable of illuminating what is true, good, and beautiful than they are of revealing the surface of Pluto. We'll never outshine the sun.

Only God can speak his truth and share more than yet another perspective. Only he can declare "let there be light" (Genesis 1:3) or "it is finished" (John 19:30), and reality itself respond to accommodate his narration. Trying to be our own light source would be comically self-defeating if our horizons of the possible weren't already set by the same story. Without a sun's worth of fuel, trying to outshine light pollution isn't sustainable. Whether we burn out quickly or slowly, collapsing into a black hole is inevitable. That's when life gets real dark, real quick.

Starving for True Light, we cope by sucking up all the lesser light and stories and meaning and news and perspectives and content (glorious content!) we're exposed to. No light can escape the event horizon of an uncritical singularity. Counterintuitively, bottomless content consumption only leaves us *emptier* of meaning, more desperate for any story that makes sense of our experience. We no longer bother trying to filter out conspiracy theories or propaganda. We'll believe any narrator or script offering the barest whiff of explanatory power, but being open to falsehood isn't any better than being closed to truth. We desperately need a way to filter out the glare.

Thankfully, there is a Story that makes sense of all our stories—all our happiness and joy, all our anger and pain, and all our hopes and fears. Understanding our place in that Grand Story and how to participate in it is where we turn our attention to next.

The True Story of the World

At its core, the Bible tells the Story of God and his mission to redeem all of creation, especially and initially through his people. The Old and New Testaments are one unified, historical narrative that tells the true story of the world in four acts:

1. **Creation:** One word sums up the picture of Genesis 1–2—shalom. The creation of the universe (generally) and Eden (especially) was God "setting the table" in cosmic preparation for creating and welcoming Adam and Eve. All creation is God's gift to humanity. God's plan and our design was to live in joyful worship of God, in harmony with one another, and stewarding the creation he entrusted to our care for eternity. In short, *everything was the way it was supposed to be.*

2. **Fall:** But not for long. Adam and Eve distrusted God's goodness and rejected his rule. Because Adam was God's covenant representative, the entire universe and all of humanity fell from grace too. Shalom was shattered. We have inherited their enmity, and in our attitudes and actions toward God and each other, we perpetuate the physical and spiritual death they welcomed into the world. Now *nothing is the way it is supposed to be.*

3. **Redemption:** Above and beyond our wildest imaginations, our loving Creator co-opted all our evil and suffering to rescue us from ourselves. The grand narrative of Scripture climaxes with the good news (or gospel) that the King of creation took on human flesh as

a new Adam; he lived the life we should have lived and died the death we deserved to die to save us by grace rather than merit. In the person of Jesus Christ, God himself came to renew the world and restore humanity. Christ's bodily resurrection is the down payment on his promise that we too will be made new at the end of history. Though we live in the "not yet" of full restoration, we are still really, truly, and "already" redeemed. And because Jesus is even now ruling and reigning and making all things new in the present tense, we can meaningfully experience intermittent shalom here and now. In other words, *some things can be as they're supposed to be.*

4. **Restoration:** But the Story isn't over. God has promised to bring that redemption into full, breathtaking completion across all creation—the spiritual and material alike. Scripture gives us a peek into this glorious future state: a new heavens and new earth, radiating with a truth, goodness, and beauty beyond our wildest dreams. This final chapter, history's epilogue, is inaugurated by Christ's judgment of all sin and evil and culminates with the full return of shalom. *Everything will be as it is supposed to be—always and forevermore.*

The best lowercase "s" stories ever written include elements of all four acts of this redemptive drama. We resonate with them to the degree that they echo the true and better story of the world. When a story underemphasizes or leaves out one or more acts, they're just not as satisfying. They feel like bad news because they're incomplete.

Individualism is one of those incomplete stories; it reverses Act 2 (the fall) and Act 3 (redemption). Our problem, individualism leads us to believe, isn't that we want to be like God but that we let anyone tell us we're not (including God). We must be the author, hero, and narrator of our own redemption. We shout our truth over and against each other because it's the only way we can matter according to individualism's script. And we are terrified of not mattering.

No one can dwell in that fantasy for long. Yet we try to anyway because we long to participate in something bigger than ourselves. This is a right and good longing, but we can't sate it by inflating our role to cosmic proportions. We have a far more freeing, satisfying, and human-sized role to play.

Discovering Our Role in the Story

Spoiler alert: We're neither author nor protagonist. We're not even the narrator—no one can narrate a story bigger than themselves. Those are shoes only Jesus can fill. Who, then, are we? What is our role, our part to play in this cosmic metanarrative of grace?

To answer, let me first introduce you to a plot device called a "MacGuffin." A MacGuffin is a person or object that provides a "why" to the primary characters in a story, the raison d'être for an event or chapter to progress into the next. Alfred Hitchcock, who popularized it, gave a lecture at Columbia University where he demonstrated how it worked:

> It might be a Scottish name, taken from a story about two men on a train. One man says, "What's that package up there in the baggage rack?" And the other answers, "Oh, that's a MacGuffin." The first one asks, "What's a MacGuffin?" "Well," the other man says, "it's an apparatus for trapping lions in the Scottish Highlands." The first man says, "But there are no lions in the Scottish Highlands," and the other one answers, "Well then, that's no MacGuffin!" So you see that a MacGuffin is actually nothing at all.[2]

Helen of Troy. The Golden Fleece. Getting home. The Holy Grail. Launch codes. The One Ring. R2-D2 (and the Death Star plans stored in him). The buried treasure. Nearly any advanced technology. The Necronomicon. The Sorcerer's Stone (and the second half of every

---

2. Swapnil Dhruv Bose, "Alfred Hitchcock Explains the Vital Cinematic Plot Device 'The MacGuffin,'" March 13, 2021, https://faroutmagazine.co.uk/alfred-hitchcock-the-macguffin-explanation/.

Harry Potter title). "Rosebud." A briefcase, especially if it contains microfilm. The Infinity Stones. The Infinity Gauntlet. E. T. Paradise Falls. A kidnapped daughter. The Magic Mirror. The AllSpark. Any cure or antidote. Genie's Lamp. The Rabbit's Foot. Grogu (a.k.a. Baby Yoda). A stolen bride, princess or otherwise.

What's my point? Just as the best storytelling adheres closely to the redemptive drama, the best MacGuffins resemble Christ's rescued bride. In the true story recorded in Scripture, Old Testament Israel and the New Testament church are the object of God's pursuit and rescue. They—*we*—are the MacGuffin:

> It was not because you were more in number than any other people that the LORD set his love on you and chose you, for you were the fewest of all peoples, but it is because the LORD loves you and is keeping the oath that he swore to your fathers, that the LORD has brought you out with a mighty hand and redeemed you from the house of slavery, from the hand of Pharaoh king of Egypt. (Deuteronomy 7:7–8)

We're the otherwise irrelevant focal point in a conflict between good and evil, over whom the hero and villain fight to claim. We are the raison d'être moving the plot forward despite our best efforts (just ask Abraham, Isaac, and Jacob). This story's author has promised to finish what he started at creation. He can and he will, even if it requires the ultimate sacrifice and comes at infinite cost to himself.

The World War II epic *Saving Private Ryan* offers a classic example of a MacGuffin. The movie centers on Captain John H. Miller's rescue and extraction of Private James Francis Ryan from behind enemy lines. Ryan didn't have any special knowledge or skills. He was just a random soldier with the lowest possible rank. Ryan is so interchangeable and not special that at one point in the movie, Miller mistakenly breaks the horrible news to the wrong "Private Ryan"—a James *Frederick* Ryan. The only thing that set him apart was that he happened to have three brothers who were recently killed in combat. That's it.

In the end, Ryan refuses to be rescued and abandon his comrades, so

Miller's squad joins them for a final, climactic battle to prevent a German unit from capturing a key bridge that the Allies needed to advance on Berlin and defeat Hitler. Miller keeps Ryan at his side, at times almost comically jerking him around by his uniform to keep him out of harm's way. He succeeds in his mission to protect Ryan and repulse the German offensive, but only barely and at the cost of his own life. Bleeding out on the bridge they fought to defend, his last whispered words to Ryan were: "James, earn this . . . *earn* it."

This is the gospel of individualism. And it isn't good news.

With those words, Miller laid a lifelong curse on Ryan. Decades later when his family visited Miller's gravesite, Ryan tearfully turns to his wife and says, "Tell me I've led a good life; tell me I'm a good man." How could anyone answer that question but the one who died so Ryan could live? With his last breath, Miller set the price of his sacrifice and robbed Ryan of any way to know whether he'd ever paid his debt. Redemption is impossible because we can't answer for ourselves whether we matter, and no one can grant absolution from beyond the grave. Paradoxically, we need both a hero's sacrifice and an author's assurance to answer that question in any deep or lasting way.

Jesus Christ gave his life to flip individualism's script for MacGuffins like you and me. With his last breath, he didn't say, "Earn it." He declared, "It is finished" (John 19:30) and answered once and for all whether we matter. In Christ and by his narration alone, there is "no guilt in life, no fear in death."[3] Apart from his relentlessly self-giving pursuit, there's nothing remarkable or special about us. We're MacGuffins. We are rescued and reborn for no reason but God's steadfast love and faithfulness.

If that doesn't sound like good news or strikes you as a little too easy, welcome. That dissonance you feel is a symptom of having been shaped by so many lesser stories. Light pollution is real, but it's possible to see by a different light. We can stop rehearsing the bad scripts and start inhabiting a true and better story. Here's how.

---

3. Keith Getty and Stuart Townend, *In Christ Alone (My Hope Is Found)* lyrics © Thankyou Music Ltd.

Rehearsing the Drama of Redemption

During my senior year of high school, I got to see legendary jazz pianist Herbie Hancock perform at the Miles Davis Arts Festival in East St. Louis. He took the stage with another jazz legend, Wayne Shorter, who played the tenor and soprano saxophone. Both played together as part of the *Miles Davis Quintet* in the 1960s and collaborated on various side projects in the decades since. They were old friends reuniting to celebrate what would have been Miles Davis's seventy-fifth birthday.

I had just started playing guitar in our high school jazz band and Hancock's "Chameleon" was one of my favorite pieces we played, so I couldn't wait to hear it live. I went with a friend and his older brother, Jonathan, who had just started his master's degree in jazz composition for trombone. Compared to either of them, I was a wide-eyed noob and couldn't even read sheet music. And it's a good thing I had them as tour guides because I had no idea what I was walking into.

About an hour into their mesmerizing set, I leaned over to Jonathan and shouted into his ear, "When do you think they'll play 'Chameleon'?" Even though it was just Hancock playing piano and Shorter playing soprano sax on stage, it was still really loud, and we were front and center. So I thought maybe he didn't hear me because, instead of answering, he doubled over laughing. I spent a long couple of minutes wondering what got lost in translation. After recovering and wiping the tears from his eyes, he said, "Young padawan, they've been playing 'Chameleon' for the last twenty minutes!" The look on my face must have made it abundantly clear that I thought he was pulling my chain, so he helped me inhabit what I was hearing. He gestured in the air with his hand, visually conducting the rhythm at the same time he scat sang[4] Chameleon's main melody into my ear. Without any explanation, Hancock and Shorter's improv suddenly made sense.

It was like magic. A whole new sonic narrative unfolded in front

---

4. "In scat singing, the singer improvises melodies and rhythms using the voice solely as an instrument rather than a speaking medium." "Scat Singing," *Wikipedia*, May 5, 2024, https://en.wikipedia.org/w/index.php?title=Scat_singing&oldid=1222283208.

of me. My very basic familiarity with the "story" called "Chameleon" became immediately dwarfed as absolute masters of their craft drew me into harmonies and settings and plotlines and riffs and characters I didn't know *existed*, never mind had the pleasure of meeting before. Despite being so newly acquainted, the music's topography was still instantly and overwhelmingly familiar. I *knew* these hills and valleys, even if the landscape teemed with a wider range of melodies and harmonies and combinations thereof than I could have ever imagined (especially with only two instruments). It's hard to put into words, but it was like I had suddenly experienced in multisensory living color what I'd only ever glimpsed in black and white. I couldn't wait to get home and play "Chameleon"[5] on my guitar and, at the same time, I couldn't imagine ever trying to play it again. Not after hearing perfection incarnate. Noticing that my jaw rested somewhere on the trampled grass at our feet, Jonathan paused his audio-visual demonstration and said simply, "Welcome."

What left me particularly awestruck was that everything I witnessed that day was all improvised. There wasn't a single printed sheet of music anywhere in sight. They didn't need it. The tapestry of sound that wrapped me up like a warm blanket was a momentary creation born from decades of musical discipleship. Their improv flowed out of intimate familiarity with the story of jazz. Hancock and Shorter are masters because they are, first and foremost, disciples dedicated to rehearsing jazz's varied liturgies for so long and so many times that jazz's grand metanarrative had become permanently imprinted upon their souls. They didn't play jazz, they embodied it.

Hancock and Shorter were so free to improvise "Chameleon" for almost thirty minutes because they immersed themselves in the original arrangement (i.e., the composer's perspective) over and over and over and over again. Each spontaneous micronarrative and riff may have sounded made up on the spot, but they stood on the shoulders of musical saints and paid homage to their legacy and tradition with every flourish.

Whether we are practicing the minor pentatonic scale, reciting

---

5. Did you catch that this was the MacGuffin in my story?

Hamlet's monologue, or memorizing the Westminster Shorter Catechism, every narrative will feel rote if we expect the natural freedom of performance without first inhabiting them, and we do that by rehearsing them. The point of rehearsal isn't freedom, but familiarity. Like all intimacy, familiarity requires an iterative cycle of immersing ourselves in another perspective—be that of an author by reading their poetry, a spouse by listening to how their day went, a chef by eating their cuisine, or a culture by living in their country. Intentionally immersing ourselves in another story enables us, over time, to see by its light and through its lens with greater acuity.

None of us can embody a cosmic drama of redemption by ourselves. It's too big. For that, we must gather for worship every Sunday morning. It's okay if the script feels unfamiliar. By grace, the Holy Spirit illuminates God's Word, attuning us to rhythms of grace. Because God's Word won't return void, we can't remain unchanged even when the sermon is subpar and the preacher is imperfect. Congregations inhabit and rehearse the gospel story by reciting liturgy, raising hands, and singing praise to God. By grace, God doesn't laugh when we confess sin or show evidence that we still don't get it. By grace, he gently convicts our hearts, exposing where we live by false fluorescence and enlightening our understanding of the true and better story. The redemptive drama comes alive as the Spirit of Christ scat-sings good news into the depths of our souls.

Simply showing up week in and week out to participate with whatever you have left in the tank will leave a grace-shaped impression on our souls. Over the clamor of a world shouting, "Strive! Strive! Earn your worth!" we'll start hearing a very different tune. We'll catch ourselves tapping our feet to the rhythm of grace. We might even develop the sneaking suspicion that God loves rather than tolerates us.

Entering the True and Better Story

Worship is never a performance (or at least it shouldn't be), but it isn't *just* rehearsal either. Whether scat-singing Herbie Hancock's "Chameleon" or shout-singing a Taylor Swift anthem, concerts offer a very real kind of participation, but one limited by time and space. And even as epic as those experiences might be, they barely scratch the surface of the reality we get to participate in every Sunday.

Unlike a theatrical production that unfolds on a stage, we aren't playacting when we worship in Christ. This isn't fiction. We don't put on masks or pull costumes from a wardrobe when we "put on Christ" (Galatians 3:27). We become our true selves. Like Peter, Susan, Edmund, and Lucy in *The Chronicles of Narnia*, we pass through the wardrobe to inhabit a world where masks aren't necessary. We enter that world initially and anew every time we participate in the sacraments.

The word "sacrament" comes from the Latin *sacramentum* ("holy oath" or "promise"), which is a translation of the Greek word *musterion* ("mystery").[6] The Romans used *sacramentum* to describe the relationship between an individual and the gods, not unlike how the Old Testament describes Israel's relationship with Yahweh as a *berit* (most often translated as "covenant"). So when Paul says the *musterion* of the gospel has been revealed, he is using a familiar analogy to explain to Gentiles that they now have access to full covenantal relationship with God (Ephesians 3:4–6) through the sacraments of baptism and Communion.

Baptism is the wardrobe, the covenant making sacrament. When we are baptized into Christ Jesus we enter the Story at the climax of history, not just symbolically but really and truly. Without Jesus, baptism is just a bath. We must still respond to his transforming grace through faith. But whether we are baptized as believing adults or as children (1 Corinthians 10:1–4) of believing parents (as Presbyterians, like myself, believe), we are grafted into an embodied story and, therefore, entitled to the church's ordinary means of grace.[7] With water and in the name of the Trinity, all God's promises are made available to MacGuffins (Acts 2:39).

Similarly, Communion is a sacrament of covenant "*participation* in the blood . . . [and] body of Christ" (1 Corinthians 10:16–17, emphasis

---

6. "Sacrament, n. Meanings, Etymology and More," *Oxford English Dictionary*, accessed May 25, 2024, https://www.oed.com/dictionary/sacrament_n.

7. See Romans 11:17–24 and 1 Corinthians 12:12–13.

added). Without Jesus, the Lord's Supper is just a snack. While not literally Christ's body and blood, Jesus is still mysteriously and especially present when we receive ordinary bread and wine as a congregation. Through this tangible and tasty mode of multisensory storytelling, we are really and truly caught up in the redemptive drama. The body of Christ is spiritually nourished just as bread and wine nourishes our physical bodies. We don't just remember and proclaim that the Lord is good, we also taste and see that he is.

The sacraments aren't magic. They don't guarantee perfect clarity or make us immune to light pollution. However, trying to navigate a deeply confused and confusing world without them is to go without important sense-making fuel and nourishment. They are existential anchors to an embodied narrative and bulwark for resisting lesser imitations. But even if we don't fully appreciate the sacraments or see the spiritual power in them as I've described, they are no less nourishing. That's the difference between magic and mystery. Magic depends on us. The mystery for which the sacraments are a sign and seal is that Jesus finished what we could never achieve. Their nourishment depends on Christ's faithfulness to us, not ours to him. By his amazing grace and through our participation therein (however weak and flagging), we will find over time that we don't need to squint against the glare quite so much. In Christ, we see everything more clearly.

Seeing Church in a New Light

On the one hand, ninety minutes of inhabiting and participating in the Story is a drop in the bucket compared to the hours and hours of light pollution we are bombarded with every week. On the other, false fluorescence can't compete with the Light of Heaven, nor flashlights with the risen Son. For anyone wondering if they matter but burning out under the pressure of self-narration, we have a "city set on a hill [that] cannot be hidden," where, in Christ, we might be "the light of the world" (Matthew 5:14).

If culture is "what we make of the world,"[8] and institutions are what we make of each other, then the worshiping church is who Christ uses to make us more like himself. Paul even uses narrative language when he describes that sanctification: "For we are God's *handiwork* (*poema*), created in Christ Jesus to do good works, which God prepared in advance for us to do" (Ephesians 2:10 NIV, emphasis added). Nothing less could be true if Jesus is "the founder (*arxegos,* also "author") and perfecter of our faith" (Hebrews 12:2). In his light, the church is not merely the sum of individuals who believe the same thing and live in the same geographic area. Every church is a living, breathing embodiment of the gospel story.

Our church uses a blessing from the French Reformed tradition in our infant baptism liturgy. Yet whether you practice infant baptism, baby dedication, or neither, it's true for MacGuffins of all ages:

> Blessed Child of the Covenant,
>> For you God made the world.
>> For you the prophets & patriarchs were sent.
>> For you the covenants & promises were given.
>> For you He came into the world as a baby like yourself.
>> For you He lived, died and rose again.
>> This Gospel is your Story, and we your church promise to
>>> tell you this Story until and beyond the time you've
>>> made it your own.[9]

Reflection Questions

1. Stories have the power to shape our moral imagination. Reflect on the dangers of light pollution created by so many false narratives. What are some of the lesser stories you live in light of (knowingly

---

8. Ken Myers, as quoted by Andy Crouch, *Culture Making: Recovering Our Creative Calling,* expanded ed. (IVP Books, 2023).

9. Adapted from Carrie Steenwyk, John D. Witvliet, and Linda Saport, *At Your Baptism,* 1st ed. (Grand Rapids: Eerdmans Books for Young Readers, 2011).

or unknowingly)? How have they been unreliable narrators for what is true, good, and beautiful?

2. Where do you see yourself through the individualistic lens of Main Character Syndrome rather than as a redeemed MacGuffin? Where do you need the drama of redemption to redefine success, identity, and purpose?

3. How might more regularly rehearsing the gospel shape you as the story of jazz shaped Herbie Hancock and Wayne Shorter? What are a few first steps you can take to more fully immerse yourself in the gospel story through your local church?

9

A Table for Belonging

*How Hospitality Redeems Obligation
and Sacrifice in the Church*

Someone once told me . . . *community* is "where people keep showing
up." Well, where is that now, exactly? Certainly not church; each
successive generation is attending less than their parents' . . . America
is suffering a kind of ritual recession, with fewer community-based
routines and more entertainment for, and empowerment of, individuals and the aloneness that they choose.

—Derek Thompson

You are no longer strangers and aliens, but you are fellow citizens with
the saints and members of the household of God . . .

—Ephesians 2:19

Outside of work, school, or church, when was the last time you made
a new friend? I don't mean merely meeting someone or learning
someone's name. Rekindling a friendship with someone you used to
know doesn't count either. They don't have to be your ride-or-die, but
they should at least get a Christmas card.

Making new friends is generally more difficult and less natural the older we get, but that challenge is now happening decades earlier than any previous generation. Countless studies and news articles proclaim that we are in the midst of a loneliness epidemic, but crises only risk becoming clichés when they grow without abatement. In 2023 the United States surgeon general, Dr. Vivek Murthy, issued an advisory "calling attention to the public health crisis of loneliness, isolation, and lack of connection in our country."[1] It was the first of its kind in the United States, but similar government-led initiatives have already been underway in Europe for several years. And for good reason. The physical health impact of insufficient connection is associated with "a 29% increased risk of heart disease, a 32% increased risk of stroke, and a 50% increased risk of developing dementia for older adults."[2]

Far more is at stake than individual medical consequences. We bear the image of a trinitarian God. Man is made for community as birds are made for the sky, trees are made for the earth, and fish are made for the sea. Even if we survive an increase in "risk of premature death by more than 60%,"[3] we certainly won't thrive. Like Bilbo in J. R. R. Tolkien's *The Fellowship of the Ring*, we will "feel thin, sort of stretched, like butter scraped over too much bread."[4] A deficit of belonging makes us less of what it means to be human.

Then why are we lonelier than ever?

Due to everything we've discussed so far, modernity is uniquely unsuitable and inhospitable to starting and strengthening the bonds of friendship. We're living through a "liminal" age—a transitional phase where established social norms and expectations are unraveling at the seams, yet what's replacing them is still TBD. We're in the sociocultural equivalent of a hallway or foyer, neither of which are designed

---

1. Office of the Assistant Secretary for Health (OASH), "New Surgeon General Advisory Raises Alarm About the Devastating Impact of the Epidemic of Loneliness and Isolation in the United States," U.S. Department of Health and Human Services, May 3, 2023, https://www.hhs.gov/about/news/2023/05/03/new-surgeon-general-advisory-raises-alarm-about-devastating-impact-epidemic-loneliness-isolation-united-states.html.

2. OASH, "New Surgeon General Advisory."

3. OASH, "New Surgeon General Advisory."

4. J. R. R. Tolkien, *The Fellowship of the Ring* (London: George Allen & Unwin, 1954), 86.

for lingering or socializing, only traveling through. They're no place to make friends.

Airports are the quintessential liminal space. Everything about an airport is meant to reduce friction and speed you along your way. Have you ever tried striking up a get-to-know-you conversation while waiting to go through security? Of course not. It's weird. Don't do that. Asking about someone's family is barely still acceptable if you're sitting next to them while trapped in the confines of a plane cabin. And then, only if they're not wearing headphones. When you're perpetually on your way to somewhere else, relational attachments are like the hair product the TSA agent discovered while searching your bag—disposable and not worth slowing down for.

Liminality is getting married, starting a family, and building a career all on one of those moving walkways at an airport. Belonging is the opposite: an anchored yet flexible state of connectedness. You're not so mobile you can't stop and smell the roses, but you're not too tied down to take a few meaningful risks. Belonging is sitting around a table with friends and losing track of time because you don't have anywhere else to be. Or because your phone died. Belonging is unbothered either way.

Right now we're stuck in a layover from hell. We need God to set a table in the midst of our liminality as much as David needed one in the midst of his enemies. But that's a lot easier said than done. We're so conditioned to a liminal existence that, now it's hard to sit still anywhere, never mind with strangers around a table. We've subsisted on individualism's crappy food court for so long that we've long lost our appetite for two essential ingredients of healthy belonging: obligation and sacrifice.

Redeeming Obligation

For most of us, obligation is a dirty word. Expressive individualism sees any social duty or pressure as mildly coercive. Obligation that requires us to sacrifice something we want is even worse. It's a threat to our individuality and fundamentally dehumanizing. That said, we don't mind being obligated if we *want* to be. That doesn't *feel* like obligation. It's also why we go through extreme measures to make sure no one does anything for us that they don't want to do.

Think about the last time someone gave you a gift. Besides "thank you," what did you say in response? It was probably something like, "Oh, you didn't *have* to do that!" When receiving a gift, we do a whole song and dance to extract assurance (e.g., "Of course not, I *wanted* to!") that the gift giver isn't being generous out of some old-fashioned sense of duty.

And our allergy to obligation goes both ways.

Now imagine that you're the gift giver. After they thank you, would you reply, "Oh, but I was *obligated* to"? Of course not! You wouldn't because gifts should never, *ever* be given with strings attached. After all, grace is unconditional. If a gift incurs reciprocity or a change in relationship, is it even still a gift? To modern Westerners, transaction is incompatible with benevolence or charity. In situations involving a power differential, it might even be corruption.

So next time you're invited to a birthday party . . .

When not fueled by genuine grace, obligation can certainly be wielded as dehumanizing social pressure. One friend of mine experienced just such a strings-attached gift in his first pastoral position. "During the interview process," he recounted, "the senior pastor told me that one of the real gifts of pastoring his church was that the congregation really honored and celebrated their pastors." He wasn't lied to, not exactly. But less than a year after taking the job, he realized that for many parishioners, "the honoring isn't just gratitude, sometimes it's also a down-payment entitling them to ministry being done how and when they want it." And when their pastors don't fulfill that obligation, it's often those who "have been most appreciative who become the most verbally abusive."

"If you scratch my back, I'll scratch yours" reciprocity can get icky at times. Not all obligation is a threat to our individuality, and without it, disposable attachments are the most we can hope for. We take for granted many positive instances of obligation (e.g. that wedding guests bring a gift) *because* we remember them positively—we *wanted* to be obligated. So to better understand how obligation is essential to belonging, we need to explore how bidirectional obligation (reciprocity) was the social cement that built the Roman Empire.

Patronage and the Gift of Reciprocity

Few books illustrate the social good of obligation as clearly as *Misreading Scripture with Individualist Eyes* by E. Randolph Richards and "Richard James" (a pseudonym to protect his identity as a cross-cultural trainer in the Middle East). The authors explain that "patronage," a social structure based on reciprocity and gifts with strings attached, was the defining social structure of the Roman Empire when the New Testament was written. Phoebe (Romans 16:1–2) is a prime example of where patronage is explicitly mentioned in Scripture: "Paul calls her a *prostatis* (benefactor), a cognate of the term *prostasian* (patronage) . . . Phoebe was an important patroness in the early church in Corinth. She opened her home to host gatherings of believers in the port of Cenchreae . . . and helped take care of the needs of traveling Christians."[5]

To explain how patronage worked, the authors tell the hypothetical story of a wealthy patron, "Diocles," who graciously chose to help out a baker, "Belen," who couldn't afford to rebuild his bakery after it tragically burned down.

> That morning, as every morning, Diocles's "friends" line up at their patron's door. Each meets to see whether Diocles needs anything done that day, to make any requests for help, and to receive any benefits he wishes to give. These "friends" all have an established relationship with Diocles as their patron. Belen joins the end of the line.[6] He explains his problem and asks for help rebuilding his bakery. Diocles is not required, either socially or morally, to help Belen. But he is able and decides to help. Patronage (benefaction) is a virtue stressed for the

---

5. E. Randolph Richards and Richard James, *Misreading Scripture with Individualist Eyes: Patronage, Honor, and Shame in the Biblical World* (IVP Academic, 2020), 92.

6. "And everyone who has left houses or brothers or sisters or father or mother or children or lands, for my name's sake, will receive a hundredfold and will inherit eternal life. But many who are first will be last, and the last first" (Matthew 19:29–30).

wealthy. So Diocles gives the baker the resources to rebuild the bakery. He might provide funds. He might ask another of his "friends" who is a builder to assist Belen, and another "friend" to provide new wood and thatch. Likely, Diocles will offer a mix of help drawn from his social network.[7]

Belen obviously did not earn this gift and will not be able to pay it back. But he will be expected to reciprocate. Diocles has invested in Belen's life, and so Belen will want to invest in Diocles's life. He will do this by showing gratitude to Diocles. Belen's gratitude is more than words. Belen will be loyal to Diocles. From now on, he bakes bread for Diocles's family and all the people who work in Diocles's extended circle. He does it because he wants to participate in Diocles's life. He is grateful. Likewise, Diocles will ensure that Belen receives a fair price for his bread and all the customers Belen can handle. From now on Belen will show up every morning at Diocles's house with all Diocles's other "friends" to ask whether Diocles needs anything and to ask for help.

By generously stewarding his resources, Diocles sparked an ongoing, reciprocal relationship that didn't just benefit Belen or himself but also his entire household—the interconnected network of people and relationships bound together by his patronage.

"It's not what you know, it's who you know" sounds very unfair to our merit-based culture, where competency is the great equalizer and, hypothetically, anyone can climb the social ladder if they work hard enough. No system is perfect. Like merit, patronage can be taken to unhealthy and dehumanizing ends. In Francis Ford Coppola's classic film, *The Godfather*, gift-giving is primarily a means of "loading someone down with beauty" to control them "by placing them into the debt of

---

7. "For by the grace given to me I say to everyone among you not to think of himself more highly than he ought to think, but to think with sober judgment, each according to the measure of *faith* that God has assigned. For as in one body we have many members, and the members do not all have the same function, so we, though many, are one body in Christ, and individually members one of another. Having *gifts* that differ according to the *grace* given to us, let us use them" (Romans 12:3–6, emphasis added).

the giver" rather than to invite them into a relationship of reciprocal blessing.[8] But we can't let misuse preclude any use at all. Water has the power to drown, but it also quenches thirst. We likewise can't quench our loneliness without obligation.

While we don't get to choose which social structure we live in, we do have the choice to live counterculturally. Paul is co-opting and re-purposing Roman patronage when he wrote, "For it is by *grace* you have been saved, through *faith*—and this is not from yourselves, it is the gift of God" (Ephesians 2:8 NIV, emphasis added). The Greek root word for "grace" (*charis*) is the same one used in antiquity to describe multiple facets of patronage: a patron's gift or "benefit" (*charis*) to their clients, the benefits themselves, and the client's responsibility to reciprocate with personal gratitude and publicly honoring their patron. "When an ancient Greek person heard the word *charis*, they would naturally think of the flow of patronage all around them" (emphasis added).[9] *Charis* held cities and societies together.

We can't save ourselves any more than Belen could rebuild his bak-ery. So when Paul says that we've been saved by *grace* and then emphasizes that this salvation is the gift of God, he's saying, "Make no mistake, you are not the patron in this relationship, you're the helpless client in need." We need a true and better Diocles to pay our debts and bring us into his kingdom. We need the only patron whose *charis* can raise the dead to new life in him—Jesus. By *charis*, we belong *in* Christ and his body.

But wait, there's more. The word we translate as "faith" (*pistis*) and its synonyms, "trust" and "loyalty," are also used to describe three more vital facets of patronage: a patron's faithful provision for their clients, their client's trust in their patron to do so, and the client's loyalty to them above any other patron. Without reciprocation, "faith" is reduced to mere belief in the gospel (i.e., cognitive assent to a statement of faith) and/or the *charis* we give back to God as praise and worship. Faith is certainly not less than that, but "grace and faith are not about me having

---

8. Richards and James, *Misreading Scripture,* 95.

9. Richards and James, *Misreading Scripture,* 104.

an individual, isolated relationship with God. Faith means swearing allegiance to Jesus *and his household* . . . I don't invite Jesus into my heart. I join his flock. I become part of his we."[10] Through *pistis*, we belong *to* Christ and his bride.

Salvation isn't conditional, but it does have strings attached. Nothing in Scripture presumes that it is even possible to separate allegiance to Jesus and loyalty to his church. He is our head (patron) and we are his body (clients). However, and I can't state this strongly enough: This reciprocal relationship is *for our good*. We're made for it. In Christ, obligation's yoke is easy and its burden is light. We don't just belong to God *as* one of his people, we also belong to God's people because that's where God has obligated himself to be.

Charis that does not meaningfully bind us all together in the household of God isn't much of a gift. Community without healthy obligation is fundamentally unable "to weave between its adherents a web of ethical responsibilities, and so of long-term commitments."[11] Diocles's generosity demonstrates the power of patronage to cultivate private and public gratitude:

> The community would have seen the fire and known Belen's plight. They all know Diocles helped the baker, and many will give Diocles honor for it.[12] Belen in particular will boast of Diocles's goodness to all who will listen. Likely his customers will hear all about how grateful he is to Diocles. This is not just transactional. They are in relationship.[13]

We are given a gift of surpassing worth in Christ, one we are obligated to reciprocate in grateful love (*charis*) for God, loyalty (*pistis*) to his household, and boasting of our patron's provision to all who will listen.

---

10. Richards and James, *Misreading Scripture,* 109, emphasis added.

11. Zygmunt Bauman, *Community: Seeking Safety in an Insecure World*, Themes for the 21st Century (Polity Press, 2011), 71.

12. "In the same way, let your light shine before others, so that they may see your good works and give glory to your Father who is in heaven" (Matthew 5:16).

13. Richards and James, *Misreading Scripture*, 71.

Christ's *charis* has *pistis* attached, and *pistis* to Christ and his household invites others into his *charis*. Take out any one ingredient and belonging will be half-baked at best. It is individualism, not Scripture, that says we can belong to God without being obligated as "members of his household" (Ephesians 2:19).

Choosing Obligation for Good

When I was still a seminary student, my wife and I had the opportunity to be part of a launch team for a church plant in the city of St. Louis. I'll never forget one meeting, when one of the co-pastors tearfully repented to all twenty of us in that group. A few months prior, he had passionately expounded on the vision for biblical community in Acts 2, and how devoting ourselves to "the fellowship" meant obligating ourselves to one another and inviting each other to speak wisdom into major life decisions that we, as twenty-first-century Americans, dogmatically treat as private.

> Should I take this new job to give our family more financial margin, or will the additional responsibilities take up bandwidth needed for loving our neighbors?
>
> Should I pop the question or am I too blinded by fear of being alone to see serious problems in our relationship?
>
> Should we send our kids to the subpar public school so our family can invest in teachers and support struggling students, or send them to private school to prioritize their long-term contribution to the common good?

That night, our pastor repented because he realized that he and his family had just gone through the lengthy process of buying a house without once practicing what he'd preached. To his credit, he invited everyone in the room to offer perspective and feedback anyway.

To be clear, I'm not arguing for Christian socialism or communism. Belen wasn't primarily grateful for his bakery being rebuilt but for the *freely chosen* generosity Diocles lavished on him. So even though I think it'd be a genuinely beautiful, countercultural embodiment of God's kingdom, I'm not saying Christians need to run every four-figure purchase by their small group. Unless, of course, you choose to. Obligation to a patron's household was freely chosen because belonging to one and participating in the free-flowing exchange of resources benefited everyone involved.

If we're skeptical, it's likely because our obsessive pursuit of ever-greater freedom has been far more successful than we realize. Behind our loneliness crisis is a kind of cultural amnesia. We've achieved enough autonomy in life that we've forgotten that all friendships need healthy, reciprocal obligation potent enough to occasionally supersede individual desires. Otherwise, community will "tend to evaporate at the moment when human bonds truly matter."[14] That's why belonging also requires a degree of sacrifice.

Redeeming Sacrifice

On December 30, 2021, unusually high winds turned a small grass fire into a countywide conflagration that burned through 1,600 acres, destroyed almost 1,100 homes, and caused more than half a billion dollars in damage in under six hours. The Marshall Fire was the most destructive fire in Colorado history (and that's saying something). Miraculously, no one in our church was injured or lost their home, though two of our families had to move out for several months to make repairs due to smoke and ash damage. With very little prompt, our congregation mobilized, collecting clothing, kitchen supplies, blankets, and everything else our neighbors might need. It was amazing.

GoFundMe and Kickstarter are so wildly successful partly because it feels good to be generous when someone is in need. The Marshall Fire was no exception. People gave millions of dollars to victims through online platforms. So much, in fact, that we struggled to find opportunities for

---

14. Bauman, *Community,* 71.

our church to offer tangible or financial support. The combination of insurance, the Federal Emergency Management Agency (FEMA), and the normalization of online charity addressed the most obvious needs, so we started working through members of our congregation (household) and encouraged them to reach out to neighbors and coworkers (Belens). We found more than a few who'd fallen through the cracks because they weren't digitally savvy enough to leverage online platforms.

Jesus taught his disciples, "And if you lend to those from whom you expect repayment, what credit is that to you? Even sinners lend to sinners, expecting to be repaid in full" (Luke 6:34 NIV). We feel good being generous toward those who can't give back because we live in a culture downstream of a New Testament ethic that subverted and exploded social obligation to include outsiders. But it wasn't always that way. Jesus's Sermon on the Mount also confronted the established norm of self-serving reciprocity—generosity based exclusively on the needs of those who already belong to their family, tribe, or community. When there aren't many resources to go around, survival depends on prioritizing generosity toward those who would be honor-bound to return the favor in *their* time of need. Reciprocal dependency was the norm in Israel, and the default assumption of all collectivist cultures. With surgical precision, Jesus affirmed that cultural norm while using it to expose a disposition of the heart that depends more on reciprocal dependency than God for provision.

We've swung the pendulum in the opposite direction, and we've swung it *hard*. Where ancient collectivist cultures couldn't fathom considering anyone a friend if you *couldn't* rely on them for financial support—and they, you—we avoid asking friends for financial help because we value the relationship too much. This sentiment wouldn't make a lick of sense to Jesus's disciples.

If Jesus preached the Sermon on the Mount today, it is very likely he would address a disposition of our hearts that uses charitable giving to avoid sacrificial generosity. You see, we also love GoFundMe and Kickstarter for selfish reasons. With the click of a button, we can play the patron without incurring any ongoing obligation. Relationship is neither included nor necessary. That social distance makes sacrifice easier to avoid, but it also reinforces the cultural firewall between social and economic relationships.

That's why it *doesn't* feel good to give or tithe to a church.

For example, any pastor will tell you it is *significantly* easier to rally a congregation for an emergency or mercy need than to cultivate regular, sacrificial generosity to their church. Why? Because most of us approach charitable giving like managing a stock portfolio—allocating funds based on a projected return on investment (ROI). That return need not be financial. It can be existentially motivated too (e.g., giving to people, organizations, or causes we have a personal passion for). While an ROI approach to giving is still charitable and contributes to the common good, it doesn't necessarily require sacrifice because it doesn't require relationship. More often than not, charitable giving is far more sacramental than sacrificial—we build a diversified giving portfolio with passion projects and causes that reflect our idealized self. It never occurs to us that we might be using the needs of others to achieve our dignity, value, and worth.

At this point (if not much earlier), the biblically astute will cite 2 Corinthians 9:7, where Paul says, "Each of you should give what you have decided in your heart to give, not reluctantly or under compulsion, for God loves a cheerful giver" (NIV). To which I say, "Yes!" and "Amen!" *Also*, note what Paul says should be the underlying motivation and context for that cheerful giving just a few verses later:

> This service that you perform is not only supplying the needs of *the Lord's people* but is also overflowing in many *expressions of thanks* to God. Because of the service by which you have proved yourselves, others will praise God for the obedience that accompanies your confession of the gospel of Christ, and for your generosity in sharing with them and with everyone else. And in their prayers for you their hearts will go out to you, because of the surpassing grace God has given you. Thanks be to God for *his indescribable gift!* (2 Corinthians 9:12–15 NIV, emphasis added)

To give cheerfully is indeed incompatible with reluctance and compulsion. That's what makes Paul's exhortation truly remarkable. Despite their many dysfunctions, the Corinthian church viewed it as an honor and privilege to sacrifice for the household Christ died to save. What could honor God more than to emulate him in such a comparatively small way? Paul isn't saying, "don't feel obligated to give if you don't want to," but that if we don't feel *pistis* to give cheerfully, we don't fully apprehend the "indescribable *charis*" we've been given. Then, we need to taste and see anew the even greater hospitality of our divine patron and host.

"Expressions of thanks" in 2 Corinthians 9:12 is the Greek word *eucharistia*, and "sharing with" in verse 13 is *koinonia*—both are key words and names used for the sacrament of Communion. "Thanksgiving is a central Christian virtue, intended to replace despair, anxiety, and worldly ways."[15] We participate (*koinōnia*) in Christ's self-sacrificial love (*charis*) by giving thanks (*eucharistia*) in fellowship (*koinōnia*) around the Lord's Table:

> The cup of blessing that we bless, is it not a participation [*koinōnia*] in the blood of Christ? The bread that we break, is it not a participation [*koinōnia*] in the body of Christ? Because there is one bread, *we who are many are one body*, for we all partake of the one bread. (1 Corinthians 10:16–17, emphasis and parentheticals added)

It is not a coincidence that Paul uses *koinonia* to describe Communion in his first letter to the church in Corinth, and then again to describe generosity in his second. Both are expressions of thanksgiving (*eucharistia*) for God's patronage (*charis*), and both are expressions of obedience (*pistis*) that strengthen belonging (*koinonia*) among members of God's household. Christ's hospitality is the fuel and engine for the church's hospitality.

We pastors are understandably reticent to know how much people in our congregations give to the church. There's wisdom in cutting off any

---

15. John Frederick, "Praise and Thanksgiving," ed. Douglas Mangum et al., *Lexham Theological Wordbook*, Lexham Bible Reference Series (Lexham Press, 2014).

temptation of partiality or prioritizing pastoral care for more generous sheep. However, there is a remarkably strong and consistent correlation between giving and belonging. It is a bit of a chicken-and-egg situation: you sacrifice for what you love, and you love what you (cheerfully!) sacrifice for. We should never coerce, but we should lovingly challenge members to give until it starts to hurt a little (i.e., sacrificially, and specific to individual circumstances). For the same reason, The Table requires members to be *willing* to serve in our children's ministry—in Christ, neither obligation nor sacrifice are transactional, but relational. Both are loving (if costly) invitations to experience more gratitude for Jesus and belonging within his body.

The Radical Hospitality of Jesus

Admittedly, while all the above is God's design and intention for hospitality, the church's hospitality often leaves much to be desired. Sometimes that gap is a sign of unhealth. But more often, it's a symptom of inexperience. We have too little practice anymore. The world's narratives of efficiency and optimization makes sacrifice and obligation even more counterintuitive than it is already. But it also fools us into thinking that hospitality is a function of belonging rather than a means thereof. So we wait for someone else to go first. That worked when most of us experienced some modicum of belonging, but we'll be waiting a long time if we're all suffering through the same loneliness crisis. And we've already waited too long as it is.

The only way to pull out of that is for all of us to more fully appreciate that Jesus already went first and continues to do so. Hospitality practiced as an outflow of gratitude for our deeper belonging to Christ will start to cultivate a sense of belonging in his church before we fully experience it. He will be steadfast and faithful to work through our incomplete and imperfect trying, and try we must.

I know that sounds like a scary leap of faith. It is. But if Jesus is our divine patron and host who has promised to generously provide all we need, our trust is well-placed. It is through that distinctly Christian *pistis* that we start to see just how radically hospitable Jesus has been toward us. It is a sacrifice for sure, but where it is cheerfully and gratefully obligated, Jesus promises resurrection on the other side.

In the summer of 2021, Mike and Tiffany, along with their two little girls, moved in with Tiffany's parents. Her mom had been battling Parkinson's disease for over a decade, but her symptoms grew increasingly severe, and she was beginning to also show signs of dementia. Her dad insisted he could care for her on his own—and he technically could—but Mike and Tiffany didn't think he should have to. Even though they lived only seven minutes apart, they felt responsible for more than coming over for dinner and helping out a few nights per week. Joining households made some financial sense and gave their girls many more tender memories with their grandparents, but they still "closed the back door" and intentionally made it harder to extract themselves because joining two households is a lot like marriage: "If divorce is an option on the table, marriage looks very different." They knew it would be painful to care for a parent deteriorating before their eyes and explain it all to their children in real time. But it was even more difficult than Tiffany expected:

> The first year or so of living with them, I had difficulty looking at my mom, much less seeing the image of God in her. The mom I remembered and the grandma I hoped she would be was gone, replaced by someone helpless. She couldn't hold my babies. She couldn't watch my kids for an hour while I ran an errand. We couldn't commiserate over the trials of parenting. She felt like a stranger. I have had so much grief and anger about what I had lost when this disease took over.

Both personally and practically, Tiffany's mom couldn't reciprocate her hospitality. But it went even deeper than that. The combination of self-giving sacrifice and inescapable obligation also forced Tiffany to recognize that she had been treating herself like she treats her cell phone and computer with too many open browser tabs. Trying to operate with superhuman capacity was taking a toll even before joining households.

Sustaining such significant hospitality meant having to kill many disintegrated wants, expectations, and ambitions that long kept her from feeling fully human anyway. She had to accept her finitude and start resting in Christ. Over time, those changes bore remarkable fruit:

> Jesus has transformed my perspective by showing me his love for her and empowering mine along the way. I've begun to see my mom again, but *in* and *through* her need rather than despite it. . . . I no longer care for her because I have to; I care for her because she's in need of care, Jesus cares for her, and so she deserves my love and care for her regardless of how she behaves or responds.

I am not exaggerating when I say that this family is, second only to Jesus, the heart and soul of hospitality at The Table. No one has so consistently or sacrificially practiced relational and creational generosity since our church launched in 2016, and long before Tiffany's mom started having health problems. When Gordy's daughter and son-in-law needed food for the reception following her dad's memorial service, Mike coordinated food from our church family, smoked eight pork shoulders, and functionally catered a meal for more than a hundred people on just a few days' notice. When I first meet a guest on Sunday morning, it is greater than 50/50 odds that they've already met Mike, Tiffany, or both of them. We had to stop sending people to their community group because so many of their non-Christian neighbors had joined. And those are just a few of the examples I am personally aware of. They don't draw attention to themselves and most of what they do likely goes entirely unnoticed. They just show up, time and time again.

It was many years of practicing such hospitality as members of God's household that prepared them for the all-in obligation and sacrifice of joining households. Likewise, they aren't the most hospitable family in our church *despite* having to care for an ailing parent, but *because* they did. Through it all, hospitality became a habit, then a posture, and finally a lifestyle freed to assume obligation and sacrifice when encountering a need. For Mike and Tiffany, that just doesn't feel all that sacrificial anymore.

Unsurprisingly, Tiffany was more than a little skeptical when I told her that their leap of faith made them more hospitable. The day-to-day logistics of their living arrangements are even more limiting than they expected. They rarely get evenings out of the house and overnight trips are a thing of the past. They don't host as much as they used to but, I assured her, frequency isn't what makes hospitality a catalyst for belonging. Frequency is the hallmark of hospitality's counterfeit: entertainment.

Like mere charitable giving, entertainment requires very little relational obligation or sacrifice. We prefer entertainment because it's easier (no ongoing commitment to others) and safer (we can appear generous without self-giving). But it can't offer more than a skin-deep and self-centered sense of belonging. As guests who already belong in Christ, we have tasted and seen divine hospitality. Because we belong to Christ and not to ourselves, we are called to reciprocate his self-giving hospitality by extending his welcome through his body. True hospitality both reinforces our belonging and relies on the nourishment Jesus provides through his people. So while Mike and Tiffany still face as many of life's challenges as anyone, a lack of belonging isn't one of them.

Every time we read Scripture and come across familial language—or words like covenant, household, etc.—it isn't saying that church is *like* a family or household, but that we *are* one. In Christ, we don't just belong *with* all Christians spiritually, we also belong *to* the body of Christians with whom we live day in and day out. Neither belonging is possible apart from the grace of Jesus, but both require a mutual reciprocation of obligation and sacrifice to experience belonging in Christ as more than disposable.[16]

If you've ever felt like you're closest to God when the proverbial fecal material hits the overhead oscillating unit, that's because self-belonging is impossible once we've come to the end of ourselves and more is still required. By our boss. By our spouse. By our parents or kids or, yes, even our church family. Nobody sleeps well in an airport for the same reason

---

16. This does not mean that we don't "belong in" Jesus unless we "belong to" a church, but that if we belong in Jesus (by grace) we *do* belong to a church (through faith) even if we insist otherwise or wait until that feels true before we start living it out.

self-belonging isn't sustainable—you can't close your eyes, you can't even blink if it all depends on you to be your own host or patron. We have to belong somewhere, *to* someone. Spiritually and manifestly. Practicing hospitality revealed new frontiers in Tiffany's life and heart where self-belonging still reigned. It was only her belonging in Christ, to both Jesus and his people, that gave her the power to colonize those frontiers with fresh hospitality.

We absolutely lack opportunities for belonging, and more than ever before. But our loneliness epidemic is significantly worsened if we never fully commit to any community for fear of not belonging as easily or deeply as we might somewhere else. Trying to be everywhere and never going anywhere only delivers us more deeply into our liminal fugue state, making us more allergic to the ordinary and healthy friction of community.

But the time and effort that it requires is worthwhile. Mike and Tiffany know from experience that embracing *pistis* to God's household on the basis of his *charis* is a powerful upstream catalyst for a life teeming with hospitality. It is better to give than to receive, not because we are especially generous, but because our divine host is. And gratuitously so.

"Feed My Sheep"

Every Sunday when we introduce Communion at The Table, we say, "On the night that he was betrayed, Jesus was with his disciples . . ." It can be easy to forget that those two clauses are inseparably linked by a table. Understandably, the disciples struggled to get over their shock when Jesus straight-up announced that one of them—one of his twelve closest followers sitting in the room that very moment—would betray him. They had sacrificed so much. They'd given their lives to this Messiah . . . how could any of them do something so evil?

But when David wrote in Psalm 23:5 that the Lord "prepare[s] a table before me in the presence of my enemies," he likely meant that God would keep him safe enough that he could let his guard down. But in

Christ, God's provision and protection is such that we can dine *with* our enemies. Jesus knew Judas would give him over to death by crucifixion. Grace gave him a seat at the table anyway.

Yet we hesitate to invite "difficult" people over for dinner.

Unless one draws a hard line between active betrayal and passive abandonment, Judas wasn't the only enemy Jesus shared a meal with. No sooner had Jesus made his announcement than Peter, never one to miss an opportunity for virtue signaling, proclaimed that he would follow Jesus even to death, if necessary (Luke 22:33). Jesus knew Peter was full of himself so he held up a mirror. He told Peter that he would publicly deny even knowing his beloved Rabbi three times before the rooster crowed. Peter was aghast in the moment. But when it unfolded exactly as Jesus foretold, Peter fled in shame.

That both episodes began around a table—around *the Lord's* table— isn't an accident. Christ's hospitality is as challenging as it is inviting; grace exposes and comforts. The difference between Judas and Peter was not how strongly they believed in Jesus or his teachings, but their answer to the question, "to whom shall we go?" (John 6:68). Judas answered by leaving the Last Supper, forsaking his patron's hospitality, and selling his soul in the clearance aisle. Crushed by the weight of his guilt, Judas hung himself from a tree, cursed and alone. He came to the end of himself but self-belonging kept him from seeing an offer worth much, much more than thirty pieces of silver—the Host's priceless gift of himself. Peter never left the Last Supper. He belonged there. And although he denied his patron in a moment (or three) of reflexive self-preservation, he repented and returned to whom he belonged just as reflexively.

One evening after Jesus's resurrection, Peter and several of the disciples decided to go fishing.[17] After they had labored all night with nothing to show for it, a man appeared on the shore and shouted that they should cast their nets on the other side of the boat. It wasn't until their net filled with more fish than they could haul in that they connected the dots. As soon as they realized it was Jesus, the text says Peter *threw*

---

17. See John 21:1–19.

himself into the sea. Not "jumped" into the sea. "Threw himself." Like Judas, Peter tried belonging to himself and relying on his own strength, and like Judas, he failed. But unlike Judas, Peter threw himself into the sea and at the mercy of his patron.

One day I'd love to ask Peter if he expected to supernaturally walk on water again, or if the thought even crossed his mind before plunging beneath the waves. Either way, Peter didn't just belong *with* Jesus, he belonged *to* him. And nothing, not even the shame of abandoning his beloved rabbi, could keep him from Jesus a moment longer.

When he reached the shore, Jesus, ever the gracious host, offered the disciples creational and relational generosity in the form of a breakfast of fish and an assurance of *charis*. For each of the three times Peter denied knowing him, Jesus asked, "Do you love me?" With the aroma of fire-roasted fish and confusion hanging thick in the air, Peter replied all three times, "Yes, of course!" If we were in Jesus's sandals, we'd probably comfort Peter and tell him "It's okay" or "I forgive you." But Jesus doesn't offer so much as a "stop beating yourself up!" Instead, he very counter-intuitively invites Peter (three times) into deeper belonging . . . through even greater obligation and sacrifice.

"Feed my sheep."

At the Last Supper, Peter insisted that he was a worthy disciple more loyal and loving than the rest, and that he would faithfully follow Jesus even if it cost his life. And so, over breakfast, Jesus reminded his weary disciple that he was a more loyal and loving patron than any other, and that he gave himself to us at infinite cost to himself. In one fell swoop, Jesus reminds Peter that his yoke is easy, his burden is light (Matthew 11:30), and his gift has strings attached: to love our Lord by serving his household.

No hospitality given or received will be without conflict, difficulty, or friction. But not forever. Like Peter, we are not worthy disciples by virtue of our faithfulness to Jesus, but by virtue of his faithfulness to us. Communion is "God's love made tasty"[18] but it's still only an appetizer

---

18. I first heard this from my dear friend Mark Smith, who is the planting pastor for City Church in Dublin, Ireland.

for the full belonging we will experience at the wedding feast of the Lamb. If we let ourselves belong to our shepherd's admittedly flawed flock (obligation) and start reciprocating our host's hospitality through them (sacrifice), we'll never look at potlucks the same way again.

Reflection Questions

1. Where do you feel like you're trying to make yourself at home in an airport? How might belonging more deeply to a church change your experience?

2. Where have you experienced obligation in a good way? How did it contribute to a sense of belonging—for you and others? How might reframing obligation as "social cement" change your attitude toward commitments to/within a church?

3. How could gratitude for Christ's hospitality fuel sacrificial generosity toward your church (both for the good of the institution and the individuals within)? How have you seen—or could you see—giving and receiving hospitality become a feedback loop that leads to deeper belonging?

10

A City on a Hill

How the Church Stewards God's Blessing for the Life of the World

"I will bless you . . . so that you will be a blessing . . . and in you all the families of the earth shall be blessed."

—Genesis 12:2–3

It is a deliberate act that will activate God's promise of blessing for them. The nations will indeed be blessed as Abraham was, but only because they will have turned to the only source of blessing, Abraham's God, and identified themselves with the story of Abraham's people. They will know the God of Abraham.

—Christopher Wright

If individualism could be said to have a purpose, or maybe even a great commission of its own, it would almost certainly be the proverb commonly attributed to Buddhist pacifist, Mahatma Gandhi: "Be the change you want to see in the world." I've heard that aspiration espoused by pro-life Christians pursuing adoption, civically engaged neighbors inspired to "think globally and act locally," political activists of all stripes trying to inspire voters, and even a life coach advertising psychic training in clairvoyant self-healing. It's everywhere. Whether expressed as a kind of neo-pagan gospel of self-help or just a common-sense proverb about how to best contribute to the common good, it taps into deeply embedded cultural narratives about an individual's power to change ourselves and the world around us.

There's much to affirm about the phrase. For example, it recognizes that we need to change and that we *should* want to change ourselves and the world for the better. No argument there. However, at the end of the day, "be the change you want to see in the world" is neither sustainable nor healthy. It suffers from at least three major problems:

- **"Be the change . . ."** presumes that it's possible to change ourselves at a deeper level without saying anything about how. Does it come from inside of us? Do we have everything we need to affect this change? If not, where do we get it and how long should transformation take?
- **". . . [we] want to see"** assumes that what we want is good (for ourselves or others), not by any objective standard outside ourselves, but *because* we want it (see chapter 2). But what if we all want different things? Whose want wins out?
- **". . . in the world"** implies that our individual transformation is potent enough to manifest local (and maybe even global) change. In which case, why haven't we accomplished world peace, solved global poverty, or cured cancer? How do we know what we want is what the world needs?

The President of the United States or a member of his cabinet might be able to point to some instances where self-improvement resulted in real world change, but that's a far cry from qualifying as an inviolable law of nature. It also ignores what is likely many more instances where "being the change" didn't have any impact at all. For the 325 million Americans who lack access to such levers of power and influence (to say nothing of citizens in nondemocratic countries), "be the change you want to see in the world" isn't good news, but a trite denial of reality that is possible to sustain only with an extraordinary heaping of privilege.

So why do so many of us insist on living it out and evangelizing others to do the same? Because individualism provides a built-in explanation for its ineffectiveness: if the world *hasn't* changed, it is because too few of us are *being* the change. Honestly, having everyone agree with my perspective sounds pretty great. Indeed, if we see things so clearly, we probably *should* insist others conform to the change we want to see in the world. If unity isn't possible, uniformity will have to do. If everyone would want what I want, maybe we could achieve the peace and harmony we all dream about. What's everyone waiting for? Let's get with the program (as I define it, of course).

Do you see the problem yet?

It isn't that too *few* of us are trying to "be the change [we] want to see in the world." We have become so deeply divided, in part, because too *many* of us are. If, as the saying goes, the proof is in the pudding, the change we want to see is a lot more coercion and a lot less collaboration.

Individualism's not-so-great commission and it's even-worse fruit eerily resemble one of the most violent and volatile periods in Israel's history. The author of Judges summarizes that vicious cycle with the refrain, "In those days . . . Everyone did what was right in his own eyes" (17:6; 21:25). Functionally, if not consciously, we have been sipping on the same Kool-Aid for long enough that we struggle to see any difference between our wants and others' needs. That's simply narcissism by any other name.

Man-Centered Versus God-Centered

Even if we haven't adopted the phrase as a motto for life or a secular great commission, "be the change you want to see in the world" summarizes the *missio singula* (mission of the individual). To make something about us even when it so obviously isn't about us is a self-deception as old as sin and Serpent. But for Christians unaware or unequipped to tell the difference, our respective *missio singulis* can come perilously close to competing with, if not supplanting the *missio Dei* in our everyday intentions. We don't have any precedent for that in living memory, nor even in modern history, and that newness makes it an especially potent blind spot. Even pastors like me can unwittingly reinforce it in our approach to ministry.

Early on in planting The Table, I started a six-week leadership intensive that I called an Emerging Leaders Incubator (ELI). Each iteration involved taking several current and potential lay leaders through a study in Nehemiah and three especially good books on biblical and common grace leadership.[1] We discussed implications for life, vocation, and the ministry of our still wet-behind-the-ears church plant. At the end of those six weeks, I met with each participant to coach them on how to start applying everything they learned, which included crafting a personal mission statement in light of how God has gifted them. It was easily everyone's favorite part of the whole intensive, and I thoroughly enjoyed it too. Also, I'll never do it again.

I started ELI to help our people see that biblical leadership is primarily discipleship that even more proactively takes up our calling to live out God's mission—in both the church and the world. It accomplished much of that purpose, and there may be some contexts where crafting a personal mission statement could still be worthwhile. But making it the culmination of a six-week leadership intensive inadvertently enabled the very self-referential, upside-down individualism I was trying to disciple out of our church. Instead of having them answer, "what kind of mission does God have for *me*?" I should have insisted we wrestle with the question, "what kind of *we* does God want for *his* mission?"[2]

American Christianity, Christopher Wright says, "translate[s] the

---

1. Ronald Heifetz and Marty Linsky, *Leadership on the Line: Staying Alive Through the Dangers of Change* (Harvard Business Review Press, 2017); Andy Crouch, *Strong and Weak: Embracing a Life of Love, Risk, and True Flourishing* (InterVarsity Press, 2016); Patrick Lencioni, *The Five Dysfunctions of a Team: A Leadership Fable, 20th Anniversary Edition* (Jossey-Bass, 2002).

2. Christopher J. H. Wright, *The Great Story and the Great Commission: Participating in the Biblical Drama of Mission*, Acadia Studies in Bible and Theology (Baker Academic, 2023), 53.

Great Commission merely into a management project for ourselves."[3] Whether we make it about "sinners in need of salvation" or "saints in need of a purpose,"[4] it still sources the "why" of God's mission in the needs of individuals. That framing makes the Great Commission inherently something we (individuals) do that God empowers, not something God is doing in which we (churches) participate. That might sound like nit-picking, but where we source purpose makes all the difference in the world.

As badly as the world needs Christians to make a difference and share the life-transforming, world-changing power of God in the gospel, the world needs Christians to prioritize the common good within and through God's city on a hill. Without a collective purpose to anchor us (individually and institutionally), we will either turn inward and make it all about our individual callings or about whatever felt needs we see in the world. Both narrow God's mission to our very subjective perspective and set us up for the same tug-of-war as "being the change you want to see in the world." Any definition of God's mission that does not explicitly prioritize church as God's primary and essential vehicle for gospel transformation will inevitably reinforce individualism's subtle but powerful bias—even when we are consciously trying to resist it!

If you're still skeptical that it's that tempting or pervasive, just make a mental list of all the various evangelism, discipleship, and other "equipping" ministries you've participated in. If you've spent any time in the church, it may be a really long list, but here are a few to get the juices flowing: spiritual gifts inventories, gospel tracts and leaflets, personality assessments, the Billy Graham crusades and the many conference experiences that have followed in their wake, and the plethora of niche parachurch ministries that have sprung up over the last several decades.

I don't have anything against these approaches (most of them, anyway), but how many even had an *implied* ecclesiology as part of their vision? How many included building up the local church as part of (and

---

3. Wright, *Great Story*, 64.
4. Wright, *Great Story*, 64.

not just a utilitarian means for) their world-changing mission? Did any of them? Most importantly, who did they functionally treat as a city on a hill—individual disciples or the local church?

We need a far greater commission than the subjective and arbitrary *missio singula* of "be the change you want to see in the world." We need the true, good, and beautiful purpose for which we were made: the *missio Dei* as laid out in God's covenant with Abraham, "I will bless you . . . so that you will be a blessing" (Genesis 12:2). That blessing is why the church exists. A *missio singula* requires us to pursue an impossible self-transformation with everything on the line, but the *missio Dei* invites all of us into God's transformative purpose to bless the world far more abundantly than all we could ask or think. The church's purpose, then, is three dimensional.

Beauty's Temple

Imagine that you were transported to Europe in the decade leading up to the Reformation, and you walked into a local parish to attend a Catholic Mass. Several things would stand out. First, you'd probably notice that many congregants are walking around and talking quietly during the service. You might wonder why it doesn't seem to bother anyone, but then you realize it's because the priests are all speaking in Latin and no one else understands Latin any better than you do! Strangely, the priests don't seem to mind the chatter either. They're so focused on conducting Mass that they don't seem particularly aware that anyone else is even in the room. It would feel more like a performance if more people were paying attention. Eventually, you realize the priests are in the middle of the Eucharist. Or at least, you think they are because they're holding up the bread and wine. But then . . . well, you wait a few extra moments to avoid rushing to judgment . . . aaaand, you were right. They did, in fact, take communion by themselves without ever offering the bread or wine to anyone in the congregation.

Suppose you lean over to ask a random peasant for help understanding why. They'd be as confused by your question as you are by the Mass. Unclean commoners don't receive Communion. Where did you hear such blasphemy? Only priests are holy enough to partake the (literal) body and blood of Christ. But don't worry, they're taking it on behalf of the congregation. That's their job as mediators between Christ and his bride.[5]

In response to the Catholic Church's doctrine that priests are spiritual mediators between congregants and Christ, Martin Luther and other leaders of the Protestant Reformation argued for "the priesthood of all believers."[6] And they were right to do so. When Jesus died as the spotless Passover Lamb, the temple curtain was torn in two. Jesus satisfied once and for all the need God addressed with the Old Testament's sacrificial system, rendering priestly mediation redundant for all time. Now, nothing separated the holy of holies (where God's presence dwelled) and the inner court (where priests cleansed themselves and received offerings). God is with us.

That no merely human mediation is necessary is one of the most wonderous implications of the gospel. But no longer needing the sacrificial system to atone for sin doesn't mean we no longer need a temple to abide with God. We, collectively, are now the temple. One body, many parts.

Luther objected to a clerical caste operating as heaven's middle managers because it put the temple curtain back up between Christians and God. Filtered through the combined influence of expressive individualism and twentieth-century spiritual pragmatism, the priesthood of all believers has come to mean something much more radical: the *self-sufficiency* of every believer. We no longer believe we need priests to access God, but we also don't think we need the church to experience or abide in him. We can do that on our own.

---

5. There is no small irony in that the modern megachurch (and yes, seeker sensitive churches) *must* operate similarly just to execute worship services at such a large scale. Professional staff and a stage separate congregants from the Lord's Table as easily as Latin and an altar rail.

6. While the phrase "priesthood of all believers" isn't explicitly from Scripture, it's a very accurate summary and implication of New Testament passages like Hebrews 4:14 (which describes Jesus as our "great high priest") and 1 Peter 2:5–9 (which describes the church as a "royal priesthood").

Luther would have more than a few choice words for us if he knew where we've taken his reforms. Not least because that interpretation cuts us off from experiencing deeper communion with God. While he was still a Catholic priest, Luther suffered from debilitating spiritual anxiety and depression. The burden of being a capital-*M* Mediator for the bride's atonement is one only her groom can bear. Without realizing or intending to, believers carry the self-sufficiency burden of having to be lowercase-*m* mediators of Christ's presence that only his bride can bear.

What does this have to do with our purpose and the *missio Dei*? In a word, everything. If we are saved because we ask Jesus into our hearts, then he becomes part of "me" instead of our "me" joining his "we." Church, then, is little more than a spiritual refueling station for the *real* front lines of individual mission and ministry. Isn't God #blessed to have us on his kickball team?

To be clear, every individual believer has a vital and essential role to play in God's mission. However, individuals aren't the locus, starting point, or primary means of God's mission. We (collectively) are a "royal priesthood" (singular), not "a group of royal priests." And the existence of a priesthood also implies the existence of a temple where God is uniquely and especially present.

As discussed at the end of chapter 6, Jesus bookended the Great Commission with reminders of his authority—"All authority in heaven and on earth has been given to me"—and presence—"I am with you always . . ." (Matthew 28:18–20). While the command to go and make disciples is at least an individual responsibility, that responsibility flows out of *belonging* to a people named Glory. Any possibility otherwise would have been totally incomprehensible to anyone in ancient Israel, Rome, or anywhere in the world until well after the Reformation. That wasn't just assumed either. Jesus explicitly bookended the imperative (make disciples) with *collective* indicatives (authority and presence) to evoke the disciples' familiarity with the temple and its role in God's redemptive mission:

Extending the boundaries of the temple by witnessing and strengthening those receiving the witness is a priestly sacrifice and offering

to God. God's presence grows among his priestly people by their knowing his word, believing it and by obeying it, and then they spread that presence [blessing] to others by living their lives faithfully and prayerfully in the world . . . *The mark of the true church is an expanding witness to the presence of God*: first to our families, then to others in the church, then to our neighborhood, then to our city, then the country and ultimately the whole earth.[7] (emphasis added)

When God told Abraham, "In you all the families of the earth shall be blessed" (Genesis 12:3), he was both promising his faithful presence to his people forever and charging them to extend his presence through his people over the face of the earth. We typically understand that God's presence is essential to his mission yet forget that God's mission is unfinished without his spreading presence. In other words, the church isn't just the means for *how* we live out God's mission, the church is herself the *fruit* of God's missional activity in time and space. Even more than a waystation for individual mission, it *is* the earthly manifestation of our High Priest extending his presence throughout the earth and every sphere of life.

Yes, every Christian also has the spirit of Christ dwelling within each of us, but that indwelling is derivative of God's presence in our midst. In the same way, the Great Commission is individually derived from Christ's collective charge—the *missio Dei*. To be a blessing isn't only a call to individual evangelism, it is also a call to devote ourselves to "being built together into a dwelling place for God by the Spirit" (Ephesians 2:22). We shouldn't just plant churches because it's the most effective way to make disciples (though it is), we should want to plant more churches because the body of Christ *is* Jesus's earthly presence until he returns. Jesus works first and foremost through churches to bring heaven to earth and God's kingdom come. If that weren't the case, then God would not be keeping his promise to Abraham, that "*in* [*him*] all the families of earth will be blessed."

---

7. G. K. Beale, *The Temple and the Church's Mission: A Biblical Theology of the Dwelling Place of God*, New Studies in Biblical Theology, vol. 17 (InterVarsity Press, 2004).

Don't be the change or change the world. Devote yourself, *fully*, to a church. Plant more churches, more outposts of God's inbreaking presence. Invite your neighbors to "taste and see that the LORD is good" (Psalm 34:8), and trust that the spreading of his presence will change the face of the earth.

God blessed the children of Abraham so that the nations peeking over the fence from afar would see Israel flourishing and think to themselves, "there must be a God around here somewhere." God's blessing is intended to spark curiosity and provoke questions about God, but presence alone can't answer them. For that, the nations need an embassy in their midst.

Truth's Embassy

When Israel was carted off to exile in Babylon, God had Jeremiah deliver a strange kind of reassurance. He told them to stop listening to the false prophets telling them not to get too comfortable because their stay in Babylon would be short-lived. God said, rather, "settle in" because they were going to be there for a while. But more than that, God told Israel to go ahead and live in Babylon *as if* they lived in Jerusalem, to "build houses and live in them; plant gardens and eat their produce" (Jeremiah 29:5). They'd even be there long enough to have children and give them away in marriage. Just as they sought the welfare ("shalom") of Jerusalem ("city of shalom"), so too should they seek Babylon's. God's message was clear: worry not, for he would still be steadfast and faithful to his promise to Abraham—not despite Israel's exile, but through it. He was, even then, restoring Israel to their God-given purpose as his people, to be witnesses and "agents of God's promise to Abraham."[8]

When Israel first entered the promised land, they were faithful, if imperfectly, in their witness and stewardship of God's blessing. But as memory of God's deliverance faded, they began turning inward, keeping

---

8. Christopher J. H. Wright, *The Mission of God: Unlocking the Bible's Grand Narrative* (IVP, 2006), 100.

God's blessing for themselves as all the comfort, stability, and wealth that tempts us with selfishness. Temptation wasn't the problem per se. Israel's problem was falling prey to the same propaganda that fooled Adam and Eve—that perhaps God was holding back some of his blessing. As happens with any hermeneutic of suspicion, they lost the plot and missed the point. And, unfortunately, there's no faster path to forgetting the purpose of God's blessing than taking it for granted and letting abundance remind you of what you don't have. Ingratitude is the first step away from faithfulness, and entitlement is the last nail in the coffin.

We Christians are no less prone to that propaganda in the modern era. What better explains our unquestioning pursuit of the American Dream and "trying to keep up with the Joneses"? Our "affluenza" is just the most recent mutation of the universal human sickness that made it necessary to include "you shall not covet your neighbor's house" in the Ten Commandments (Exodus 20:17). Unfortunately, withholding God's blessing from their neighbors compromised more than their God-given mission. It compromised their worship too.

Wanting still more blessing for themselves, Israel adopted the habits and practices of neighboring nations—thinking it would satisfy—and then their worship and liturgies. Eventually, Israel became so much like the nations that there was nothing that set them apart anymore. God's royal embassy was just another mailing address, indistinguishable from their neighbors. Once Israel lost their God in the white noise of idolatry, they also lost any ability to serve as God's royal embassy or represent his interests in the world.

Through exile, they'd regain it.

Exile wasn't punitive, but restorative. It was as if God said, "Because I am faithful to both the promise and purpose of my blessing, I will move you to where you can't *help* but be my royal embassy among the nations." Just as God scattered Babel for building the tower, he exiled Israel for losing their witness. But where Babel's builders were divided by confusion, when God exiled Israel he preserved a remnant and kept them from scattering. At the very beginning of Israel's exile, God removed their confusion by reiterating his promise to bless them and restored their purpose by moving them to the ground zero of their diplomatic mission. In Israel, God gave Israel's enemies an embassy of his shalom.

Individually, God's people are ambassadors who represent his interests among the nations, but only inasmuch as we embody the kingdom and embassy from which we come. An ambassador without an embassy is just a lobbyist, and I think we can all agree we have more than enough of those already. The *missio Dei* is bigger than any of us. Without God, it's too big for all of us.

If "being a blessing" or even just evangelism is on our individual shoulders, our witness hangs on our personal experience and capacity. No matter how much we are prepared or equipped to share gospel truth with our neighbors, they're as blinded by light pollution as we are. Because social media filters everything through an unending stream of individual perspectives, our value of truth is experiencing hyperinflation. Heart-numbing distraction, rather than confusion, is the source of our division. It's never been easier to disregard or explain away personal testimonies— both online and in person. The gospel is still the power of God and can supernaturally transform the most hardened of hearts, but it still has to be seen and heard to be believed.

But a *people's* witness . . . ? A city can't be hidden. Lived experience can't hold a candle to shared experience. A politically, ethnically, and socioeconomically diverse people living in improbable shalom and imperfect obedience is a whole lot harder to disregard or explain away. Nothing could be a more compelling contrast to the world's or representative of our king's interests than a people whose life together is fueled and shaped by gospel truth. In fact, it is so rare, so counterculturally strange in a society being torn apart by radical individualism, that our neighbors couldn't help but think, "There must be a God around here somewhere."

Besides, why would anyone forsake the world for a kingdom whose citizens don't seem to believe is worth embodying? Not only does that fail to represent our king's interests, it is quite literally individualism. So don't pursue what you want to see in the world but what *God wants the world to see in us*—a community whose devotion reflects and requires a God of steadfast love and faithfulness.

Without a church to inoculate us from the perennial temptation of keeping God's blessing for ourselves, we won't fully experience or faithfully steward our king's blessing. But that blessing is more than an experience of psychological or spiritual well-being, it's also material. To seek the welfare of nations and neighbors alike, we need a way to pool our resources and integrate our effort that adds up to more than the sum of our parts.

Goodness Storehouse

Jesus taught the disciples that "Everyone to whom much [is] given, of him much will be required" (Luke 12:48), but that obligation is not bad news for a city on a hill. Our greatest good is found in pursuing our neighbor's good because it requires us to go back for more blessing from the One who delights in giving it. It is that trust and reliance on God that pushes us to exercise in all our sacrificial generosity:

> Bring the full tithe into the storehouse, that there may be food in my house. And thereby put me to the test, says the LORD of hosts, if I will not open the windows of heaven for you and pour down for you a blessing until there is no more need. (Malachi 3:10)

God doesn't call us to anything he won't abundantly provide for. We are thus poor and foolish stewards of God's blessing if we aren't devoting all our faculties and resources to tangibly cultivate goodness in our broader community. That will look different for every congregation based on their context, but our bias toward individualism radically underestimates the social, economic, and civic good that churches, not just Christians, contribute to their local community—especially indirectly.

Despite frequent calls to start taxing churches, revoking the nonprofit status of religious institutions wouldn't help their broader communities—it would cause them very real harm. With very few exceptions, local churches generate exponentially more social and economic good than whatever property or capital gains taxes might be gleaned from treating them like a for-profit corporation. But don't worry, you don't have to take a pastor's word for it. The data overwhelmingly supports my case.

One study, titled "The Economic Halo Effect of Sacred Places"— conducted in partnership with the University of Pennsylvania's School of Social Policy and Practice—found that "the average urban historic sacred place generates over $1.7 million in economic impact annually." Quantified in that total are, among others, all the ways a church and its congregation contribute "volunteer time; space at below market rates; and cash and in-kind donations to community-serving programs." Of those who benefited from those programs, four out of five were members of the broader community, *not congregants*.[9] To be clear, this study limited their scope to the direct, institutional programming offered by a sacred place (i.e., a building). They intentionally excluded from their analysis any social or economic good that may have been indirectly contributed by individual congregants.

The UNC Charlotte Urban Institute conducted a similar study across eighty-seven rural United Methodist churches across North Carolina and discovered that "they provide an average annual contribution to their local economies of over $735,000."[10] Multiplying that average impact across all of the state's 1,283 UMC churches translates to $944 million in economic value *per year*. They also found that, eerily consistent with their urban counterparts, 72% of those who benefited were *not* members of a congregation. It's true that the church is a community, not a building, but a church with a building is an incredible storehouse of goodness and a tangible blessing to their community.

I could go on, but all of this illustrates a historic principle of social organization originally developed by Thomas Aquinas, called

9. "Economic Halo Effect," Partners for Sacred Places, accessed May 26, 2024, https://sacredplaces.org/info/publications/halo-studies/.

10. "An 'Economic Halo' for Rural Churches in North Carolina," UNC Charlotte Urban Institute, January 11, 2022, https://ui.charlotte.edu/story/economic-halo-rural-churches-north-carolina/.

subsidiarity. The principle is simple, but profoundly underappreciated in an era that idealizes efficiency and mass, at-scale solutions: social and economic problems are most effectively resolved at the most local level possible. Some needs require national solutions (e.g., the federal tax code or national security), but it's not a coincidence that many of our most vitriolic disagreements don't have one-size-fits-all solutions. Scale just isn't all it's cracked up to be, especially for many of our most pressing economic problems because they have very immaterial root causes that vary by geographic region. Because social capital can't be generated with financial capital, churches can address needs that no government could dream of resolving with unanimous bipartisan agreement.

To underscore my point, consider the state of another bedrock American institution: families. "We've made life freer for individuals," David Brooks wrote in a provocatively titled article in *The Atlantic*, "but more unstable for families."

> We've moved from big, interconnected, and extended families, which helped protect the most vulnerable people in society from the shocks of life, to smaller, detached nuclear families (a married couple and their children), which give the most privileged people in society room to maximize their talents and expand their options. The shift . . . liberates the rich and ravages the working-class and the poor.[11]

How many marriages end in divorce because they lack a community where both spouses might be fully known and fully loved? How many couples don't have people around them to offer the challenge, structure, and support needed to grow out of unhealthy relational patterns before conflict becomes unreconcilable? How many families break down into dysfunction, abuse, or neglect under the unyielding weight of economic grind? Federal funding for mental health programs can't help those couples. Instead, imagine how "all the families of the earth [might]

---

11. David Brooks, "The Nuclear Family Was a Mistake," *The Atlantic*, February 10, 2020, https://www.theatlantic.com/magazine/archive/2020/03/the-nuclear-family-was-a-mistake/605536/.

be blessed" through God's provision of an extended spiritual family (Genesis 12:3).

That said, I am painfully aware of how much I am leaving out. Entire books and volumes can (and should still) be written about the church's flourishing presence and her catalytic role in mediating justice, mercy, and peace. But I am focusing on these more interpersonal and intangible dimensions of goodness because they are often the least sexy and most neglected needs that public policy has no way to meaningfully address. This relational and creational goodness is the entire reason common grace institutions exist in the first place, and why our abandonment of institutions is leaving us without a way to generate social capital anywhere near as quickly as we're burning through it. As the only redemptive institution ordained for the life of the world, the body of Christ is uniquely equipped to steward blessing, strengthen bonds, and mediate tangible goodness that everyone everywhere needs.

If we *really* followed the data and took it seriously, municipalities would be actively courting new and existing churches to establish deeper roots in their cities. Established churches would be climbing over themselves to help every church buy their first building. And yes, I'm aware that I have a conflict of interest, but the sheer amount of data backing it up shouts louder than my most passionately delivered pitch. It is, in fact, perfectly aligned with *all* our interests because there is no more powerful engine or storehouse for social, economic, and civic good than the local church.

The Blessing of Shalom

So if you want to be a world-changer, stop. Please. That's way above our pay grade. Even if you could change the world, human society is too sprawling and complex for any number of mere mortals to have a clue regarding what to change, how to change it, or where to start. And even if we did have a clue, even if nothing that we propose to do is out of our reach (Genesis 11:6–7), that isn't necessarily a good thing. Remember:

it was both Babel's sinful folly and *potential ability* that God frustrated by confusing their language. He loved Babel too much to let them succeed without him or (by extension) apart from his people.

If the survival, never mind flourishing, of human civilization is on our individual shoulders, then of course we are going to feel an acute sense of urgency, even crisis. We'll be ruled by shalom's opposite—anxiety. But if it is Jesus's job to make all things new—and he promises that the gates of hell will not withstand the church—what could possibly threaten us? We should be celebrating outside the empty tomb, not whistling past the graveyard. The *missio Dei* is the only purpose that offers both lasting transformation and rest in this life. By planting, establishing, and building up God's city on a hill we can bless our neighbors and experience everyday meaning and mattering without being crushed under the weight of that responsibility. God promises to bless the church and, through her, bless the world. God's blessing is never merely for the church, nor can we bless the world apart from the church.

So much of our anxiety and division, it seems, flows not out of an under-realized appreciation of what God can do, but an over-realized expectation of what we think we can do without a city on a hill.

Whether the garden of Eden, temple Israel, or your local church, each foreshadow and spiritually connect us to the New Jerusalem—the restored "city of shalom" that comes down to reunite the new heaven and new earth in Revelation 21–22. Every local church is a socio-spiritual manifestation of God's presence in a particular time and space. That means that your broken, messy, often painful and sometimes scandal-ridden congregation is the firstfruits of Christ's cosmic mission to make all things new. It's not the family I'd choose either but, by grace, God has chosen to work among and through us for the life of the world. Go figure.

Far from making individual Christians irrelevant in the *missio Dei*, the church's centrality supercharges individual purpose. We church planters love saying that "the Church is God's 'Plan A,' and there is no 'Plan B.'" We say it often enough that it risks becoming a cliché (if it hasn't already). But it's also true. It is *only* through "we" that God changes the world, first by blessing us in and through the body of Christ, and then through our stewardship thereof. We can't do that on our own, and even if we could, it wouldn't be satisfying. But when "we" is for the glory of God and the good of our neighbor, individuals are freed from self-interest to seek the welfare of everywhere God has placed us. Setting up chairs and serving in children's ministry echoes into eternity if for no other reason than because the first step in seeking the welfare of any city is planting and establishing a city on a hill from within.

That fundamental change in perspective is not easy, but let's bring that down to earth. In very practical terms, if "the medium is the message," how can we ever fully talk about the gospel message without utilizing (or even mentioning) the medium God designed for its transmission? Do we believe the body of Christ embodies anything beyond our ken, or is it just a trite metaphor? What have we lost in treating individuals as the medium and the church as a separate dimension or relational circumstance? At the very least, we've lost how the body of Christ is not just a means to God's ends, but also an end to all our spiritual emptiness. In not knowing the existential and institutional reasons for church, we have deprived ourselves of an invaluable opportunity to taste and see that the Lord is not only true, but also good and beautiful. Second only to God's gift of himself, there simply is no greater blessing in this age, for us or our neighbors, than the body of Christ.

Reflection Questions

1. How do you reconcile the statement, "the mark of the true church is an expanding witness to the presence of God"[12] with truisms like "it's not about the numbers"? If God's presence is among a people named Glory, how does our witness expand without inviting our neighbors to church? What's stopping you from doing so?
2. How has individualism influenced your view of Christian mission? Do you operate more as a freelancer (representing yourself), lobbyist

---

12. Beale, *The Temple and the Church's Mission*.

(extracting shalom), or an embassy-anchored ambassador (stewarding God's blessing)? What steps can you take to cooperate with the mission of the institutional church (versus individual Christians or parachurch ministries) as an embassy of God's kingdom?

3. Where do you believe that shalom (welfare) is found in personal success rather than by seeking the welfare of your neighbors through the church?

Bonus Questions

1. Reflect on how the themes in part 2—identity, exile, narrative, belonging, and mission—combine to form a comprehensive "reason for church." What was most new or surprising? Do you believe that the local church is the institution best suited for human flourishing on this side of the new heaven and new earth? Why, or why not?

2. Take some time to consider where you hold church at arm's length and how this vision of church could help you more fully devote yourself "to the apostles' teaching and the fellowship, to the breaking of bread and the prayers" (Acts 2:42).

Epilogue

A Love Letter to the Local Church

As you come to him, a living stone rejected by men but in the sight of
God chosen and precious, you yourselves like living stones are being
built up as a spiritual house, to be a holy priesthood, to offer spiritual
sacrifices acceptable to God through Jesus Christ.

—1 Peter 2:4–5

I'm so confused. When did we become a normie church?"

Lindsay and her family had to move away in June 2020 so her
husband, Jake, could take a job in another part of the country. They had
been dear friends of ours for more than eight years and had been part
of The Table since before we even had a launch team or a name. Saying
goodbye to them was one of the hardest things we had to do in a year of
incredibly hard things.

On paper, their move should have been a dream come true for them.
Jake landed a dream job that paid for their dream house. Outdoor lovers,
they were surrounded by a natural beauty to (almost) rival Colorado's.
If they had to move away from home, there was a lot to be legitimately
excited about.

Instead, they fought a growing sense of loneliness and depression.
Jake's workload was grinding his soul into dust. Lindsay, an accomplished

teacher, couldn't find a position in an area desperate for teachers because she didn't check a long list of ideological boxes. Their kids struggled to navigate the influence and pressure of peers with deeply misguided intuitional beliefs about sexuality and gender. It was somewhat comforting to remember that they didn't necessarily choose this. Jake's job required them to relocate, so the alternative was not being able to pay the mortgage or buy groceries. Following their dreams quickly became a slow-motion train wreck (albeit a very common one). And it was all exponentially harder because, as hard as they tried, they never found a church.

They weren't seeking a perfect spiritual family—being long-suffering friends with a church planter and his wife had quicky dispelled such naïve expectations. They were no strangers to the sometimes painful and awkward reality of what it takes to rebuild community from scratch. But they had tasted God's blessing through that work, so they were up for moving to a city with even fewer churches per capita than they were used to. Yet the few churches they could find within a forty-minute drive had largely become "holy huddles" as polarized and inhospitable as their surrounding culture. Knowing them as well as I do, their experience made it even more clear to me that not all who dechurch after moving to a new place do so for apathetic or selfish reasons. Every place seems to work against us now.

My wife and I connected with them over Zoom at what was probably their lowest point, about a year and a half after they'd moved away. They said they felt conflicted and confused. This wasn't their first time going through a hard season and they could point to more than a few reasons for gratitude, but they couldn't shake an existential emptiness that verged on despair. God had never felt more distant, and they badly wanted someone to tell them how to close the gap.

We were good enough friends that I didn't need to sugarcoat my response. I told them that, though they didn't choose it, they were living their best (secular) life now. For reasons above and beyond any of our understanding, God was allowing them to experience the full implications of living without church in an inhumane and inhospitable world. Despite doing so in almost ideal circumstances, life "under the sun" was still as fruitless and empty as chasing after the wind. The good news, I shared, is that they weren't crazy. In fact, theirs was a right and reasonable reaction of anyone who understood and valued the truth, goodness, and beauty of the church. They were feeling *exactly* as an image bearer should. Their experience was not symptomatic of a distant or absent God, but of One who is immanently near and present in their distress.

As you can tell, I have the spiritual gift of encouragement.

Self-deprecating humor aside, our conversation bled off some of their distress by naming, validating, and pointing to the very good reasons for their experience. Some of it must have resonated because, after our conversation and a few months of prayer, they decided to move back home to Colorado.

All of that was part of the context and background when Lindsay, shortly after moving back, asked about The Table becoming a "normie church." She didn't mean it as a complaint or criticism either. Far from it and even more than she realized at the time, she was describing a very real shift that The Table went through in the two years they'd been away.

Pre-pandemic and with the best of intentions, I regularly invited our people to "do church differently." We avoided many of the churchier rhythms and practices we thought would be alienating to our non-Christian friends and neighbors. Now we embrace them. We do a lot of potlucks. We still do our text-in sermon Q&A every Sunday morning, but now we also recite the Communion liturgy from the *Book of Common Prayer*. At the beginning of our Passing of the Peace, we now invite our older kids up front to answer catechism questions before we send them to our children's ministry. We hired a pastor of spiritual formation to help us grow in areas that don't come naturally to an entrepreneurial church planter like me. My preaching has changed too. I still appeal to areas of agreement with secular culture, but I now spend even more time highlighting the differences that make secularism so inhumane and unsatisfying.

We didn't set out to become a "normie" church, but prioritizing institutional health and depth of spiritual formation rather than reinventing the wheel across a hundred different decisions added up to exactly that. And The Table is all the better for it.

I wrote this book, in part, because I was banging my head against a cultural wall and expecting the wall to surrender. It didn't. Our culture is only growing more radically individualistic and hostile toward institutions, and I needed new language and categories to explain why church still matters. Our congregations and church members feel that need too, but our unchurched and dechurched neighbors are often even more lonely, more discontent, more desperate for meaning and identity only found in Christ. Without reasons for church that speak to a new generation's defeater beliefs and offer sanctuary from individualism, inviting our neighbors felt almost misleading—like we were inviting them to experience something we hadn't fully grasped ourselves. I shared this concern with the members of our church and invited them to pray boldly that God would shift our perspective.

I'm finishing *The Reason for Church* in the midst of an incredible series of answers to that prayer. Three months ago, we learned that we were getting kicked out of the building we'd been meeting in since pandemic lockdowns ended. Two months ago, another local pastor called me out of the blue to ask if we were still looking for a home, and our people have spent the last month renovating the fifty-year-old church building they're leasing to us. Even more incredibly, because we're renting it 24/7 and not just on Sundays, we're able to support a small Hispanic congregation by sharing space and subleasing to them for half their previous monthly rent. Congregants from both our churches worked side by side in cleaning up and renovating the space we all now call home. And so, ten days before our eighth anniversary, our church worshiped in a church building for the first time. Ever. I couldn't tell how many dry eyes were in the room because mine weren't, but our move shifted more than our physical address. God is answering our prayers and planting many of the seeds we've needed to change and deepen how we abide in the body of Christ.

No, the church isn't a building, but a building is a lot more than an irrelevant tool or distraction from "real" ministry. That well-meaning but gnostic mindset has too often disembodied life "in Christ," precluding many from "devoting themselves" to the church. It has only deepened our sense of exile. Without a physical, tangible place to call home, it's hard to experience, let alone steward, God's blessing.

God promises the body of Christ, "I will bless you . . . so that you will be a blessing" (Genesis 12:2). Because one church chose to faithfully steward that promise and bless The Table, we are more able to be a blessing to our neighbors. We now have a natural opportunity to support and co-labor with a congregation trying to reach the first and second generation immigrants who make up almost 20% of our broader community—an opportunity we started praying for several years ago but sadly dropped at some point in all the chaos of 2020. By pouring themselves into needed renovations, our people get a real-life illustration of how devoting themselves to The Table leads to "glad and generous hearts, praising God and having favor with all the people" (Acts 2:46). By grace, and no merit or achievement of our own, we have been caught up in a cascade of God's blessing beyond what any of us could achieve on our own. We have a *very* long way to go in becoming the embodied hospitality of Jesus, but these are significant steps in a church's journey that will (and must) outlast any of us.

That's the dream.

Imagine if we didn't just invite our neighbors to church but also gave them true, good, and beautiful reasons to accept our invitation. Imagine if, from firsthand experience and before they even walked through the doors, we could describe to them that a call to worship isn't just a content-based reminder for why we gather, but a call to abide in the presence of One from whom we are no longer separated—not by a curtain, nor by time or space, nor even by sin and death. Imagine the difference it would make if, rather than a Coldplay concert followed by a TED Talk, our neighbors expected every local church to be a strange, thin place between a fallen world and the God who helps us make sense of it all. Imagine a refuge saturated in shalom not because it's easy or natural, but because our devotion to each other in Christ is more than theological head knowledge; it's also a life-reordering embrace of Christ's steadfast love for his bride. Imagine not needing to achieve our identity through spiritual pragmatism, the sacred self, counterfeit institutions, (un)civil religions, or virtuous victimhood because they pale in comparison to the true, good, and beautiful identity freely offered and received in Christ. Imagine seeing God's glory so clearly, without any light pollution.

These reasons for church—for being bound to one another in Christ not just individually and spiritually, but institutionally and covenantally—have never mattered more. Yet as in liminal ages past, Jesus will work among his body and through his bride despite our best intentions and brilliant plans—thank God!

So whether we meet in a gothic cathedral, a renovated warehouse, or a public school cafetorium, a church gathered to worship our Great High Priest on the basis of his once-for-all sacrifice is nothing less than an inbreaking of the new heaven and new earth into our here and now. We don't have to fully believe that for it to be true, good, or beautiful. It simply is. The rest, God will open our eyes to see and our ears to hear.